FOREIGN AFFAIRS AGENDA

FOREIGN AFFAIRS AGENDA

The New Shape of World Politics

(Revised Edition)

Contending Paradigms in International Relations

FOREIGN AFFAIRS
NEW YORK

W·W·NORTON
NEW YORK · LONDON

Published by Foreign Affairs, New York.
Distributed by W.W. Norton & Company, Inc.,
500 Fifth Avenue, New York, NY 10110.

FOREIGN AFFAIRS AGENDA

THE NEW SHAPE OF WORLD POLITICS
(Revised Edition)

ISBN 0-87609-244-X

Contents

Introduction

THE CHINESE curse, "May you live in interesting times," is a blessing for scholars. What makes it a curse (change and unpredictability) are prime conditions under which to test theories and arguments about the nature of international life. In this sense, the world after the Cold War is very interesting indeed. It may not have the drama and life-threatening urgency of a nuclear arms race, but it raises fascinating and fundamental issues about international politics, economics and society.

Foreign Affairs has sought to put together a reader comprising the most stimulating and informative debates about the world we are living in. In order to reflect the very best of the wide-ranging debate that has taken place since the collapse of the Soviet Union, we decided not to arbitrarily limit the reader to articles from *Foreign Affairs* but instead to add in any essay that seemed indispensable. The result, as you can see, is a "greatest hits" of international relations.

The End of Politics? Francis Fukuyama set the stage for these debates by arguing in a now-legendary essay in *The National Interest* that the collapse of Communism represents not just the end of the Cold War but the end of History, by which he meant the end of the great ideological battles of the last three centuries. For Fukuyama, the political realm would no longer be one of conflict but rather of bland consensus. International conflict—if there was great international conflict—would have to come from other sources. A different view of the world with similar overtones can be found in Michael Doyle's *American Political Science Review* article on the "Democratic Peace." It presents what many now regard as the strongest "empirical law" in international relations.

Many disagreed with Fukuyama's teleology, most directly Samuel P. Huntington in a response, but in other ways writers as diverse as John Mearsheimer, Fouad Ajami, Ethan Kapstein and Kim Dae Jung all stressed the importance of politics and the political goals of states and statesmen. The Cold War is over, but in Mearsheimer's formulation in *International Security* we are going "back to the future," into a world characterized by balance-of-power rivalries.

Introduction

Economics triumphant. Globalization may well be the next wave — but it could well mean new and different conflicts. Perhaps the first new paradigm of the post-Cold War world to be named was "Geo-economics," a term coined by Edward Luttwak in an article by the same name. If Clausewitz said war is a continuation of politics by other means, Luttwak stressed that economics was really a continuation of politics by other means. States would no longer compete for bases and sea lanes but for market share and import quotas. The mercantilism of the Far East Asian economies was the model of the future; the laissez faire of the West the self-indulgent decadence of the past. Paul Krugman, one of the world's leading theoretical economists, took exception to this viewpoint and made the case that economics, unlike politics, was not a zero-sum game and to apply a political lens to questions of national economies produced, in his words, " a dangerous obsession."

In a very different vein, scholars like Robert Keohane have argued that economics may well be the driving force of international politics today. The nature and extent of economic interdependence and the rise of international institutions have tamed the fires of international conflict. Nations are learning to cooperate and resolve tensions in incremental ways that will have benign international consequences. Economics has not become like politics; instead politics has become like economics.

Democracy triumphant? President Clinton has proudly proclaimed that more people live under democratic governments today that at any previous time in history. And indeed, since the fall of the Berlin Wall, democracy, unrivalled and unchallenged, has seemed to move inexorably across the world. But in a much discussed and reprinted essay, Fareed Zakaria raises uncomfortable questions about democracy and its worldwide spread. "The Rise of Illiberal Democracy" asks whether elections constitute genuine democracy and whether their premature adoption actually hurts the cause of individual rights and the rule of law. Zakaria and, in his response, Marc Plattner debate the tension between democracy and liberty in theory and practise.

Is Culture Destiny? Perhaps the most controversial essay of the post-Cold War world has been Samuel Huntington's "The Clash of Civilizations?" in which he argued that the dominating force of the future was neither politics nor economics but culture. While Huntington's analysis—not to say his prose—were most dramatic and far reaching, the argument that culture—religion, language, custom, national identity—is the key to understanding human affairs is currently in vogue. Businessmen speak of the cultural traits of groups that succeed; military scholars study strategic culture; political scientists look to culture and civil society to explain why some countries do well and others badly. Like Huntington, Lee Kuan Yew adopts a variation of this view.

Does Sex Matter? (No not in that sense.) If there is anything more fundamental than culture it is surely biology, and Francis Fukuyama argues that biology is destiny. Surveying the vast literature on the subject, he concludes that the feminists are right, male aggression is an important cause of international conflict. But because it is so deep rooted, changing this will prove difficult. Fukuyama's wide-ranging essay has already produced considerable debate.

Fareed Zakaria
Managing Editor
Foreign Affairs

The End of History?

Francis Fukuyama

IN WATCHING the flow of events over the past decade or so, it is hard to avoid the feeling that something very fundamental has happened in world history. The past year has seen a flood of articles commemorating the end of the Cold War, and the fact that "peace" seems to be breaking out in many regions of the world. Most of these analyses lack any larger conceptual framework for distinguishing between what is essential and what is contingent or accidental in world history, and are predictably superficial. If Mr. Gorbachev were ousted from the Kremlin or a new Ayatollah proclaimed the millennium from a desolate Middle Eastern capital, these same commentators would scramble to announce the rebirth of a new era of conflict.

And yet, all of these people sense dimly that there is some larger process at work, a process that gives coherence and order to the daily headlines. The twentieth century saw the developed world descend into a paroxysm of ideological violence, as liberalism contended first with the remnants of absolutism, then bolshevism and fascism, and finally an updated Marxism that threatened to lead to the ultimate apocalypse of nuclear war. But the century that began full of self-confidence in the ultimate triumph of Western liberal democracy seems at its close to be returning full circle to where it started: not to an "end of ideology" or a convergence between capitalism and socialism, as earlier predicted, but to an unabashed victory of economic and political liberalism.

The triumph of the West, of the Western *idea*, is evident first of all in the total exhaustion of viable systematic alternatives to Western liberal-

FRANCIS FUKUYAMA is Professor of Political Science at George Mason University. This article appeared in the Summer 1989 issue of *The National Interest*. © 1989 by National Affairs, Inc.

ism. In the past decade, there have been unmistakable changes in the intellectual climate of the world's two largest communist countries, and the beginnings of significant reform movements in both. But this phenomenon extends beyond high politics and it can be seen also in the ineluctable spread of consumerist Western culture in such diverse contexts as the peasants' markets and color television sets now omnipresent throughout China, the cooperative restaurants and clothing stores opened in the past year in Moscow, the Beethoven piped into Japanese department stores, and the rock music enjoyed alike in Prague, Rangoon, and Tehran.

What we may be witnessing is not just the end of the Cold War, or the passing of a particular period of postwar history, but the end of history as such: that is, the end point of mankind's ideological evolution and the universalization of Western liberal democracy as the final form of human government. This is not to say that there will no longer be events to fill the pages of *Foreign Affairs'* yearly summaries of international relations, for the victory of liberalism has occurred primarily in the realm of ideas or consciousness and is as yet incomplete in the real or material world. But there are powerful reasons for believing that it is the ideal that will govern the material world *in the long run.* To understand how this is so, we must first consider some theoretical issues concerning the nature of historical change.

I

THE NOTION of the end of history is not an original one. Its best known propagator was Karl Marx, who believed that the direction of historical development was a purposeful one determined by the interplay of material forces, and would come to an end only with the achievement of a communist utopia that would finally resolve all prior contradictions. But the concept of history as a dialectical process with a beginning, a middle, and an end was borrowed by Marx from his great German predecessor Georg Wilhelm Friedrich Hegel.

For better or worse, much of Hegel's historicism has become part of our contemporary intellectual baggage. The notion that mankind has progressed through a series of primitive stages of consciousness on his path to the present, and that these stages corresponded to concrete forms of social organization, such as tribal, slave-owning, theocratic, and finally democratic-egalitarian societies, has become inseparable from the modern understanding of man. Hegel was the first philosopher to speak the language of modern social science, insofar as man for him was the product of his concrete historical and social environment and not, as earlier natural right theorists would have it, a collection of more or less fixed "natural" attributes. The mastery and transformation of man's natural environment through the application of science and technology was originally not a Marxist concept, but a Hegelian one. Unlike later historicists whose historical relativism degenerated into relativism *tout court,* however, Hegel believed that history culminated in an absolute moment—a moment in which a final, rational form of society and state became victorious.

It is Hegel's misfortune to be known now primarily as Marx's precursor, and it is our misfortune that few of us are familiar with Hegel's work from direct study, but only as it has been filtered through the distorting lens of Marxism. In France, however, there has been an effort to save Hegel from his Marxist interpreters and to resurrect him as the philosopher who most correctly speaks to our time. Among those modern French interpreters of Hegel, the greatest was certainly Alexandre Kojève, a brilliant Russian emigre who taught a highly influential series of seminars in Paris in the 1930s at the *Ecole Practique des Hautes Etudes*[1] While largely unknown in the United States, Kojève had a major impact on the intellectual life of the continent. Among his students ranged such future luminaries as Jean-Paul Sartre on the Left and Raymond Aron on the Right; postwar existentialism borrowed many of its basic categories from Hegel via Kojève.

Kojève sought to resurrect the Hegel of the *Phenomenology of Mind,* the Hegel who proclaimed history to be at an end in 1806. For as early as this Hegel saw in Napoleon's defeat of the Prussian monarchy at the Battle of Jena the victory of the ideals of the French Revolution, and the imminent universalization of the state incorporating the principles of liberty and equality. Kojève, far from rejecting Hegel in light of the turbulent events of the next century and a half, insisted that the latter had been es-

---

1. Kojève best-known work is his *Introduction à la lecture de Hegel* (Paris: Editions Gallimard, 1947), which is a transcript of the *Ecole Practique* lectures from the 1930s. This book is available in English entitled *Introduction to the Reading of Hegel* arranged by Raymond Queneau, edited by Allan Bloom, and translated by James Nichols (New York: Basic Books, 1969).

sentially correct.[2] The Battle of Jena marked the end of history because it was at that point that the *vanguard* of humanity (a term quite familiar to Marxists) actualized the principles of the French Revolution. While there was considerable work to be done after 1806—abolishing slavery and the slave trade, extending the franchise to workers, women, blacks, and other racial minorities, etc.—the basic *principles* of the liberal democratic state could not be improved upon. The two world wars in this century and their attendant revolutions and upheavals simply had the effect of extending those principles spatially, such that the various provinces of human civilization were brought up to the level of its most advanced outposts, and of forcing those societies in Europe and North America at the vanguard of civilization to implement their liberalism more fully.

The state that emerges at the end of history is liberal insofar as it recognizes and protects through a system of law man's universal right to freedom, and democratic insofar as it exists only with the consent of the governed. For Kojève, this so-called "universal homogenous state" found real-life embodiment in the countries of postwar Western Europe— precisely those flabby, prosperous, self-satisfied, inward-looking, weak-willed states whose grandest project was nothing more heroic than the creation of the Common Market.[3] But this was only to be expected. For human history and the conflict that characterized it was based on the existence of "contradictions": primitive man's quest for mutual recognition, the dialectic of the master and slave, the transformation and mastery of nature, the struggle for the universal recognition of rights, and the dichotomy between proletarian and capitalist. But in the universal homogenous state, all prior contradictions are resolved and all human needs are satisfied. There is no struggle or conflict over "large" issues, and consequently no need for generals or statesmen; what remains is primarily economic activity. And indeed, Kojève's life was consistent with his teaching. Believing that there was no more work for philosophers as well, since Hegel (correctly understood) had already achieved absolute knowledge, Kojève left teaching after the war and spent the remainder of his life working as a bureaucrat in the European Economic Community, until his death in 1968.

2. In this respect Kojève stands in sharp contrast to contemporary German interpreters of Hegel like Herbert Marcuse who, being more sympathetic to Marx, regarded Hegel ultimately as an historically bound and incomplete philosopher.

3. Kojève alternatively identified the end of history with the postwar "American way of life," toward which he thought the Soviet Union was moving as well.

The End of History?

To his contemporaries at mid-century, Kojève's proclamation of the end of history must have seemed like the typical eccentric solipsism of a French intellectual, coming as it did on the heels of World War II and at the very height of the Cold War. To comprehend how Kojève could have been so audacious as to assert that history has ended, we must first of all understand the meaning of Hegelian idealism.

II

FOR HEGEL, the contradictions that drive history exist first of all in the realm of human consciousness, i.e. on the level of ideas[4]—not the trivial election year proposals of American politicians, but ideas in the sense of large unifying world views that might best be understood under the rubric of ideology. Ideology in this sense is not restricted to the secular and explicit political doctrines we usually associate with the term, but can include religion, culture, and the complex of moral values underlying any society as well.

Hegel's view of the relationship between the ideal and the real or material worlds was an extremely complicated one, beginning with the fact that for him the distinction between the two was only apparent.[5] He did not believe that the real world conformed or could be made to conform to ideological preconceptions of philosophy professors in any simple-minded way, or that the "material" world could not impinge on the ideal. Indeed, Hegel the professor was temporarily thrown out of work as a result of a very material event, the Battle of Jena. But while Hegel's writing and thinking could be stopped by a bullet from the material world, the hand on the trigger of the gun was motivated in turn by the ideas of liberty and equality that had driven the French Revolution.

For Hegel, all human behavior in the material world, and hence all human history, is rooted in a prior state of consciousness—an idea similar to the one expressed by John Maynard Keynes when he said that the views of men of affairs were usually derived from defunct economists and academic scribblers of earlier generations. This consciousness may not be

---

4. This notion was expressed in the famous aphorism from the preface to the *Philosophy of History* to the effect that "everything that is rational is real, and everything that is real is rational."

5. Indeed, for Hegel the very dichotomy between the ideal and material worlds was itself only an apparent one that was ultimately overcome by the self-conscious subject; in his system, the material world is itself only an aspect of mind.

explicit and self-aware, as are modern political doctrines, but may rather take the form of religion or simple cultural or moral habits. And yet this realm of consciousness in the long run necessarily becomes manifest in the material world, indeed creates the material world in its own image. Consciousness is cause and not effect, and can develop autonomously from the material world; hence the real subtext underlying the apparent jumble of current events is the history of ideology.

Hegel's idealism has fared poorly at the hands of later thinkers. Marx reversed the priority of the real and the ideal completely, relegating the entire realm of consciousness— religion, art, culture, philosophy itself—to a "superstructure" that was determined entirely by the prevailing material mode of production. Yet another unfortunate legacy of Marxism is our tendency to retreat into materialist or utilitarian explanations of political or historical phenomena, and our disinclination to believe in the autonomous power of ideas. A recent example of this is Paul Kennedy's hugely successful *The Rise and Fall of the Great Powers,* which ascribes the decline of great powers to simple economic overextension. Obviously, this is true on some level: an empire whose economy is barely above the level of subsistence cannot bankrupt its treasury indefinitely. But whether a highly productive modern industrial society chooses to spend 3 or 7 percent of its GNP on defense rather than consumption is entirely a matter of that society's political priorities, which are in turn determined in the realm of consciousness.

The materialist bias of modern thought is characteristic not only of people on the Left who may be sympathetic to Marxism, but of many passionate anti-Marxists as well. Indeed, there is on the Right what one might label the *Wall Street Journal* school of deterministic materialism that discounts the importance of ideology and culture and sees man as essentially a rational, profit-maximizing individual. It is precisely this kind of individual and his pursuit of material incentives that is posited as the basis for economic life as such in economic textbooks.[6] One small example will illustrate the problematic character of such materialist views.

Max Weber begins his famous book, *The Protestant Ethic and the Spirit of Capitalism,* by noting the different economic performance of

---

6. In fact, modern economists, recognizing that man does not always behave as a profit-maximizer, posit a "utility" function, utility being either income or some other good that can be maximized: leisure, sexual satisfaction, or the pleasure of philosophizing. That profit must be replaced with a value like utility indicates the cogency of the idealist perspective.

Protestant and Catholic communities throughout Europe and America, summed up in the proverb that Protestants eat well while Catholics sleep well. Weber notes that according to any economic theory that posited man as a rational profit-maximizer, raising the piece-work rate should increase labor productivity. But in fact, in many traditional peasant communities, raising the piece-work rate actually had the opposite effect of *lowering* labor productivity: at the higher rate, a peasant accustomed to earning two and one-half marks per day found he could earn the same amount by working less, and did so because he valued leisure more than income. The choices of leisure over income, or of the militaristic life of the Spartan hoplite over the wealth of the Athenian trader, or even the ascetic life of the early capitalist entrepreneur over that of a traditional leisured aristocrat, cannot possibly be explained by the impersonal working of material forces, but come preeminently out of the sphere of consciousness—what we have labeled here broadly as ideology. And indeed, a central theme of Weber's work was to prove that contrary to Marx, the material mode of production, far from being the "base," was itself a "superstructure" with roots in religion and culture, and that to understand the emergence of modern capitalism and the profit motive one had to study their antecedents in the realm of the spirit.

As we look around the contemporary world, the poverty of materialist theories of economic development is all too apparent. The *Wall Street Journal* school of deterministic materialism habitually points to the stunning economic success of Asia in the past few decades as evidence of the viability of free market economics, with the implication that all societies would see similar development were they simply to allow their populations to pursue their material self-interest freely. Surely free markets and stable political systems are a necessary precondition to capitalist economic growth. But just as surely the cultural heritage of those Far Eastern societies, the ethic of work and saving and family, a religious heritage that does not, like Islam, place restrictions on certain forms of economic behavior, and other deeply ingrained moral qualities, are equally important in explaining their economic performance.[7] And yet the intellectual weight of materialism is such that not a single respectable contemporary

---

7. One need look no further than the recent performance of Vietnamese immigrants in the U.S. school system when compared to their black or Hispanic classmates to realize that culture and consciousness are absolutely crucial to explain not only economic behavior but virtually every other important aspect of life as well.

theory of economic development addresses consciousness and culture seriously as the matrix within which economic behavior is formed.

FAILURE TO understand that the roots of economic behavior lie in the realm of consciousness and culture leads to the common mistake of attributing material causes to phenomena that are essentially ideal in nature. For example, it is commonplace in the West to interpret the reform movements first in China and most recently in the Soviet Union as the victory of the material over the ideal—that is, a recognition that ideological incentives could not replace material ones in stimulating a highly productive modern economy, and that if one wanted to prosper one had to appeal to baser forms of self-interest. But the deep defects of socialist economies were evident thirty or forty years ago to anyone who chose to look. Why was it that these countries moved away from central planning only in the 1980s? The answer must be found in the consciousness of the elites and leaders ruling them, who decided to opt for the "Protestant" life of wealth and risk over the "Catholic" path of poverty and security.[8] That change was in no way made inevitable by the material conditions in which either country found itself on the eve of the reform, but instead came about as the result of the victory of one idea over another.[9]

For Kojève, as for all good Hegelians, understanding the underlying processes of history requires understanding developments in the realm of consciousness or ideas, since consciousness will ultimately remake the material world in its own image. To say that history ended in 1806 meant that mankind's ideological evolution ended in the ideals of the French or American Revolutions: while particular regimes in the real world might not implement these ideals fully, their theoretical truth is absolute and could not be improved upon. Hence it did not matter to Kojève that the

---

8. I understand that a full explanation of the origins of the reform movements in China and Russia is a good deal more complicated than this simple formula would suggest. The Soviet reform, for example, was motivated in good measure by Moscow's sense of *insecurity* in the technological-military realm. Nonetheless, neither country on the eve of its reforms was in such a state of *material* crisis that one could have predicted the surprising reform paths ultimately taken.

9. It is still not clear whether the Soviet peoples are as "Protestant" as Gorbachev and will follow him down that path.

consciousness of the postwar generation of Europeans had not been universalized throughout the world; if ideological development had in fact ended, the homogenous state would eventually become victorious throughout the material world.

I have neither the space nor, frankly, the ability to defend in depth Hegel's radical idealist perspective. The issue is not whether Hegel's system was right, but whether his perspective might uncover the problematic nature of many materialist explanations we often take for granted. This is not to deny the role of material factors as such. To a literal-minded idealist, human society can be built around any arbitrary set of principles regardless of their relationship to the material world. And in fact men have proven themselves able to endure the most extreme material hardships in the name of ideas that exist in the realm of the spirit alone, be it the divinity of cows or the nature of the Holy Trinity.[10]

But while man's very perception of the material world is shaped by his historical consciousness of it, the material world can clearly affect in return the viability of a particular state of consciousness. In particular, the spectacular abundance of advanced liberal economies and the infinitely diverse consumer culture made possible by them seem to both foster and preserve liberalism in the political sphere. I want to avoid the materialist determinism that says that liberal economics inevitably produces liberal politics, because I believe that both economics and politics presuppose an autonomous prior state of consciousness that makes them possible. But that state of consciousness that permits the growth of liberalism seems to stabilize in the way one would expect at the end of history if it is underwritten by the abundance of a modern free market economy. We might summarize the content of the universal homogenous state as liberal democracy in the political sphere combined with easy access to VCRS and stereos in the economic.

---

10. The internal politics of the Byzantine Empire at the time of Justinian revolved around a conflict between the so-called monophysites and monothelites, who believed that the unity of the Holy Trinity was alternatively one of nature or of will. This conflict corresponded to some extent to one between proponents of different racing teams in the Hippodrome in Byzantium and led to a not insignificant level of political violence. Modern historians would tend to seek the roots of such conflicts in antagonisms between social classes or some other modern economic category, being unwilling to believe that men would kill each other over the nature of the Trinity.

III

HAVE WE in fact reached the end of history? Are tnere, in other words, any fundamental "contradictions" in human life that cannot be resolved in the context of modern liberalism, that would be resolvable by an alternative political-economic structure? If we accept the idealist premises laid out above, we must seek an answer to this question in the realm of ideology and consciousness. Our task is not to answer exhaustively the challenges to liberalism promoted by every crackpot messiah around the world, but only those that are embodied in important social or political forces and movements, and which are therefore part of world history. For our purposes, it matters very little what strange thoughts occur to people in Albania or Burkina Faso, for we are interested in what one could in some sense call the common ideological heritage of mankind.

In the past century, there have been two major challenges to liberalism, those of fascism and of communism. The former[11] saw the political weakness, materialism, anomie, and lack of community of the West as fundamental contradictions in liberal societies that could only be resolved by a strong state that forged a new "people" on the basis of national exclusiveness. Fascism was destroyed as a living ideology by World War II. This was a defeat, of course, on a very material level, but it amounted to a defeat of the idea as well. What destroyed fascism as an idea was not universal moral revulsion against it, since plenty of people were willing to endorse the idea as long as it seemed the wave of the future, but its lack of success. After the war, it seemed to most people that German fascism as well as its other European and Asian variants were bound to self-destruct. There was no material reason why new fascist movements could not have sprung up again after the war in other locales, but for the fact that expansionist ultranationalism, with

---

11. I am not using the term "fascism" here in its most precise sense, fully aware of the frequent misuse of this term to denounce anyone to the right of the user. "Fascism" here denotes any organized ultra-nationalist movement with universalistic pretensions—not universalistic with regard to its nationalism, of course, since the latter is exclusive by definition, but with regard to the movement's belief in its right to rule other people. Hence Imperial Japan would qualify as fascist while former strongman Stoessner's Paraguay or Pinochet's Chile would not. Obviously fascist ideologies cannot be universalistic in the sense of Marxism or liberalism, but the structure of the doctrine can be transferred from country to country.

its promise of unending conflict leading to disastrous military defeat, had completely lost its appeal. The ruins of the Reich chancellory as well as the atomic bombs dropped on Hiroshima and Nagasaki killed this ideology on the level of consciousness as well as materially, and all of the proto-fascist movements spawned by the German and Japanese examples like the Peronist movement in Argentina or Subhas Chandra Bose's Indian National Army withered after the war.

The ideological challenge mounted by the other great alternative to liberalism, communism, was far more serious. Marx, speaking Hegel's language, asserted that liberal society contained a fundamental contradiction that could not be resolved within its context, that between capital and labor, and this contradiction has constituted the chief accusation against liberalism ever since. But surely, the class issue has actually been successfully resolved in the West. As Kojève (among others) noted, the egalitarianism of modern America represents the essential achievement of the classless society envisioned by Marx. This is not to say that there are not rich people and poor people in the United States, or that the gap between them has not grown in recent years. But the root causes of economic inequality do not have to do with the underlying legal and social structure of our society, which remains fundamentally egalitarian and moderately redistributionist, so much as with the cultural and social characteristics of the groups that make it up, which are in turn the historical legacy of premodern conditions. Thus black poverty in the United States is not the inherent product of liberalism, but is rather the "legacy of slavery and racism" which persisted long after the formal abolition of slavery.

As a result of the receding of the class issue, the appeal of communism in the developed Western world, it is safe to say, is lower today than any time since the end of the First World War. This can be measured in any number of ways: in the declining membership and electoral pull of the major European communist parties, and their overtly revisionist programs; in the corresponding electoral success of conservative parties from Britain and Germany to the United States and Japan, which are unabashedly pro-market and antistatist; and in an intellectual climate whose most "advanced" members no longer believe that bourgeois society is something that ultimately needs to be overcome. This is not to say that the opinions of progressive intellectuals in Western countries are not deeply pathological in any number of ways. But those who believe that the future must inevitably be socialist tend to be very old, or very marginal to the real political discourse of their societies.

ONE MAY argue that the socialist alternative was never terribly plausible for the North Atlantic world, and was sustained for the last several decades primarily by its success outside of this region. But it is precisely in the non-European world that one is most struck by the occurrence of major ideological transformations. Surely the most remarkable changes have occurred in Asia. Due to the strength and adaptability of the indigenous cultures there, Asia became a battleground for a variety of imported Western ideologies early in this century. Liberalism in Asia was a very weak reed in the period after World War I; it is easy today to forget how gloomy Asia's political future looked as recently as ten or fifteen years ago. It is easy to forget as well how momentous the outcome of Asian ideological struggles seemed for world political development as a whole.

The first Asian alternative to liberalism to be decisively defeated was the fascist one represented by Imperial Japan. Japanese fascism (like its German version) was defeated by the force of American arms in the Pacific war, and liberal democracy was imposed on Japan by a victorious United States. Western capitalism and political liberalism when transplanted to Japan were adapted and transformed by the Japanese in such a way as to be scarcely recognizable.[12] Many Americans are now aware that Japanese industrial organization is very different from that prevailing in the United States or Europe, and it is questionable what relationship the factional maneuvering that takes place with the governing Liberal Democratic Party bears to democracy. Nonetheless, the very fact that the essential elements of economic and political liberalism have been so successfully grafted onto uniquely Japanese traditions and institutions guarantees their survival in the long run. More important is the contribution that Japan has made in turn to world history by following in the

---

12. I use the example of Japan with some caution, since. Kojève late in his life came to conclude that Japan, with its culture based on purely formal arts, proved that the universal homogenous state was not victorious and that history had perhaps not ended. See the long note at the end of the second edition of *Introduction à la Lecture de Hegel*, 462-3.

footsteps of the United States to create a truly universal consumer culture that has become both a symbol and an underpinning of the universal homogenous state. V.S. Naipaul traveling in Khomeini's Iran shortly after the revolution noted the omnipresent signs advertising the products of Sony, Hitachi, and JVC, whose appeal remained virtually irresistible and gave the lie to the regime's pretensions of restoring a state based on the rule of the *Shariah*. Desire for access to the consumer culture, created in large measure by Japan, has played a crucial role in fostering the spread of economic liberalism throughout Asia, and hence in promoting political liberalism as well.

The economic success of the other newly industrializing countries (NICs) in Asia following on the example of Japan is by now a familiar story. What is important from a Hegelian standpoint is that political liberalism has been following economic liberalism, more slowly than many had hoped but with seeming inevitability. Here again we see the victory of the idea of the universal homogenous state. South Korea had developed into a modern, urbanized society with an increasingly large and well-educated middle class that could not possibly be isolated from the larger democratic trends around them. Under these circumstances it seemed intolerable to a large part of this population that it should be ruled by an anachronistic military regime while Japan, only a decade or so ahead in economic terms, had parliamentary institutions for over forty years. Even the former socialist regime in Burma, which for so many decades existed in dismal isolation from the larger trends dominating Asia, was buffeted in the past year by pressures to liberalize both its economy and political system. It is said that unhappiness with strongman Ne Win began when a senior Burmese officer went to Singapore for medical treatment and broke down crying when he saw how far socialist Burma had been left behind by its ASEAN neighbors.

BUT THE power of the liberal idea would seem much less impressive if it had not infected the largest and oldest culture in Asia, China. The simple existence of communist China created an alternative pole of ideological attraction, and as such constituted a threat to liberalism. But the past fifteen years have seen an almost total discrediting of Marxism-Leninism as an economic system. Beginning with the famous third plenum of the

Tenth Central Committee in 1978, the Chinese Communist party set about decollectivizing agriculture for the 800 million Chinese who still lived in the countryside. The role of the state in agriculture was reduced to that of a tax collector, while production of consumer goods was sharply increased in order to give peasants a taste of the universal homogenous state and thereby an incentive to work. The reform doubled Chinese grain output in only five years, and in the process created for Deng Xiao-ping a solid political base from which he was able to extend the reform to other parts of the economy. Economic statistics do not begin to describe the dynamism, initiative, and openness evident in China since the reform began.

China could not now be described in any way as a liberal democracy. At present, no more than 20 percent of its economy has been marketized, and most importantly it continues to be ruled by a self-appointed Communist party which has given no hint of wanting to devolve power. Deng has made none of Gorbachev's promises regarding democratization of the political system and there is no Chinese equivalent of *glasnost*. The Chinese leadership has in fact been much more circumspect in criticizing Mao and Maoism than Gorbachev with respect to Brezhnev and Stalin, and the regime continues to pay lip service to Marxism-Leninism as its ideological underpinning. But anyone familiar with the outlook and behavior of the new technocratic elite now governing China knows that Marxism and ideological principle have become virtually irrelevant as guides to policy, and that bourgeois consumerism has a real meaning in that country for the first time since the revolution. The various slowdowns in the pace of reform, the campaigns against "spiritual pollution" and crackdowns on political dissent are more properly seen as tactical adjustments made in the process of managing what is an extraordinarily difficult political transition. By ducking the question of political reform while putting the economy on a new footing, Deng has managed to avoid the breakdown of authority that has accompanied Gorbachev's *perestroika*. Yet the pull of the liberal idea continues to be very strong as economic power devolves and the economy becomes more open to the outside world. There are currently over 20,000 Chinese students studying in the U.S. and other Western countries, almost all of them the children of the Chinese elite. It is hard to believe that when they return home to run the country they will be content for China to be the only country in Asia unaffected by the larger democratizing trend. The student demonstrations in Beijing that broke out first in December 1986 and recurred recently on the occasion of Hu Yao-bang's death were only the beginning of what will inevitably be mounting pressure for change in the political system as well.

What is important about China from the standpoint of world history is not the present state of the reform or even its future prospects. The central issue is the fact that the People's Republic of China can no longer act as a beacon for illiberal forces around the world, whether they be guerrillas in some Asian jungle or middle class students in Paris. Maoism, rather than being the pattern for Asia's future, became an anachronism, and it was the mainland Chinese who in fact were decisively influenced by the prosperity and dynamism of their overseas co-ethnics—the ironic ultimate victory of Taiwan.

Important as these changes in China have been, however, it is developments in the Soviet Union—the original "homeland of the world proletariat"—that have put the final nail in the coffin of the Marxist-Leninist alternative to liberal democracy. It should be clear that in terms of formal institutions, not much has changed in the four years since Gorbachev has come to power: free markets and the cooperative movement represent only a small part of the Soviet economy, which remains centrally planned; the political system is still dominated by the Communist party, which has only begun to democratize internally and to share power with other groups; the regime continues to assert that it is seeking only to modernize socialism and that its ideological basis remains Marxism-Leninism; and, finally, Gorbachev faces a potentially powerful conservative opposition that could undo many of the changes that have taken place to date. Moreover, it is hard to be too sanguine about the chances for success of Gorbachev's proposed reforms, either in the sphere of economics or politics. But my purpose here is not to analyze events in the short-term, or to make predictions for policy purposes, but to look at underlying trends in the sphere of ideology and consciousness. And in that respect, it is clear that an astounding transformation has occurred.

Emigres from the Soviet Union have been reporting for at least the last generation now that virtually nobody in that country truly believed in Marxism-Leninism any longer, and that this was nowhere more true than in the Soviet elite, which continued to mouth Marxist slogans out of sheer cynicism. The corruption and decadence of the late Brezhnev-era Soviet state seemed to matter little, however, for as long as the state itself refused to throw into question any of the fundamental principles underlying Soviet society, the system was capable of functioning adequately out of sheer inertia and could even muster some dynamism in the realm of foreign and defense policy. Marxism-Leninism was like a magical incantation which, however absurd and devoid of meaning, was the only common basis on which the elite could agree to rule Soviet society.

WHAT HAS happened in the four years since Gorbachev's coming to power is a revolutionary assault on the most fundamental institutions and principles of Stalinism, and their replacement by other principles which do not amount to liberalism *per se* but whose only connecting thread is liberalism. This is most evident in the economic sphere, where the reform economists around Gorbachev have become steadily more radical in their support for free markets, to the point where some like Nikolai Shmelev do not mind being compared in public to Milton Friedman. There is a virtual consensus among the currently dominant school of Soviet economists now that central planning and the command system of allocation are the root cause of economic inefficiency, and that if the Soviet system is ever to heal itself, it must permit free and decentralized decision-making with respect to investment, labor, and prices. After a couple of initial years of ideological confusion, these principles have finally been incorporated into policy with the promulgation of new laws on enterprise autonomy, cooperatives, and finally in 1988 on lease arrangements and family farming. There are, of course, a number of fatal flaws in the current implementation of the reform, most notably the absence of a thoroughgoing price reform. But the problem is no longer a *conceptual* one: Gorbachev and his lieutenants seem to understand the economic logic of marketization well enough, but like the leaders of a Third World country facing the IMF, are afraid of the social consequences of ending consumer subsidies and other forms of dependence on the state sector.

In the political sphere, the proposed changes to the Soviet constitution, legal system, and party rules amount to much less than the establishment of a liberal state. Gorbachev has spoken of democratization primarily in the sphere of internal party affairs, and has shown little intention of ending the Communist party's monopoly of power; indeed, the political reform seeks to legitimize and therefore strengthen the CPSU's rule.[13]

---

13. This is not true in Poland and Hungary, however, whose Communist parties have taken moves toward true power-sharing and pluralism.

Nonetheless, the general principles underlying many of the reforms—that the "people" should be truly responsible for their own affairs, that higher political bodies should be answerable to lower ones, and not vice versa, that the rule of law should prevail over arbitrary police actions, with separation of powers and an independent judiciary, that there should be legal protection for property rights, the need for open discussion of public issues and the right of public dissent, the empowering of the Soviets as a forum in which the whole Soviet people can participate, and of a political culture that is more tolerant and pluralistic—come from a source fundamentally alien to the USSR's Marxist-Leninist tradition, even if they are incompletely articulated and poorly implemented in practice.

Gorbachev's repeated assertions that he is doing no more than trying to restore the original meaning of Leninism are themselves a kind of Orwellian doublespeak. Gorbachev and his allies have consistently maintained that intraparty democracy was somehow the essence of Leninism, and that the various liberal practices of open debate, secret ballot elections, and rule of law were all part of the Leninist heritage, corrupted only later by Stalin. While almost anyone would look good compared to Stalin, drawing so sharp a line between Lenin and his successor is questionable. The essence of Lenin's democratic centralism was centralism, not democracy; that is, the absolutely rigid, monolithic, and disciplined dictatorship of a hierarchically organized vanguard Communist party, speaking in the name of the *demos*. All of Lenin's vicious polemics against Karl Kautsky, Rosa Luxemburg, and various other Menshevik and Social Democratic rivals, not to mention his contempt for "bourgeois legality" and freedoms, centered around his profound conviction that a revolution could not be successfully made by a democratically run organization.

Gorbachev's claim that he is seeking to return to the true Lenin is perfectly easy to understand: having fostered a thorough denunciation of Stalinism and Brezhnevism as the root of the USSR's present predicament, he needs some point in Soviet history on which to anchor the legitimacy of the CPSU's continued rule. But Gorbachev's tactical requirements should not blind us to the fact that the democratizing and decentralizing principles which he has enunciated in both the economic and political spheres are highly subversive of some of the most fundamental precepts of both Marxism and Leninism. Indeed, if the bulk of the present economic reform proposals were put into effect, it is hard to know how the Soviet economy would be more socialist than those of other Western countries with large public sectors.

The Soviet Union could in no way be described as a liberal or democratic country now, nor do I think that it is terribly likely that *perestroika* will succeed such that the label will be thinkable any time in the near future. But at the end of history it is not necessary that all societies become successful liberal societies, merely that they end their ideological pretensions of representing different and higher forms of human society. And in this respect I believe that something very important has happened in the Soviet Union in the past few years: the criticisms of the Soviet system sanctioned by Gorbachev have been so thorough and devastating that there is very little chance of going back to either Stalinism or Brezhnevism in any simple way. Gorbachev has finally permitted people to say what they had privately understood for many years, namely, that the magical incantations of Marxism-Leninism were nonsense, that Soviet socialism was not superior to the West in any respect but was in fact a monumental failure. The conservative opposition in the USSR, consisting both of simple workers afraid of unemployment and inflation and of party officials fearful of losing their jobs and privileges, is outspoken and may be strong enough to force Gorbachev's ouster in the next few years. But what both groups desire is tradition, order, and authority; they manifest no deep commitment to Marxism-Leninism, except insofar as they have invested much of their own lives in it.[14] For authority to be restored in the Soviet Union after Gorbachev's demolition work, it must be on the basis of some new and vigorous ideology which has not yet appeared on the horizon.

IF WE ADMIT for the moment that the fascist and communist challenges to liberalism are dead, are there any other ideological competitors left? Or put another way, are there contradictions in liberal society beyond that of class that are not resolvable? Two possibilities suggest themselves, those of religion and nationalism.

---

14. This is particularly true of the leading Soviet conservative, former Second Secretary Yegor Ligachev, who has publicly recognized many of the deep defects of the Brezhnev period.

The End of History?

The rise of religious fundamentalism in recent years within the Christian, Jewish, and Muslim traditions has been widely noted. One is inclined to say that the revival of religion in some way attests to a broad unhappiness with the impersonality and spiritual vacuity of liberal consumerist societies. Yet while the emptiness at the core of liberalism is most certainly a defect in the ideology—indeed, a flaw that one does not need the perspective of religion to recognize[15]—it is not at all clear that it is remediable through politics. Modern liberalism itself was historically a consequence of the weakness of religiously-based societies which, failing to agree on the nature of the good life, could not provide even the minimal preconditions of peace and stability. In the contemporary world only Islam has offered a theocratic state as a political alternative to both liberalism and communism. But the doctrine has little appeal for non-Muslims, and it is hard to believe that the movement will take on any universal significance. Other less organized religious impulses have been successfully satisfied within the sphere of personal life that is permitted in liberal societies.

The other major "contradiction" potentially unresolvable by liberalism is the one posed by nationalism and other forms of racial and ethnic consciousness. It is certainly true that a very large degree of conflict since the Battle of Jena has had its roots in nationalism. Two cataclysmic world wars in this century have been spawned by the nationalism of the developed world in various guises, and if those passions have been muted to a certain extent in postwar Europe, they are still extremely powerful in the Third World. Nationalism has been a threat to liberalism historically in Germany, and continues to be one in isolated parts of "post-historical" Europe like Northern Ireland.

But it is not clear that nationalism represents an irreconcilable contradiction in the heart of liberalism. In the first place, nationalism is not one single phenomenon but several, ranging from mild cultural nostalgia to the highly organized and elaborately articulated doctrine of National Socialism. Only systematic nationalisms of the latter sort can qualify as a formal ideology on the level of liberalism or communism. The vast majority of the world's nationalist movements do not have a political pro-

---

15. I am thinking particularly of Rousseau and the Western philosophical tradition that flows from him that was highly critical of Lockean or Hobbesian liberalism, though one could criticize liberalism from the standpoint of classical political philosophy as well.

gram beyond the negative desire of independence *from* some other group or people, and do not offer anything like a comprehensive agenda for socio-economic organization. As such, they are compatible with doctrines and ideologies that do offer such agendas. While they may constitute a source of conflict for liberal societies, this conflict does not arise from liberalism itself so much as from the fact that the liberalism in question is incomplete. Certainly a great deal of the world's ethnic and nationalist tension can be explained in terms of peoples who are forced to live in unrepresentative political systems that they have not chosen.

While it is impossible to rule out the sudden appearance of new ideologies or previously unrecognized contradictions in liberal societies, then, the present world seems to confirm that the fundamental principles of socio-political organization have not advanced terribly far since 1806. Many of the wars and revolutions fought since that time have been undertaken in the name of ideologies which claimed to be more advanced than liberalism, but whose pretensions were ultimately unmasked by history. In the meantime, they have helped to spread the universal homogenous state to the point where it could have a significant effect on the overall character of international relations.

IV

WHAT ARE the implications of the end of history for international relations? Clearly, the vast bulk of the Third World remains very much mired in history, and will be a terrain of conflict for many years to come. But let us focus for the time being on the larger and more developed states of the world who after all account for the greater part of world politics. Russia and China are not likely to join the developed nations of the West as liberal societies any time in the foreseeable future, but suppose for a moment that Marxism-Leninism ceases to be a factor driving the foreign policies of these states—a prospect which, if not yet here, the last few years have made a real possibility. How will the overall characteristics of a de-ideologized world differ from those of the one with which we are familiar at such a hypothetical juncture?

The most common answer is—not very much. For there is a very widespread belief among many observers of international relations that underneath the skin of ideology is a hard core of great power national interest that guarantees a fairly high level of competition and conflict between nations.

Indeed, according to one academically popular school of international relations theory, conflict inheres in the international system as such, and to understand the prospects for conflict one must look at the shape of the system—for example, whether it is bipolar or multipolar— rather than at the specific character of the nations and regimes that constitute it. This school in effect applies a Hobbesian view of politics to international relations, and assumes that aggression and insecurity are universal characteristics of human societies rather than the product of specific historical circumstances.

Believers in this line of thought take the relations that existed between the participants in the classical nineteenth century European balance of power as a model for what a de-ideologized contemporary world would look like. Charles Krauthammer, for example, recently explained that if as a result of Gorbachev's reforms the USSR is shorn of Marxist-Leninist ideology, its behavior will revert to that of nineteenth century imperial Russia.[16] While he finds this more reassuring than the threat posed by a communist Russia, he implies that there will still be a substantial degree of competition and conflict in the international system, just as there was say between Russia and Britain or Wilhelmine Germany in the last century. This is, of course, a convenient point of view for people who want to admit that something major is changing in the Soviet Union, but do not want to accept responsibility for recommending the radical policy redirection implicit in such a view. But is it true?

In fact, the notion that ideology is a superstructure imposed on a substratum of permanent great power interest is a highly questionable proposition. For the way in which any state defines its national interest is not universal but rests on some kind of prior ideological basis, just as we saw that economic behavior is determined by a prior state of consciousness. In this century, states have adopted highly articulated doctrines with explicit foreign policy agendas legitimizing expansionism, like Marxism-Leninism or National Socialism.

THE EXPANSIONIST and competitive behavior of nineteenth-century European states rested on no less ideal a basis; it just so happened that the ideology driving it was less explicit than the doctrines of the twentieth cen-

---

16. See his article, "Beyond the Cold War," *New Republic,* December 19, 1988.

tury. For one thing, most "liberal" European societies were illiberal insofar as they believed in the legitimacy of imperialism, that is, the right of one nation to rule over other nations without regard for the wishes of the ruled. The justifications for imperialism varied from nation to nation, from a crude belief in the legitimacy of force, particularly when applied to non-Europeans, to the White Man's Burden and Europe's Christianizing mission, to the desire to give people of color access to the culture of Rabelais and Molière. But whatever the particular ideological basis, every "developed" country believed in the acceptability of higher civilizations ruling lower ones—including, incidentally, the United States with regard to the Philippines. This led to a drive for pure territorial aggrandizement in the latter half of the century and played no small role in causing the Great War.

The radical and deformed outgrowth of nineteenth-century imperialism was German fascism, an ideology which justified Germany's right not only to rule over non-European peoples, but over *all* non-German ones. But in retrospect it seems that Hitler represented a diseased by-path in the general course of European development, and since his fiery defeat, the legitimacy of any kind of territorial aggrandizement has been thoroughly discredited.[17] Since the Second World War, European nationalism has been defanged and shorn of any real relevance to foreign policy, with the consequence that the nineteenth-century model of great power behavior has become a serious anachronism. The most extreme form of nationalism that any Western European state has mustered since 1945 has been Gaullism, whose self-assertion has been confined largely to the realm of nuisance politics and culture. International life for the part of the world that has reached the end of history is far more preoccupied with economics than with politics or strategy.

The developed states of the West do maintain defense establishments and in the postwar period have competed vigorously for influence to meet a worldwide communist threat. This behavior has been driven, however, by an external threat from states that possess overtly expansionist ideologies, and would not exist in their absence. To take the "neo-realist" theory seriously, one would have to believe that "natural" com-

---

17. It took European colonial powers like France several years after the war to admit the illegitimacy of their empires, but decolonialization was an inevitable consequence of the Allied victory which had been based on the promise of a restoration of democratic freedoms.

petitive behavior would reassert itself among the OECD states were Russia and China to disappear from the face of the earth. That is, West Germany and France would arm themselves against each other as they did in the 1930s, Australia and New Zealand would send military advisers to block each others' advances in Africa, and the U.S.-Canadian border would become fortified. Such a prospect is, of course, ludicrous: minus Marxist-Leninist ideology, we are far more likely to see the "Common Marketization" of world politics than the disintegration of the EEC into nineteenth-century competitiveness. Indeed, as our experience in dealing with Europe on matters such as terrorism or Libya prove, they are much further gone than we down the road that denies the legitimacy of the use of force in international politics, even in self-defense.

The automatic assumption that Russia shorn of its expansionist communist ideology should pick up where the czars left off just prior to the Bolshevik Revolution is therefore a curious one. It assumes that the evolution of human consciousness has stood still in the meantime, and that the Soviets, while picking up currently fashionable ideas in the realm of economics, will return to foreign policy views a century out of date in the rest of Europe. This is certainly not what happened to China after it began its reform process. Chinese competitiveness and expansionism on the world scene have virtually disappeared: Beijing no longer sponsors Maoist insurgencies or tries to cultivate influence in distant African countries as it did in the 1960s. This is not to say that there are not troublesome aspects to contemporary Chinese foreign policy, such as the reckless sale of ballistic missile technology in the Middle East; and the PRC continues to manifest traditional great power behavior in its sponsorship of the Khmer Rouge against Vietnam. But the former is explained by commercial motives and the latter is a vestige of earlier ideologically-based rivalries. The new China far more resembles Gaullist France than pre-World War I Germany.

The real question for the future, however, is the degree to which Soviet elites have assimilated the consciousness of the universal homogenous state that is post-Hitler Europe. From their writings and from my own personal contacts with them, there is no question in my mind that the liberal Soviet intelligentsia rallying around Gorbachev has arrived at the end-of-history view in a remarkably short time, due in no small measure to the contacts they have had since the Brezhnev era with the larger European civilization around them. "New political thinking," the general rubric for their views, describes a world dominated by economic concerns, in which there are no ideological grounds for major conflict between nations, and in which, consequently, the use of military force becomes less legitimate. As Foreign Minister Shevardnadze put it in mid-1988:

> The struggle between two opposing systems is no longer a determining tendency of the present-day era. At the modern stage, the ability to build up material wealth at an accelerated rate on the basis of front-ranking science and high-level techniques and technology, and to distribute it fairly, and through joint efforts to restore and protect the resources necessary for mankind's survival acquires decisive importance.[18]

The post-historical consciousness represented by "new thinking" is only one possible future for the Soviet Union, however. There has always been a very strong current of great Russian chauvinism in the Soviet Union, which has found freer expression since the advent of *glasnost*. It may be possible to return to traditional Marxism-Leninism for a while as a simple rallying point for those who want to restore the authority that Gorbachev has dissipated. But as in Poland, Marxism-Leninism is dead as a mobilizing ideology: under its banner people cannot be made to work harder, and its adherents have lost confidence in themselves. Unlike the propagators of traditional Marxism-Leninism, however, ultra-nationalists in the USSR believe in their Slavophile cause passionately, and one gets the sense that the fascist alternative is not one that has played itself out entirely there.

The Soviet Union, then, is at a fork in the road: it can start down the path that was staked out by Western Europe forty-five years ago, a path that most of Asia has followed, or it can realize its own uniqueness and remain stuck in history. The choice it makes will be highly important for us, given the Soviet Union's size and military strength, for that power will continue to preoccupy us and slow our realization that we have already emerged on the other side of history.

---

18. *Vestnik Ministerstva Inostrannikh Del SSSR* no. 15 (August 1988), 27-46. "New thinking" does of course serve a propagandistic purpose in persuading Western audiences of Soviet good intentions. But the fact that it is good propaganda does not mean that its formulators do not take many of its ideas seriously.

V

THE PASSING of Marxism-Leninism first from China and then from the Soviet Union will mean its death as a living ideology of world historical significance. For while there may be some isolated true believers left in places like Managua, Pyongyang, or Cambridge, Massachusetts, the fact that there is not a single large state in which it is a going concern undermines completely its pretensions to being in the vanguard of human history. And the death of this ideology means the growing "Common Marketization" of international relations, and the diminution of the likelihood of large-scale conflict between states.

This does not by any means imply the end of international conflict *per se*. For the world at that point would be divided between a part that was historical and a part that was post-historical. Conflict between states still in history, and between those states and those at the end of history, would still be possible. There would still be a high and perhaps rising level of ethnic and nationalist violence, since those are impulses incompletely played out, even in parts of the post-historical world. Palestinians and Kurds, Sikhs and Tamils, Irish Catholics and Walloons, Armenians and Azeris, will continue to have their unresolved grievances. This implies that terrorism and wars of national liberation will continue to be an important item on the international agenda. But large-scale conflict must involve large states still caught in the grip of history, and they are what appear to be passing from the scene.

The end of history will be a very sad time. The struggle for recognition, the willingness to risk one's life for a purely abstract goal, the worldwide ideological struggle that called forth daring, courage, imagination, and idealism, will be replaced by economic calculation, the endless solving of technical problems, environmental concerns, and the satisfaction of sophisticated consumer demands. In the post-historical period there will be neither art nor philosophy, just the perpetual caretaking of the museum of human history. I can feel in myself, and see in others around me, a powerful nostalgia for the time when history existed. Such nostalgia, in fact, will continue to fuel competition and conflict even in the post-historical world for some time to come. Even though I recognize its inevitability, I have the most ambivalent feelings for the civilization that has been created in Europe since 1945, with its north Atlantic and Asian offshoots. Perhaps this very prospect of centuries of boredom at the end of history will serve to get history started once again. ☯

No Exit:
The Errors of Endism

Samuel P. Huntington

FOR A SECOND YEAR serious discussion of international affairs has been dominated by a major theoretical and academic issue. In 1988 the issue was American decline. The theory of declinism, articulated by many thinkers, but most notably by Paul Kennedy, became the focus of extended and intense debate. Was the United States following in the path of Great Britain and declining as a great power? To what extent was its economic base being undermined by spending too much on defense and/or too much on consumption?

The major issue in 1989 is very different. The theory of declinism has been displaced by the theory of endism. Its central element is that bad things are coming to an end.[1] Endism manifests itself in at least three ways. At its most specific level, endism hails the end of the Cold War. In the spring of 1989 the *New York Times* and the International Institute for Strategic Studies, George Kennan and George Bush, all set forth this proposition in one form or another. The end of the Cold War became the Foreign Policy Establishment's Established Truth.

At a second level, endism manifested itself in the more academic and more general proposition that wars among nation states, or at least among some types of nation states, were coming to an end. Many scholars pointed to the historical absence of wars between democratic countries and saw the multiplication of democratic regimes since 1974 as evidence that the probability of war was declining. In a related but somewhat different version of this proposition, Michael Doyle argued that wars were impossible between liberal states. In a still more sweeping

---

SAMUEL P. HUNTINGTON is Weatherland University Professor and Director of the John M. Olin Institute of Strategic Studies at Harvard University. This article appeared in the Fall 1989 issue of *The National Interest.*

formulation, John Mueller contended that the advance of civilization was making war obsolescent and that it would disappear the same way that slavery and dueling had disappeared in advanced societies.[2] Wars still might occur among backward Third World countries, but among developed countries, communist or capitalist, war was unthinkable.

The third and most extreme formulation of endism was advanced by Francis Fukuyama in a brilliant essay called "The End of History?" in the Summer issue of this journal. Fukuyama celebrates not just the end of the Cold War or the end of wars among developed nation states, but instead "the end of history as such." This results from the "unabashed victory of economic and political liberalism" and the "exhaustion of viable systematic alternatives." Like Mueller, Fukuyama concedes that wars may occur among Third World states still caught up in the historical process. But for the developed countries, the Soviet Union, and China, history is at an end.

Endism—the intellectual fad of 1989—contrasts rather dramatically with declinism—the intellectual fad of 1988. Declinism is conditionally pessimistic. It is rooted in the study of history and draws on the parallels between the United States in the late twentieth century, Britain in the late nineteenth century, and France, Spain, and other powers in earlier centuries. Its proponents and its critics debate the relevance of these parallels and argue over detailed, historical data concerning economic growth, productivity, defense spending, savings,

---

[1]Some have raised the question as to what extent endist writers are really serious in their arguments. The time and intellectual effort they have devoted to elaborating those arguments suggest that they are, and I will assume this to be the case. The arguments also deserve to be taken seriously because of their widespread popularity.

[2]Michael W. Doyle, "Kant, Liberal Legacies, and Foreign Affairs," *Philosophy and Public Affairs*, vol. 12 (Summer, Fall 1983), pp. 205-235, 323-353, and "Liberalism and World Politics," *American Political Science Review*, vol. 80 (December 1986), pp. 1151-1169; John Mueller, *Retreat from Doomsday: The Obsolescence of Major War* (New York: Basic Books, 1989). Also see Dean V. Babst, "A Force for Peace," *Industrial Research*, vol. 14 (April 1972), pp. 55-58; R.J. Rummel, "Libertarianism and International Violence, "*Journal of Conflict Resolution*, vol. 27 (March 1983), pp. 27-71; Ze'ev Maoz and Nasrin Abdolali, "Regime Types and International Conflict, 1816-1976," *Journal of Conflict Resolution*, vol. 33 (March 1989), pp. 3-35; Bruce Russett, "The Politics of an Alternative Security System: Toward a More Democratic and Therefore More Peaceful World," in Burns Weston, ed., *Alternatives to Nuclear Deterrence* (Boulder: Westview Press, 1989).

and investment.[3] Endism, on the other hand, is oriented to the future rather than the past and is unabashedly optimistic. In its most developed form, as with Fukuyama, it is rooted in philosophical speculation rather than historical analysis. It is based not so much on evidence from history as on assumptions about history. In its extreme form, declinism is historically deterministic: nations naturally, and perhaps inevitably, evolve through phases of rise, expansion, and decline. They are caught in the inexorable grip of history. In the extreme form of endism, in contrast, nations escape from history.

The message of declinism for Americans is "We're losing"; the message of endism is "We've won!" Despite or perhaps even because of its deterministic strand, declinism performs a useful historical function. It provides a warning and a goad to action in order to head off and reverse the decline that it says is taking place. It serves that purpose now as it did in its earlier manifestations in the 1950s, 1960s, and 1970s. Endism, in contrast, provides not a warning of danger but an illusion of well-being. It invites not corrective action but relaxed complacency. The consequences of its thesis being in error, hence, are far more dangerous and subversive than those that would result if the declinist thesis should be wrong.

THE END OF THE COLD WAR

"THE COLD WAR is over" was the prevailing cry in the spring of 1989. What does this mean? It typically referred to two related developments: the changes usually referred to as glasnost and perestroika in the Soviet Union and the improvements that were occurring in Soviet-American relations. "The cold war," as the *New York Times* put it, "of poisonous Soviet-American feelings, of domestic political hysteria, of events enlarged and distorted by East-West confrontation, of almost perpetual diplomatic deadlock is over."[4] Several questions can be raised about this proposition.

First, is it really true? The easing in Soviet-American relations in the late 1950s was followed by the Berlin and Cuban crises; detente in the early 1970s was followed by Angola and Afghanistan. How do we know that the current relaxation is not simply another swing of the cycle? One answer is that the changes occurring within the Soviet Union are far more funda-

---

[3]For a careful analysis of the evidence and arguments on this issue, see Joseph S. Nye, Jr.'s forthcoming book, *American Power: Past and Future* (New York: Basic Books).
[4]"The Cold War Is Over," *The New York Times*, April 2, 1989, p. E30.

mental than those that have occurred in the past, and this is certainly the case. The opening up of political debate, limited but real competition in elections, the formation of political groups outside the Party, the virtual abandonment, indeed, of the idea of a monolithic party, the assertion of power by the Supreme Soviet—all these will, if continued, lead to a drastically different Soviet political system. The price of attempting to reverse them increases daily, but it would be rash to conclude that they are as yet irreversible, and the costs of reversing them could decline in the future.

On the international level, the Soviets have cooperated in resolving regional conflicts in the Persian Gulf, southern Africa, and Indochina. They have promised to reduce their overall military forces and their deployments in Eastern Europe. As yet, however, no perceptible changes have taken place in Soviet force structure, Soviet deployments, or Soviet output of military equipment. Even if these do occur, the competition between the United States and the Soviet Union for influence and power in world affairs will still go on. It has been continuing as President Bush and President Gorbachev attempt to woo Eastern and Western European publics. Europe, it is well to remember, is where the Cold War started. It is the overwhelmingly preeminent stake in the Cold War, and Gorbachev's public relations can be as much a threat to American interests in Europe as were Brezhnev's tanks (which, for the moment at any rate, Gorbachev also has).

Let us, however, concede that in some meaningful and not transitory sense the Cold War is over and that a real change has occurred in Soviet-American relations. How do the proponents of this thesis see the post-Cold War world? The "we-they world" that has existed, the editors of the *New York Times* assure us, is giving way "to the more traditional struggles of great powers." In a similar vein, George Kennan alleges that the Soviet Union "should now be regarded essentially as another great power, like other great powers." Its interests may differ from ours but these differences can be "adjusted by the normal means of compromise and accommodation."[5]

Russia was, however, just "another great power" for several centuries before it became a communist state. As a great power, Russia frequently deployed its armies into Europe and repeatedly crushed popular uprisings in central Europe. Soviet troops bloodily suppressed the Hungarian

---

[5]"Just Another Great Power," *The New York Times,* April 9, 1989, p. E25.

Revolution in 1956 and trampled the embryonic Czech democracy in 1968. Russian troops bloodily suppressed the Hungarian revolution of 1848-49 and violently put down uprisings in Poland in 1831 and again in 1863-64. Soviet forces occupied Berlin in 1945; Russian troops occupied and burnt Berlin in 1760. In pursuit of Russia's interests as a great power, Russian troops appeared many places where as yet Soviet troops have not. In 1799 Russian troops occupied Milan and Turin and fought a battle on the outskirts of Zurich. The same year, they occupied the Ionian islands off Greece and stayed there until 1807. These excursions preceded Napoleon's invasion of Russia. As a great power, Russia regularly participated in the partitions of Poland. In 1914 Nicholas II directly ruled more of Europe (including most of Poland) than Gorbachev does today.

The past record of Russia as a "normal" great power, therefore, is not reassuring for either the liberty of Eastern Europe or the security of Western Europe. Some suggest that the liberalizing and democratizing trends in the Soviet Union will prevent that country from bludgeoning other countries in the manner of the tsars. One cannot assume, Fukuyama argues, that "the evolution of human consciousness has stood still" and that "the Soviets will return to foreign policy views a century out of date in the rest of Europe." Fukuyama is right: one cannot assume that the Soviets will revert to the bad old ways of the past. One also cannot assume that they will not. Gorbachev may be able to discard communism but he cannot discard geography and the geopolitical imperatives that have shaped Russian and Soviet behavior for centuries. And, as any Latin American will quickly point out, even a truly democratic superpower is capable of intervening militarily in the affairs of its smaller neighbors.

The era of the Cold War, John Lewis Gaddis reminds us, has also been the era of the Long Peace, the longest period in history without hot war between major powers. Does the end of the Cold War mean the end of the Long Peace? Two central elements of both have been bipolarity and nuclear weapons: they have in considerable measure defined both the Soviet-American rivalry and its limits. The end of the Cold War will mean a loosening of bipolarity even if it does not mean, as some declinists predict, a world of five or more roughly equal major powers. The delegitimation of nuclear weapons and the increasing constraints on their deployment and potential use could increase the probability of conventional war.

Active American involvement in world affairs has been substantially limited to two world wars and one prolonged and ideologically-driven cold war. In the absence of the Kaiser, Hitler, Stalin, and Brezhnev, the American inclination may well be to relax and to assume that peace, goodwill, and international cooperation will prevail: that if the Cold War is over, American relations with the Soviet Union will be similar to its relations with Canada, France, or Japan. Americans tend to see competition and conflict as normal and even desirable features of their domestic economy and politics and yet perversely assume them to be abnormal and undesirable in relations among states. In fact, however, the history of the relations among great powers, when it has not been the history of hot wars, has usually been the history of cold wars.

The end of the Cold War does not mean the end of political, ideological, diplomatic, economic, technological, or even military rivalry among nations. It does not mean the end of the struggle for power and influence. It very probably does mean increased instability, unpredictability, and violence in international affairs. It could mean the end of the Long Peace.

THE END OF WAR

A SECOND manifestation of endism postulates the end of war between certain types of nation states. A number of authors, including Dean V. Babst, R.J. Rummel, and Bruce Russett, have pointed to the fact that no significant interstate wars have occurred between democratic regimes since the emergence of such regimes in the early nineteenth century. Michael Doyle has similarly argued that a "pacific union" exists among liberal regimes (which includes and is slightly broader than the class of democratic regimes, as defined by most scholars). *"[C]onstitutionally secure liberal states,"* he says, *"have yet to engage in war with each other. Even threats of war have been regarded as illegitimate."*

Given the large number of wars between non-democratic regimes and between democratic regimes and non-democratic regimes, the almost total absence of armed conflict between democratic regimes is indeed striking. It is, as Bruce Russett says, "perhaps the strongest nontrivial or non-tautological statement that can be made about international relations." It is also plausible to believe that this absence of war may stem from the nature of the regime. Democracy is a means for the peaceful resolution of disputes, involving negotiation and compromise as well as elections and voting. The leaders of democracies may well expect that they ought to be able to resolve through peaceful means their differences with the leaders of other democracies. In the years since World War II, for instance, several conflicts which could or did lead to war between countries tended to moderate when the countries became democratic. The controversies between Britain and Argentina, Guatemala, and Spain over the remnants of empire (one of which did lead to war and one of which produced significant military deployment) moderated considerably when those three countries became democratic. The conflict between Greece and Turkey similarly seemed to ease in the 1980s after both countries had democratically elected regimes.

The democratic "zone of peace" is a dramatic historical phenomenon. If that relationship continues to hold and if democracy continues to spread, wars should become less frequent in the future than they have been in the past. This is one endist argument that has a strong empirical base. Three qualifications have to be noted, however, to its implications for the end of war.

First, democracies are still a minority among the world's regimes. The 1989 Freedom House survey classified 60 out of 167 sovereign states as "free" according to its rather generous definition of freedom. Multiple possibilities for war thus continue to exist among the 107 states that are not free, and between those states and the democratic states.

Second, the number of democratic states has been growing, but it tends to grow irregularly in a two-step forward, one-step backward pattern. A major wave of democratization occurred in the nineteenth century, but then significant reversals to authoritarianism took place in the 1920s and 1930s. A second wave of democratization after World War II was followed by several reversals in the 1960s and 1970s. A third wave of democratization began in 1974, with fifteen to twenty countries shifting in a democratic direction since then. If the previous pattern prevails, some of these new democracies are likely to revert to authoritarianism. Hence the possibility of war could increase rather than decrease in the immediate future, although still remaining less than it was prior to 1974.

Finally, peace among democratic states could be related to extraneous accidental factors and not to the nature of democracy. In the nineteenth century, for instance, wars tended to occur between geographical neighbors. Democratic states were few in number and seldom bordered on each other. Hence the absence of war could be caused by the absence of propinquity.[6] Since World War II most democratic countries have been members of the alliance system led by the United States, which has been directed against an alliance of non-democratic regimes and within which the hegemonic position of the U.S. has precluded war between other alliance members (e.g., between Greece and Turkey). If American leadership weakens and the alliance system loosens, the probability of war between its erstwhile members, democratic or otherwise, could well increase.

The "democratic zone of peace" argument is thus valid as far as it goes, but it may not go all that far. In his book, *Retreat from Doomsday*, John Mueller argues for the growing obsolescence of war on more general grounds. He sees the Long Peace since 1945 not as the result of bipolarity or nuclear weapons but rather as the result of a learning experience that wars do not pay and that there are few conflicts of interest among countries where it would be reasonable for either side to resort to war to achieve its goals. World War II was an aberration from the twentieth-century trend away from war due largely to the idiosyncratic and irrational personality of Hitler. As countries become more developed and civilized, they will become more peaceful. Denmark is the future model for individual countries, U.S.-Canadian relations the future model for relations between countries.

Mueller makes much of the argument that war will become "obsolete, subrationally unthinkable," and unacceptable in civilized society in the way slavery and dueling have become. Why, however, are those social practices the appropriate parallels to war? Why not murder? Murder has been unacceptable in civilized societies for millennia, and yet it seems unlikely that the murder rate in twentieth-century New York is less than it was in fifth-century Athens. While major wars between developed countries have not occurred since World War II, interstate and intrastate violence has been widespread with the casualties numbering in the tens of millions.

Mueller himself substantially qualifies his case. He agrees that wars will continue among less developed countries. He also concedes that irrational leaders on the Hitler model could involve their countries in future wars. Economic considerations motivate strongly against war, he says, but economic prosperity "is not always an overriding goal even now." Territo-

---

[6]See J. David Singer and Melvin Small, "The War-Proneness of Democratic Regimes, 1815-1965," *Jerusalem Journal of International Relations*, vol. I (Summer 1976), p. 67.

rial issues exist even in the developed world that "could lead to wars of expansion or territorial readjustment." The Cold War is being resolved peacefully, "but there is no firm guarantee that this trend will continue. "

A more general problem may also exist with the end-of-war or even a decline-in-war thesis. As Michimi Muranushi of Yale has pointed out, peace can be self-limiting rather than cumulative. If relations between two countries become more peaceful, this may, in some circumstances, increase the probability that either or both of those countries will go to war with a third country. The Hitler-Stalin pact paves the way for the attacks on Poland; normalization of U.S.-China relations precipitates China's war with Vietnam. If the Soviet threat disappears, so also does an inhibitor of Greek-Turkish war.

In addition, if more countries become like Denmark, forswearing war and committing themselves to material comfort, that in itself may produce a situation which other countries will wish to exploit. History is full of examples of leaner, meaner societies overrunning richer, less martial ones.

THE END OF HISTORY

"THE END OF history" is a sweeping, dramatic, and provocative phrase. What does Fukuyama mean by it? The heart of Fukuyama's argument is an alleged change in political consciousness throughout the principal societies in the world and the emergence of a pervasive consensus on liberal-democratic principles. It posits the triumph of one ideology and the consequent end of ideology and ideological conflict as significant factors in human existence. His choice of language suggests, however, that he may have something more sweeping in mind than simply the obsolescence of war highlighted by Mueller or the end of ideology predicted by Daniel Bell twenty-five years ago.

Insofar as it is focused on war, Fukuyama's argument suffers all the weaknesses that Mueller's does. He admits that "conflict between states still in history, and between those states and those at the end of history, would still be possible." At the same time he includes China and the Soviet Union among those states that are out of history. Current Soviet leaders, he says, have arrived at the "end-of-history view" and "assimilated the consciousness of the universal homogenous state that is post-Hitler Europe"; yet he also admits that the Soviet Union could turn to Slavophile Russian chauvinism and thus remain stuck in history.

The Errors of Endism

Fukuyama ridicules the idea that Germany and France might fight each other again. That is a valid but irrelevant point. A hundred years ago one could have validly made the point that Pennsylvania and Virginia would not fight each other again. That did not prevent the United States, of which each was a part, from engaging in world wars in the subsequent century. One trend in history is the amalgamation of smaller units into larger ones. The probability of war between the smaller units declines but the probability of war between the larger amalgamated units does not necessarily change. A united European community may end the possibility of Franco-German war; it does not end the possibility of war between that community and other political units.

With respect to China, Fukuyama argues that "Chinese competitiveness and expansionism on the world scene have virtually disappeared" and, he implies strongly, will not reappear. A more persuasive argument, however, could be made for exactly the opposite proposition that Chinese expansionism has yet to appear on the world scene. Britain and France, Germany and Japan, the United States and the Soviet Union, all became expansionist and imperialist powers in the course of industrialization. China is just beginning seriously to develop its industrial strength. Maybe China will be different from all the other major powers and not attempt to expand its influence and control as it industrializes. But how can one be confident that it will pursue this deviant course? And if it follows the more familiar pattern, a billion Chinese engaged in imperial expansion are likely to impose a lot of history on the rest of the world.

Fukuyama quite appropriately emphasizes the role of consciousness, ideas, and ideology in motivating and shaping the actions of men and nations. He is also right in pointing to the virtual end of the appeal of communism as an ideology. Ideologically, communism has been "the grand failure" that Brzezinski labels it. It is erroneous, however, to jump from the decline of communism to the global triumph of liberalism and the disappearance of ideology as a force in world affairs.

First, revivals are possible. A set of ideas or an ideology may fade from the scene in one generation only to reappear with renewed strength a generation or two later. From the 1940s to the 1960s, dominant currents in economic thinking were Keynesianism, welfare statism, social democracy, and planning. It was hard to find much support for classical economic liberalism. By the late 1970s, however, the latter had staged an amazing comeback: economists and economic institutions were devoted to The Plan in the 1950s; they have been devoted to The Market in the 1980s. Somewhat similarly, social scientists in the decades immediately after World War II argued that religion, ethnic consciousness, and nationalism would all be done in by economic development and modernization. But in the 1980s these have been the dominant bases of political action in most societies. The revival of religion is now a global phenomenon. Communism may be down for the moment, but it is rash to assume that it is out for all time.

Second, the universal acceptance of liberal democracy does not preclude conflicts within liberalism. The history of ideology is the history of schism. Struggles between those who profess different versions of a common ideology are often more intense and vicious than struggles between those espousing entirely different ideologies. To a believer the heretic is worse than the nonbeliever. An ideological consensus on Christianity existed in Europe in 1500 but that did not prevent Protestants and Catholics from slaughtering each other for the next century and a half. Socialists and communists, Trotskyites and Leninists, Shi'ites and Sunnis have treated each other in similar fashion.

Third, the triumph of one ideology does not preclude the emergence of new ideologies. Nations and societies presumably will continue to evolve. New challenges to human well-being will emerge, and people will develop new concepts, theories, and ideologies as to how those challenges should be met. Unless all social, economic, and political distinctions disappear, people will also develop belief systems that legitimate what they have and justify their getting more. Among its other functions, for instance, communism historically legitimized the power of intellectuals and bureaucrats. If it is gone for good, it seems highly likely that intellectuals and bureaucrats will develop new sets of ideas to rationalize their claims to power and wealth.

Fourth, has liberal democracy really triumphed? Fukuyama admits that it has not won out in the Third World. To what extent, however, has it really been accepted in the Soviet Union and China? Between them these societies encompass well over one quarter of the world's population. If any one trend is operative in the world today it is for societies to turn back toward their traditional cultures, values, and patterns of behavior. This trend is manifest in the revival of traditional identities and characters of Eastern European countries, escaping from the deadly uniformity of Soviet-imposed communism, and also in the increasing differentiation among the republics within the Soviet Union itself. Russia and China do not lack elements of liberalism and democracy in their histories. These are, however, minor chords, and their subordinate importance is underlined by the contemporary problems facing economic liberalism in the Soviet Union and political democracy in communist China.

More generally, Fukuyama's thesis itself reflects not the disappearance of Marxism but its pervasiveness. His image of the end of history is straight from Marx. Fukuyama speaks of the "universal homogeneous state," in which "all prior contradictions are resolved and all human needs are satisfied." What is this but the Marxist image of a society without class conflict or other contradictions organized on the basis of from each according to his abilities and to each according to his needs? The struggles of history, Fukuyama says, "will be replaced by economic calculation, the endless solving of technical problems, environmental concerns, and the satisfaction of sophisticated consumer demands." Engels said it even more succinctly: "The government of persons is replaced by the administration of things and the direction of the process of production." Fukuyama says liberalism is the end of history. Marx says communism "is the solution to the riddle of history." They are basically saying the same thing and, most importantly, they are thinking the same way. Marxist ideology is alive and well in Fukuyama's arguments to refute it.

TWO FALLACIES

THE SOVIET UNION is increasingly preoccupied with its own problems and a significant political loosening has occurred in that country. The ideological intensity of the early Cold War has virtually disappeared, and the probability of hot war between the two superpowers is as low as it has ever been. War is even more unlikely between any of the advanced industrialized democracies. On these points, endist propositions are accurate. The more extensive formulations of the endist argument, however, suffer from two basic fallacies.

First, endism overemphasizes the predictability of history and the permanence of the moment. Current trends may or may not continue into the future. Past experience certainly suggests that they are unlikely to do so. The record of past predictions by social scientists is not a happy one. Fifteen years ago, just as the democratic wave was beginning, political analysts were elaborating fundamental reasons why authoritarianism had to prevail in the Third World. Ten years ago foreign policy journals

Samuel P. Huntington

Samuel P. Huntington

were filled with warnings of the rise of Soviet military power and political influence throughout the world. Five years ago what analyst of the Soviet Union predicted the extent of the political changes that have occurred in that country? Given the limitations of human foresight, endist predictions of the end of war and ideological conflict deserve a heavy dose of skepticism. Indeed, in the benign atmosphere of the moment, it is sobering to speculate on the possible future horrors that social analysts are now failing to predict.

Second, endism tends to ignore the weakness and irrationality of human nature. Endist arguments often assume that because it would be rational for human beings to focus on their economic well-being, they will act in that way, and therefore they will not engage in wars that do not meet the tests of cost-benefit analysis or in ideological conflicts that are much ado about nothing. Human beings are at times rational, generous, creative, and wise, but they are also often stupid, selfish, cruel, and sinful. The struggle that is history began with the eating of the forbidden fruit and is rooted in human nature. In history there may be total defeats, but there are no final solutions. So long as human beings exist, there is no exit from the traumas of history.

To hope for the benign end of history is human. To expect it to happen is unrealistic. To plan on it happening is disastrous.

Liberalism and World Politics

Michael W. Doyle

PROMOTING FREEDOM will produce peace, we have often been told. In a speech before the British Parliament in June of 1982, President Reagan proclaimed that governments founded on a respect for individual liberty exercise "restraint" and "peaceful intentions" in their foreign policy. He then announced a "crusade for freedom" and a "campaign for democratic development" (Reagan, June 9, 1982).

In making these claims the president joined a long list of liberal theorists (and propagandists) and echoed an old argument: the aggressive instincts of authoritarian leaders and totalitarian ruling parties make for war. Liberal states, founded on such individual rights as equality before the law, free speech and other civil liberties, private property, and elected representation are fundamentally against war this argument asserts. When the citizens who bear the burdens of war elect their governments, wars become impossible. Furthermore, citizens appreciate that the benefits of trade can be enjoyed only under conditions of peace. Thus the very existence of liberal states, such as the U.S., Japan, and our European allies, makes for peace.

Building on a growing literature in international political science, I reexamine the liberal claim President Reagan reiterated for us. I look at three distinct theoretical traditions of liberalism, attributable to three

MICHAEL DOYLE is Professor of Political Science at Princeton University. This article appeared in the December 1986 issue of the *American Political Science Review*. © 1986 by the American Political Science Association.

theorists: Schumpeter, a brilliant explicator of the liberal pacifism the president invoked; Machiavelli, a classical republican whose glory is an imperialism we often practice; and Kant.

Despite the contradictions of liberal pacifism and liberal imperialism, I find, with Kant and other liberal republicans, that liberalism does leave a coherent legacy on foreign affairs. Liberal states are different. They are indeed peaceful, yet they are also prone to make war, as the U.S. and our "freedom fighters" are now doing, not so covertly, against Nicaragua. Liberal states have created a separate peace, as Kant argued they would, and have also discovered liberal reasons for aggression, as he feared they might. I conclude by arguing that the differences among liberal pacifism, liberal imperialism, and Kant's liberal internationalism are not arbitrary but rooted in differing conceptions of the citizen and the state.

LIBERAL PACIFISM

THERE IS NO canonical description of liberalism. What we tend to call liberal resembles a family portrait of principles and institutions, recognizable by certain characteristics—for example, individual freedom, political participation, private property, and equality of opportunity— that most liberal states share, although none has perfected them all. Joseph Schumpeter clearly fits within this family when he considers the international effects of capitalism and democracy.

Schumpeter's "Sociology of Imperialisms," published in 1919, made a coherent and sustained argument concerning the pacifying (in the sense of nonaggressive) effects of liberal institutions and principles (Schumpeter, 1955; see also Doyle, 1986, pp. 155-59). Unlike some of the earlier liberal theorists who focused on a single feature such as trade (Montesquieu, 1949, vol. 1, bk. 20, chap. 1) or failed to examine critically the arguments they were advancing, Schumpeter saw the interaction of capitalism and democracy as the foundation of liberal pacifism, and he tested his arguments in a sociology of historical imperialisms.

He defines *imperialism* as "an objectless disposition on the part of a state to unlimited forcible expansion" (Schumpeter, 1955, p. 6). Excluding imperialisms that were mere "catchwords" and those that were "objectful" (e.g., defensive imperialism), he traces the roots of objectless imperialism to three sources, each an atavism. Modern imperialism, according to Schumpeter, resulted from the combined impact of a "war machine," warlike instincts, and export monopolism.

Once necessary, the war machine later developed a life of its own and took control of a state's foreign policy: "Created by the wars that required it, the machine now created the wars it required" (Schumpeter, 1955, p. 25). Thus, Schumpeter tells us that the army of ancient Egypt, created to drive the Hyksos out of Egypt, took over the state and pursued militaristic imperialism. Like the later armies of the courts of absolutist Europe, it fought wars for the sake of glory and booty, for the sake of warriors and monarchs—wars *gratia* warriors.

A warlike disposition, elsewhere called "instinctual elements of bloody primitivism," is the natural ideology of a war machine. It also exists independently; the Persians, says Schumpeter (1955, pp. 25-32), were a warrior nation from the outset.

Under modern capitalism, export monopolists, the third source of modern imperialism, push for imperialist expansion as a way to expand their closed markets. The absolute monarchies were the last clear-cut imperialisms. Nineteenth-century imperialisms merely represent the vestiges of the imperialisms created by Louis XIV and Catherine the Great. Thus, the export monopolists are an atavism of the absolute monarchies, for they depend completely on the tariffs imposed by the monarchs and their militaristic successors for revenue (Schumpeter, 1955, p. 82-83). Without tariffs, monopolies would be eliminated by foreign competition.

Modern (nineteenth century) imperialism, therefore, rests on an atavistic war machine, militaristic attitudes left over from the days of monarchical wars, and export monopolism, which is nothing more than the economic residue of monarchical finance. In the modern era, imperialists gratify their private interests. From the national perspective, their imperialistic wars are objectless.

Schumpeter's theme now emerges. Capitalism and democracy are forces for peace. Indeed, they are antithetical to imperialism. For Schumpeter, the further development of capitalism and democracy means that imperialism will inevitably disappear. He maintains that capitalism produces an unwarlike disposition; its populace is "democratized, individualized, rationalized" (Schumpeter, 1955, p. 68). The people's energies are daily absorbed in production., The disciplines of industry and the market train people in "economic rationalism"; the instability of industrial life necessitates calculation. Capitalism also "individualizes"; "subjective opportunities" replace the "immutable factors" of traditional, hierarchical society. Rational individuals demand democratic governance.

Democratic capitalism leads to peace. As evidence, Schumpeter claims that throughout the capitalist world an opposition has arisen to "war, expansion, cabinet diplomacy"; that contemporary capitalism is associated with peace parties; and that the industrial worker of capitalism is "vigorously anti-imperialist." In addition, he points out that the capitalist world has developed means of preventing war, such as the Hague Court and that the least feudal, most capitalist society— the United States—has demonstrated the least imperialistic tendencies (Schumpeter, 1955, pp. 95-96). An example of the lack of imperialistic tendencies in the U.S., Schumpeter thought, was our leaving over half of Mexico unconquered in the war of 1846-48.

Schumpeter's explanation for liberal pacifism is quite simple: Only war profiteers and military aristocrats gain from wars. No democracy would pursue a minority interest and tolerate the high costs of imperialism. When free trade prevails, "no class" gains from forcible expansion because

> foreign raw materials and food stuffs are as accessible to each nation as though they were in its own territory. Where the cultural backwardness of a region makes normal economic intercourse dependent on colonization it does not matter, assuming free trade, which of the "civilized" nations undertakes the task of colonization. (Schumpeter, 1955, pp. 75-76)

Schumpeter's arguments are difficult to evaluate. In partial tests of quasi-Schumpeterian propositions, Michael Haas (1974, pp. 464-65) discovered a cluster that associates democracy, development, and sustained modernization with peaceful conditions. However, M. Small and J. D. Singer (1976) have discovered that there is no clearly negative correlation between democracy and war in the period 1816-1965—the period that would be central to Schumpeter's argument (see also Wilkenfeld, 1968, Wright, 1942, p. 841).

Later in his career, in *Capitalism, Socialism, and Democracy*, Schumpeter, (1950, pp. 127-28) acknowledged that "almost purely bourgeois commonwealths were often aggressive when it seemed to pay—like the Athenian or the Venetian commonwealths." Yet he stuck to his pacifistic guns, restating the view that capitalist democracy "steadily tells . . . against the use of military force and for peaceful arrangements, even when the balance of pecuniary advantage is clearly on the side of war which, under modern circumstances, is not in general very likely" (Schumpeter, 1950, p. 128).[1] A recent study by R. J. Rummel (1983) of "libertarianism" and international violence is the closest test Schumpeterian pacifism has received. "Free" states (those enjoying political and economic freedom) were shown to have considerably less conflict at or above the level of economic sanctions than "nonfree" states. The free states, the partly free states (including the democratic socialist countries such as Sweden), and the nonfree states accounted for 24%, 26%, and 61%, respectively, of the international violence during the period examined.

These effects are impressive but not conclusive for the Schumpeterian thesis. The data are limited, in this test, to the period 1976 to 1980. It includes, for example, the Russo-Afghan War, the Vietnamese invasion of Cambodia, China's invasion of Vietnam, and Tanzania's invasion of Uganda but just misses the U.S.' quasi-covert intervention in Angola (1975) and our not so covert war against Nicaragua (1981). More importantly, it excludes the cold war period, with its numerous interventions, and the long history of colonial wars (the Boer War, the Spanish-American War, the Mexican Intervention, etc.) that marked the history of liberal, including democratic capitalist, states (Doyle, 1983b; Chan, 1984; Weede, 1984).

The discrepancy between the warlike history of liberal states and Schumpeter's pacifistic expectations highlights three extreme assumptions. First, his "materialistic monism" leaves little room for noneconomic objectives, whether espoused by states or individuals. Neither glory, nor prestige, nor ideological justification, nor the pure power of ruling shapes policy. These nonmaterial goals leave little room for positive-sum gains, such as the comparative advantages of trade. Second, and relatedly, the same is true for his states. The political life of individuals seems to have been homogenized at the same time as the individuals were "rationalized, individualized, and democratized." Citizens—capitalists and workers, rural and urban—seek material welfare. Schumpeter seems to presume that ruling makes no difference. He also presumes that no one is prepared to take those measures (such as stirring up foreign quarrels to preserve a

---

1. He notes that testing this proposition is likely to be very difficult, requiring "detailed historical analysis." However, the bourgeois attitude toward the military, the spirit and manner by which bourgeois societies wage war, and the readiness with which they submit to military rule during a prolonged war are "conclusive in themselves" (Schumpeter, 1950, p. 129).

domestic ruling coalition) that enhance one's political power, despite detrimental effects on mass welfare. Third, like domestic politics, world politics are homogenized. Materially monistic and democratically capitalist, all states evolve toward free trade and liberty together. Countries differently constituted seem to disappear from Schumpeter's analysis. "Civilized" nations govern "culturally backward" *regions*. These assumptions are not shared by Machiavelli's theory of liberalism.

LIBERAL IMPERIALISM

MACHIAVELLI ARGUES, not only that republics are not pacifistic, but that they are the best form of state for imperial expansion. Establishing a republic fit for imperial expansion is, moreover, the best way to guarantee the survival of a state.

Machiavelli's republic is a classical mixed republic. It is not a democracy— which he thought would quickly degenerate into a tyranny—but is characterized by social equality, popular liberty, and political participation (Machiavelli, 1950, bk. 1, chap. 2, p. 112; see also Huliung 1983, chap. 2; Mansfield, 1970; Pocock, 1975, pp. 198-99; Skinner, 1981, chap. 3). The consuls serve as "kings," the senate as an aristocracy managing the state, and the people in the assembly as the source of strength.

Liberty results from "disunion"—the competition and necessity for compromise required by the division of powers among senate, consuls, and tribunes (the last representing the common people). Liberty also results from the popular veto. The powerful few threaten the rest with tyranny, Machiavelli says, because they seek to dominate. The mass demands not to be dominated, and their veto thus preserves the liberties of the state (Machiavelli, 1950, bk. 1, chap. 5, p.122). However, since the people and the rulers have different social characters, the people need to be "managed" by the few to avoid having their recklessness overturn or their fecklessness undermine the ability of the state to expand (Machiavelli, 1950, bk. 1, chap. 53, pp. 249-50). Thus the senate and the consuls plan expansion, consult oracles, and employ religion to manage the resources that the energy of the people supplies. Strength, and then imperial expansion, results from the way liberty encourages increased population and property, which grow when the citizens know their lives and goods are secure from arbitrary seizure. Free citizens equip large armies and provide soldiers who fight for public glory and the common good because these are, in fact, their own (Machiavelli, 1950, bk. 2, chap. 2, pp. 287-90). If you seek the honor of having your state expand, Machiavelli advises, you should organize it as a free and popular republic like Rome rather than as an aristocratic republic like Sparta or Venice. Expansion thus calls for a free republic.

"Necessity"—political survival—calls for expansion. If a stable aristocratic republic is forced by foreign conflict "to extend her territory, in such a case we shall see her foundations give way and herself quickly brought to ruin"; if, on the other hand, domestic security prevails, "the continued tranquillity would enervate her, or provoke internal dissensions, which together, or either of them separately, will apt to prove her ruin" (Machiavelli, 1950, bk. 1, chap. 6, p. 129). Machiavelli therefore believes it is necessary to take the constitution of Rome, rather than that of Sparta or Venice, as our model.

Hence, this belief leads to liberal imperialism. We are lovers of glory, Machiavelli announces. We seek to rule or, at least, to avoid being oppressed. In either case, we want more for ourselves and our states than just material welfare (materialistic monism). Because other states with similar aims thereby threaten us, we prepare ourselves for expansion. Because our fellow citizens threaten us if we do not allow them either to satisfy their ambition or to release their political energies through imperial expansion, we expand.

There is considerable historical evidence for liberal imperialism. Machiavelli's (Polybius's) Rome and Thucydides' Athens both were imperial republics in the Machiavellian sense (Thucydides, 1954, bk. 6). The historical record of numerous U.S. interventions in the postwar period supports Machiavelli's argument (Aron, 1973, chaps. 3-4; Barnet, 1968, chap. 11), but the current record of liberal pacifism, weak as it is, calls some of his insights into question. To the extent that the modern populace actually controls (and thus unbalances) the mixed republic, its diffidence may outweigh elite ("senatorial") aggressiveness.

We can conclude either that (1) liberal pacifism has at least taken over with the further development of capitalist democracy, as Schumpeter predicted it would or that (2) the mixed record of liberalism—pacifism and imperialism— indicates that some liberal states are Schumpeterian democracies while others are Machiavellian republics. Before we accept either conclusion, however, we must consider a third apparent regularity of modern world politics.

Michael W. Doyle

MODERN LIBERALISM carries with it two legacies. They do not affect liberal states separately, according to whether they are pacifistic or imperialistic, but simultaneously.

The first of these legacies is the pacification of foreign relations among liberal states.[2] During the nineteenth century, the United States and Great Britain engaged in nearly continual strife; however, after the Reform Act of 1832 defined actual representation as the formal source of the sovereignty of the British parliament, Britain and the United States negotiated their disputes. They negotiated despite, for example, British grievances during the Civil War against the North's blockade of the South, with which Britain had close economic ties. Despite severe Anglo-French colonial rivalry, liberal France and liberal Britain formed an entente against illiberal Germany before World War I. And from 1914 to 1915, Italy, the liberal member of the Triple Alliance with Germany and Austria, chose not to fulfill its obligations under that treaty to support its allies. Instead, Italy joined in an alliance with Britain and France, which prevented it from having to fight other liberal states and then declared war on Germany and Austria. Despite generations of Anglo-American tension and Britain's wartime restrictions on American trade with Germany, the United States leaned toward Britain and France from 1914 to 1917 before entering World War I on their side.

Beginning in the eighteenth century and slowly growing since then, a zone of peace, which Kant called the "pacific federation" or "pacific union," has begun to be established among liberal societies. More than 40 liberal

---

2. Clarence Streit (1938, pp. 88, 90–92) seems to have been the first to point out (in contemporary foreign relations) the empirical tendency of democracies to maintain peace among themselves, and he made this the foundation of his proposal for a (non-Kantian) federal union of the 15 leading democracies of the 1930s. In a very interesting book, Ferdinand Hermens (1944) explored some of the policy implications of Streit's analysis. D. V. Babst (1972, pp. 55–58) performed a quantitative study of this phenomenon of "democratic peace," and R. J. Rummel (1983) did a similar study of "libertarianism" (in the sense of laissez faire) focusing on the postwar period that drew on an unpublished study (Project No. 48) noted in Appendix 1 of his *Understanding Conflict and War* (1979, p. 386). I use the term *liberal* in a wider, Kantian sense in my discussion of this issue (Doyle, 1983a). In that essay I survey the period from 1790 to the present and find no war among liberal states.

states currently make up the union. Most are in Europe and North America, but they can be found on every continent, as Appendix 1 indicates.

Here the predictions of liberal pacifists (and President Reagan) are borne out: liberal states do exercise peaceful restraint, and a separate peace exists among them. This separate peace provides a solid foundation for the United States' crucial alliances with the liberal powers, e.g., the North Atlantic Treaty Organization and our Japanese alliance. This foundation appears to be impervious to the quarrels with our allies that bedeviled the Carter and Reagan administrations. It also offers the promise of a continuing peace among liberal states and as the number of liberal states increases, it announces the possibility of global peace this side of the grave or world conquest.

Of course, the probability of the outbreak of war in any given year between any two given states is low. The occurrence of a war between any two adjacent states, considered over a long period of time, would be more probable. The apparent absence of war between liberal states, whether adjacent or not, for almost 200 years thus may have significance. Similar claims cannot be made for feudal, fascist, communist, authoritarian, or totalitarian forms of rule (Doyle, 1983a, pp. 222), nor for pluralistic or merely similar societies. More significant perhaps is that when states are forced to decide on which side of an impending world war they will fight, liberal states all wind up on the same side despite the complexity of the paths that take them there. These characteristics do not prove that the peace among liberals is statistically significant nor that liberalism is the sole valid explanation for the peace.[3] They do suggest that we consider the possibility that liberals have indeed established a separate peace—but only among themselves.

Liberalism also carries with it a second legacy: international "imprudence" (Hume, 1963, pp. 346 47). Peaceful restraint only seems to work in liberals' relations with other liberals. Liberal states have fought numerous wars with non-liberal states. (For a list of international wars since 1816 see Appendix 2.)

---

3. Babst (1972) did make a preliminary test of the significance of the distribution of alliance partners in World War I. He found that the possibility that the actual distribution of alliance partners could have occurred by chance was less than 1% (Babst, 1972, p. 56). However, this assumes that there was an equal possibility that any two nations could have gone to war with each other, and this is a strong assumption. Rummel (1983) has a further discussion of the issue of statistical significance as it applies to his libertarian thesis.

Many of these wars have been defensive and thus prudent by necessity. Liberal states have been attacked and threatened by nonliberal states that do not exercise any special restraint in their dealings with the liberal states. Authoritarian rulers both stimulate and respond to an international political environment in which conflicts of prestige, interest, and pure fear of what other states might do all lead states toward war. War and conquest have thus characterized the careers of many authoritarian rulers and ruling parties, from Louis XIV and Napoleon to Mussolini's fascists, Hitler's Nazis, and Stalin's communists. Yet we cannot simply blame warfare on the authoritarians or totalitarians, as many of our more enthusiastic politicians would have us do.[4] Most wars arise out of calculations and miscalculations of interest, misunderstandings, and mutual suspicions, such as those that characterized the origins of World War I. However, aggression by the liberal state has also characterized a large number of wars. Both France and Britain fought expansionist colonial wars throughout the nineteenth century. The United States fought a similar war with Mexico from 1846 to 1848, waged a war of annihilation against the American Indians, and intervened militarily against sovereign states many times before and after World War II. Liberal states invade weak nonliberal states and display striking distrust in dealings with powerful nonliberal states (Doyle, 1983b).

Neither realist (statist) nor Marxist theory accounts well for these two legacies. While they can account for aspects of certain periods of international stability (Aron, 1968, pp. 151-54; Russett, 1985), neither the

---

4. There are serious studies showing that Marxist regimes have higher military spending per capita than non-Marxist regimes (Payne, n.d.), but this should not be interpreted as a sign of the inherent aggressiveness of authoritarian or totalitarian governments or of the inherent and global peacefulness of liberal regimes. Marxist regimes, in particular, represent a minority in the current international system; they are strategically encircled, and due to their lack of domestic legitimacy, they might be said to "suffer" the twin burden of needing defenses against both external and internal enemies. Andreski (1980), moreover, argued that (purely) military dictatorships, due to their domestic fragility have little incentive to engage in foreign military adventures. According to Walter Clemens (1982, pp. 117-18), the United States intervened in the Third World more than twice as often during the period 1946-1976 as the Soviet Union did in 1946-79. Relatedly, Posen and VanEvera (1980, p. 105; 1983, pp. 86-89) found that the United States devoted one quarter and the Soviet Union one tenth of their defense budgets to forces designed for Third World interventions (where responding to perceived threats would presumably have a less than purely defensive character).

logic of the balance of power nor the logic of international hegemony explains the separate peace maintained for more than 150 years among states sharing one particular form of governance—liberal principles and institutions. Balance-of-power theory expects—indeed is premised upon—flexible arrangements of geostrategic rivalry that include preventive war. Hegemonies wax and wane, but the liberal peace holds. Marxist "ultra-imperialists" expect a form of peaceful rivalry among capitalists, but only liberal capitalists maintain peace. Leninists expect liberal capitalists to be aggressive toward nonliberal states, but they also (and especially) expect them to be imperialistic toward fellow liberal capitalists.

Kant's theory of liberal internationalism helps us understand these two legacies. The importance of Immanuel Kant as a theorist of international ethics has been well appreciated (Armstrong, 1931; Friedrich, 1948; Gallie, 1978, chap. 1; Galston, 1975; Hassner, 1972; Hinsley, 1967, chap. 4; Hoffmann, 1965; Waltz, 1962; Williams, 1983), but Kant also has an important analytical theory of international politics. *Perpetual Peace*, written in 1795 (Kant, 1970, pp. 93-130), helps us understand the interactive nature of international relations. Kant tries to teach us methodologically that we can study neither the systemic relations of states nor the varieties of state behavior in isolation from each other. Substantively, he anticipates for us the ever-widening pacification of a liberal pacific union, explains this pacification, and at the same time suggests why liberal states are not pacific in their relations with nonliberal states. Kant argues that perpetual peace will be guaranteed by the ever-widening acceptance of three "definitive articles" of peace. When all nations have accepted the definitive articles in a metaphorical "treaty" of perpetual peace he asks them to sign, perpetual peace will have been established.

The First Definitive Article requires the civil constitution of the state to be republican. By *republican* Kant means a political society that has solved the problem of combining moral autonomy, individualism, and social order. A private property and market-oriented economy partially addressed that dilemma in the private sphere. The public, or political, sphere was more troubling. His answer was a republic that preserved juridical freedom—the legal equality of citizens as subjects—on the basis of a representative government with a separation of powers. Juridical freedom is preserved because the morally autonomous individual is by means of representation a self-legislator making laws that apply to all cit-

izens equally, including himself or herself. Tyranny is avoided because
the individual is subject to laws he or she does not also administer (Kant,
PP, pp. 99102; Riley, 1985, chap. 5).[5]

Liberal republics will progressively establish peace among themselves by means of the pacific federation, or union *(foedus pacificum)*,
described in Kant's Second Definitive Article. The pacific union will
establish peace within a federation of free states and securely maintain
the rights of each state. The world will not have achieved the "perpetual peace" that provides the ultimate guarantor of republican freedom
until "a late stage and after many unsuccessful attempts" (Kant, *UH*, p.
47). At that time, all nations will have learned the lessons of peace
through right conceptions of the appropriate constitution, great and
sad experience, and good will. Only then will individuals enjoy perfect
republican rights or the full guarantee of a global and just peace. In the
meantime, the "pacific federation" of liberal republics—"an enduring
and gradually expanding federation likely to prevent war"—brings
within it more and more republics—despite republican collapses, backsliding, and disastrous wars—creating an ever-expanding separate
peace (Kant, *PP,* p. 105).[6] Kant emphasizes that

> it can be shown that this idea of federalism, extending gradually to en-
> compass all states and thus leading to perpetual peace, is practicable and
> has objective reality. For if by good fortune one powerful and enlight-
> ened nation can form a republic (which is by nature inclined to seek
> peace), this will provide a focal point for federal association among other
> states. These will join up with the first one, thus securing the freedom of
> each state in accordance with the idea of international right, and the

---

5. All citations from Kant are from Kant's *Political Writings* (Kant, 1970), the H.
B. Nisbet translation edited by Hans Reiss. The works discussed and the abbrevia-
tions by which they are identified in the text are as follows:

PP   Perpetual Peace (1795)

UH   The Idea for a Universal History with a Cosmopolitan Purpose (1784)

CF   The Contest of Faculties (1798)

MM   The Metaphysics of Morals (1797)

6. I think Kant meant that the peace would be established among liberal regimes
and would expand by ordinary political and legal means as new liberal regimes appeared. By a process of gradual extension the peace would become global and then
perpetual; the occasion for wars with nonliberals would disappear as nonliberal
regimes disappeared.

whole will gradually spread further and further by a series of alliances of this kind. (Kant, PP p. 104)

The pacific union is not a single peace treaty ending one war, a world state, nor a state of nations. Kant finds the first insufficient. The second and third are impossible or potentially tyrannical. National sovereignty precludes reliable subservience to a state of nations; a world state destroys the civic freedom on which the development of human capacities rests (Kant, *UH*, p. 50). Although Kant obliquely refers to various classical interstate confederations and modern diplomatic congresses, he develops no systematic organizational embodiment of this treaty and presumably does not find institutionalization necessary (Riley, 1983, chap. 5; Schwarz, 1962, p. 77). He appears to have in mind a mutual nonaggression pact, perhaps a collective security agreement, and the cosmopolitan law set forth in the Third Definitive Article.7

The Third Definitive Article establishes a cosmopolitan law to operate in conjunction with the pacific union. The cosmopolitan law "shall be limited to conditions of universal hospitality." In this Kant call for the recognition of the "right of a foreigner not to be treated with hostility when he arrives on someone else's territory." This "does not extend beyond those conditions which make it possible for them [foreigners] to attempt to enter into relations [commerce] with the native inhabitants" (Kant, *PP,* p. 106). Hospitality does not require extending to foreigners either the right to citizenship or the right to settlement, unless the foreign visitors would perish if they were expelled. Foreign conquest and plunder also find no justification under this right. Hospitality does appear to include the right of access and the obligation of maintaining the opportunity for citizens to exchange goods and ideas without imposing the obligation to trade (a voluntary act in all cases under liberal constitutions).

Perpetual peace, for Kant, is an epistemology, a condition for ethical action, and, most importantly, an explanation of how the "mechanical

---

7. Kant's *foedus pacificum* is thus neither a *pactum pacis* (a single peace treaty) nor a *civitas gentium* (a world state). He appears to have anticipated something like a less formally institutionalized League of Nations or United Nations. One could argue that in practice, these two institutions worked for liberal states and only for liberal states, but no specifically liberal "pacific union" was institutionalized. Instead, liberal states have behaved for the past 180 years as if such a Kantian pacific union and treaty of perpetual peace had been signed.

process of nature visibly exhibits the purposive plan of producing concord among men, even against their will and indeed by means of their very discord" (Kant, *PP,* p. 108; *UH,* pp. 44-45). Understanding history requires an epistemological foundation, for without a teleology, such as the promise of perpetual peace, the complexity of history would overwhelm human understanding (Kant, *UH,* pp. 51-53). Perpetual peace, however, is not merely a heuristic device with which to interpret history. It is guaranteed, Kant explains in the "First Addition" to *Perpetual Peace* ("On the Guarantee of Perpetual Peace"), to result from men fulfilling their ethical duty or, failing that, from a hidden plan.[8] Peace is an ethical duty because it is only under conditions of peace that all men can treat each other as ends, rather than means to an end (Kant, *UH,* p. 50; Murphy, 1970, chap. 3). In order for this duty to be practical, Kant needs, of course, to show that peace is in fact possible. The widespread sentiment of approbation that he saw aroused by the early success of the French revolutionaries showed him that we can indeed be moved by ethical sentiments with a cosmopolitan reach (Kant, *CF,* pp. 181-82; Yovel, 1980, pp. 153-54). This does not mean, however, that perpetual peace is certain ("prophesiable"). Even the scientifically regular course of the planets could be changed by a wayward comet striking them out of orbit. Human freedom requires that we allow for much greater reversals in the course of history. We must, in fact, anticipate the possibility of backsliding and destructive wars—though these will serve to educate nations to the importance of peace (Kant, *UH,* pp. 47-48).

In the end, however, our guarantee of perpetual peace does not rest on ethical conduct. As Kant emphasizes,

---

8. In the *Metaphysics of Morals* (the *Rechtslehre*) Kant seems to write as if perpetual peace is only an epistemological device and, while an ethical duty, is empirically merely a "pious hope" (*MM,* pp. 164-75)—though even here he finds that the pacific union is not "impracticable" (*MM,* p. 171). In the *Universal History (UH),* Kant writes as if the brute force of physical nature drives men toward inevitable peace. Yovel (1980, pp. 168 ff.) argues that from a post-critical (post-*Critique of Judgment*) perspective, *Perpetual Peace* reconciles the two views of history. "Nature" is human-created nature (culture or civilization). Perpetual peace is the "*a priori* of the *a posteriori*"— a critical perspective that then enables us to discern causal, probabilistic patterns in history. Law and the "political technology" of republican constitutionalism are separate from ethical development, but both interdependently lead to perpetual peace—the first through force, fear, and self-interest; the second through progressive enlightenment—and both together lead to perpetual peace through the widening of the circumstances in which engaging in right conduct poses smaller and smaller burdens.

we now come to the essential question regarding the prospect of perpetual peace. What does nature do in relation to the end which man's own reason prescribes to him as a duty, i.e. how does nature help to promote his moral purpose? And how does nature guarantee that what man ought to do by the laws of his freedom (but does not do) will in fact be done through nature's compulsion, without prejudice to the free agency of man?... This does not mean that nature imposes on us a duty to do it, for duties can only be imposed by practical reason. On the contrary, nature does it herself, whether we are willing or not: *facta volentem ducunt, nolentem tradunt.* (PP, p. 112)

The guarantee thus rests, Kant argues, not on the probable behavior of moral angels, but on that of "devils, so long as they possess understanding" (*PP,* p. 112). In explaining the sources of each of the three definitive articles of the perpetual peace, Kant then tells us how we (as free and intelligent devils) could be motivated by fear, force, and calculated advantage to undertake a course of action whose outcome we could reasonably anticipate to be perpetual peace. Yet while it is possible to conceive of the Kantian road to peace in these terms, Kant himself recognizes and argues that social evolution also makes the conditions of moral behavior less onerous and hence more likely (*CF,* pp. 187-89; Kelly, 1969, pp. 106-13). In tracing the effects of both political and moral development, he builds an account of why liberal states do maintain peace among themselves and of how it will (by implication, has) come about that the pacific union will expand. He also explains how these republics would engage in wars with nonrepublics and therefore suffer the "sad experience" of wars that an ethical policy might have avoided.

The first source of the three definitive articles derives from a political evolution—from a constitutional law. Nature (providence) has seen to it that human beings can live in all the regions where they have been driven to settle by wars. (Kant, who once taught geography, reports on the Lapps, the Samoyeds, the Pescheras.) "Asocial sociability" draws men together to fulfill needs for security and material welfare as it drives them into conflicts over the distribution and control of social products (Kant, *UH,* p. 44-45; *PP,* pp. 110-11). This violent natural evolution tends towards the liberal peace because "asocial sociability" inevitably leads toward republican governments, and republican governments are a source of the liberal peace.

Republican representation and separation of powers are produced because they are the means by which the state is "organized well" to prepare for and meet foreign threats (by unity) and to tame the ambitions of self-ish and aggressive individuals (by authority derived from representation, by general laws, and by nondespotic administration) (Kant, *PP,* pp. 112-13). States that are not organized in this fashion fail. Monarchs thus encourage commerce and private property in order to increase national wealth. They cede rights of representation to their subjects in order to strengthen their political support or to obtain willing grants of tax revenue (Hassner, 1972, pp. 583-86).

Kant shows how republics, once established, lead to peaceful relations. He argues that once the aggressive interests of absolutist monarchies are tamed and the habit of respect for individual rights engrained by republican government, wars would appear as the disaster to the people's welfare that he and the other liberals thought them to be. The fundamental reason is this:

> If, as is inevitably the case under this constitution, the consent of the citizens is required to decide whether or not war should be declared, it is very natural that they will have a great hesitation in embarking on so dangerous an enterprise. For this would mean calling down on themselves all the miseries of war, such as doing the fighting themselves, supplying the costs of the war from their own resources, painfully making good the ensuing devastation, and, as the crowning evil, having to take upon themselves a burden of debts which will embitter peace itself and which can never be paid off on account of the constant threat of new wars. But under a constitution where the subject is not a citizen, and which is therefore not republican, it is the simplest thing in the world to go to war. For the head of state is not a fellow citizen, but the owner of the state, and war will not force him to make the slightest sacrifice so far as his banquets, hunts, pleasure palaces and court festivals are concerned. He can thus decide on war, without any significant reason as a kind of amusement, and unconcernedly leave it to the diplomatic corps (who are always ready for such purposes) to justify the war for the sake of propriety. (Kant, PP, p. 100)

Yet these domestic republican restraints do not end war. If they did, liberal states would not be warlike, which is far from the case. They do introduce republican caution—Kant's "hesitation"—in place of monarchical caprice. Liberal wars are only fought for popular, liberal purposes. The historical liberal legacy is laden with popular wars fought to promote freedom, to protect private property, or to support liberal allies against nonliberal enemies. Kant's position is ambiguous. He regards these wars as unjust and warns liberals of their susceptibility to them (Kant, *PP,* p. 106). At the same time, Kant argues that each nation "can and ought to" demand that its neighboring nations enter into the pacific union of liberal states (*PP,* p. 102). Thus to see how the pacific union removes the occasion of wars among liberal states and not wars between liberal and nonliberal states, we need to shift our attention from constitutional law to international law, Kant's second source.

Complementing the constitutional guarantee of caution, international law adds a second source for the definitive articles: a guarantee of respect. The separation of nations that asocial sociability encourages is reinforced by the development of separate languages and religions. These further guarantee a world of separate states—an essential condition needed to avoid a "global, soul-less despotism." Yet, at the same time, they also morally integrate liberal states: "as culture grows and men gradually move towards greater agreement over their principles, they lead to mutual understanding and peace" (Kant, *PP,* p. 114). As republics emerge (the first source) and culture progresses, an understanding of the legitimate rights of all citizens and of all republics comes into play; and this, now that caution characterizes policy, sets up the moral foundations for the liberal peace. Correspondingly, international law highlights the importance of Kantian publicity. Domestically, publicity helps ensure that the officials of republics act according to the principles they profess to hold just and according to the interests of the electors they claim to represent. Internationally, free speech and the effective communication of accurate conceptions of the political life of foreign peoples is essential to establishing and preserving the understanding on which the guarantee of respect depends. Domestically just republics, which rest on consent, then presume foreign republics also to be consensual, just, and therefore deserving of accommodation. The experience of cooperation helps engender further cooperative behavior when the consequences of state policy are unclear but (potentially) mutually beneficial. At the same time, liberal states assume that nonliberal states, which do not rest on free consent, are not just. Because nonliberal governments are in a state of aggression with their own people, their foreign relations become for liberal governments deeply suspect. In short, fellow liberals benefit from a presumption of amity; nonliberals suffer from a presumption of enmity. Both presumptions may be accurate; each, however, may also be self-confirming.

Lastly, cosmopolitan law adds material incentives to moral commitments. The cosmopolitan right to hospitality permits the "spirit of commerce" sooner or later to take hold of every nation, thus impelling states to promote peace and to try to avert war. Liberal economic theory holds that these cosmopolitan ties derive from a cooperative international division of labor and free trade according to comparative advantage. Each economy is said to be better off than it would have been under autarky; each thus acquires an incentive to avoid policies that would lead the other to break these economic ties. Because keeping open markets rests upon the assumption that the next set of transactions will also be determined by prices rather than coercion, a sense of mutual security is vital to avoid security-motivated searches for economic autarky. Thus, avoiding a challenge to another liberal state's security or even enhancing each other's security by means of alliance naturally follows economic interdependence.

A further cosmopolitan source of liberal peace is the international market's removal of difficult decisions of production and distribution from the direct sphere of state policy. A foreign state thus does not appear directly responsible for these outcomes, and states can stand aside from, and to some degree above, these contentious market rivalries and be ready to step in to resolve crises. The interdependence of commerce and the international contacts of state officials help create crosscutting transnational ties that serve as lobbies for mutual accommodation. According to modern liberal scholars, international financiers and transnational and transgovernmental organizations create interests in favor of accommodation. Moreover, their variety has ensured that no single conflict sours an entire relationship by setting off a spiral of reciprocated retaliation (Brzezinski and Huntington, 1963, chap. 9; Keohane and Nye, 1977, chap. 7; Neustadt, 1970; Polanyi, 1944, chaps. 1-2). Conversely, a sense of suspicion, such as that characterizing relations between liberal and nonliberal governments, can lead to restrictions on the range of contacts between societies, and this can increase the prospect that a single conflict will determine an entire relationship.

No single constitutional, international, or cosmopolitan source is alone sufficient, but together (and only together) they plausibly connect the characteristics of liberal polities and economies with sustained liberal peace. Alliances founded on mutual strategic interest among liberal and nonliberal states have been broken; economic ties between liberal and nonliberal states have proven fragile; but the political bonds of liberal rights and interests have proven a remarkably firm foundation for mutual nonaggression. A separate peace exists among liberal states.

In their relations with nonliberal states, however, liberal states have not escaped from the insecurity caused by anarchy in the world political system considered as a whole. Moreover, the very constitutional restraint, international respect for individual rights, and shared commercial interests that establish grounds for peace among liberal states establish grounds for additional conflict in relations between liberal and nonliberal societies.

CONCLUSION

KANT'S LIBERAL INTERNATIONALISM, Machiavelli's liberal imperialism, and Schumpeter's liberal pacifism rest on fundamentally different views of the nature of the human being, the state, and international relations.[9] Schumpeter's humans are rationalized, individualized, and democratized. They are also homogenized, pursuing material interests "monistically." Because their material interests lie in peaceful trade, they and the democratic state that these fellow citizens control are pacifistic. Machiavelli's citizens are splendidly diverse in their goals but fundamentally unequal in them as well, seeking to rule or fearing being dominated. Extending the rule of the dominant elite or avoiding the political collapse of their state, each calls for imperial expansion.

Kant's citizens, too, are diverse in their goals and individualized and rationalized, but most importantly, they are capable of appreciating the moral equality of all individuals and of treating other individuals as ends rather than as means. The Kantian state thus is governed publicly according to law, as a republic. Kant's is the state that solves the problem of governing individualized equals, whether they are the "rational devils" he says we often find ourselves to be or the ethical agents we can and should become. Republics tell us that

> in order to organize a group of rational beings who together require universal laws for their survival, but of whom each separate individual is secretly inclined to exempt himself from them, the constitution must be so

---

9. For a comparative discussion of the political foundations of Kant's ideas, see Shklar (1984, pp. 232–38).

designed so that although the citizens are opposed to one another in their private attitudes, these opposing views may inhibit one another in such a way that the public conduct of the citizens will be the same as if they did not have such evil attitudes. (Kant, *PP,* p. 113)

Unlike Machiavelli's republics, Kant's republics are capable of achieving peace among themselves because they exercise democratic caution and are capable of appreciating the international rights of foreign republics. These international rights of republics derive from the representation of foreign individuals, who are our moral equals. Unlike Schumpeter's capitalist democracies, Kant's republics—including our own—remain in a state of war with nonrepublics. Liberal republics see themselves as threatened by aggression from nonrepublics that are not constrained by representation. Even though wars often cost more than the economic return they generate, liberal republics also are prepared to protect and promote—sometimes forcibly—democracy, private property, and the rights of individuals overseas against nonrepublics, which, because they do not authentically represent the rights of individuals, have no rights to noninterference. These wars may liberate oppressed individuals overseas; they also can generate enormous suffering.

Preserving the legacy of the liberal peace without succumbing to the legacy of liberal imprudence is both a moral and strategic challenge. The bipolar stability of the international system, and the near certainty of mutual devastation resulting from a nuclear war between the superpowers, have created a "crystal ball effect" that has helped to constrain the tendency toward miscalculation present at the outbreak of so many wars in the past (Carnesale, Doty, Hoffmann, Huntington, Nye, and Sagan, 1983, p. 44; Waltz, 1964). However, this "nuclear peace" appears to be limited to the superpowers. It has not curbed military interventions in the Third World. Moreover, it is subject to a desperate technological race designed to overcome its constraints and to crises that have pushed even the superpowers to the brink of war. We must still reckon with the war fevers and moods of appeasement that have almost alternately swept liberal democracies.

Yet restraining liberal imprudence, whether aggressive or passive, may not be possible without threatening liberal pacification. Improving the strategic acumen of our foreign policy calls for introducing steadier strategic calculations of the national interest in the long run and more flexible responses to changes in the international political environment.

Constraining the indiscriminate meddling of our foreign interventions calls for a deeper appreciation of the "particularism of history, culture, and membership" (Walzer, 1983, p. 5), but both the improvement in strategy and the constraint on intervention seem, in turn, to require an executive freed from the restraints of a representative legislature in the management of foreign policy and a political culture indifferent to the universal rights of individuals. These conditions, in their turn, could break the chain of constitutional guarantees, the respect for representative government, and the web of transnational contact that have sustained the pacific union of liberal states.

Perpetual peace, Kant says, is the end point of the hard journey his republics will take. The promise of perpetual peace, the violent lessons of war, and the experience of a partial peace are proof of the need for and the possibility of world peace. They are also the grounds for moral citizens and statesmen to assume the duty of striving for peace.

Michael W. Doyle

Appendix 1. Liberal Regimes and the Pacific Union, 1700–1982

18th Century
Swiss Cantons[a]
French Republic. 1790–1795
United States,[a] 1776–
  Total = 3

1800–1850
Swiss Confederation
United States
France, 1830–1849
Belgium, 1830–
Great Britain, 1832–
Netherlands, 1848
Piedmont, 1848–
Denmark, 1849–
  Total = 8

1850–1900
Switzerland
United States
Belgium
Great Britain
Netherlands
Piedmont, –1861
Italy, 1861–
Denmark, –1866
Sweden, 1864–
Greece, 1864–
Canada, 1867–
France, 1871–
Argentina, 1880–
Chile, 1891–
  Total = 13

1900–1945
Switzerland
United States
Great Britain
Sweden
Canada
Greece, –1911; 1928–1936
Italy, –1922
Belgium, –1940
Netherlands, –1940
Argentina, –1943
France, –1940
Chile, –1924, 1932–
Australia, 1901
Norway, 1905–1940
New Zealand, 1907–
Colombia, 1910–1949
Denmark, 1914–1940
Poland, 1917–1935
Latvia, 1922–1934
Germany, 1918–1932
Austria, 1918–1934
Estonia, 1919–1934
Finland, 1919–
Uruguay, 1919–
Costa Rica, 1919–
Czechoslovakia, 1920–1939
Ireland, 1920–
Mexico, 1928–
Lebanon, 1944–
  Total = 29

Note: I have drawn up this approximate list of "Liberal Regimes" according to the four institutions Kant described as essential: market and private property economies; polities that are externally sovereign; citizens who possess juridical rights; and "republican" (whether republican or parliamentary monarchy), representative government. This latter includes the requirement that the legislative branch have an effective role in public policy and be formally and competitively (either inter- or intra-party) elected. Furthermore, I have taken into account whether male suffrage is wide (i.e., 30%) or, as Kant (*MM*, p. 139) would have had it, open by "achievement" to inhabitants of the national or metropolitan territory (e.g., to poll-tax payers or householders). This list of liberal regimes is thus more inclusive than a list of democratic regimes, or polyarchies (Powell, 1982, p. 5). Other conditions taken into account here are that female suffrage is granted within a generation of its being demanded by an extensive female suffrage movement and that representative government is internally sovereign (e.g., including, and especially over military and foreign affairs) as well as stable (in existence for at least three years). Sources for these data are Banks and Overstreet (1983), Gastil (1985). *The Europa Yearbook, 1985* (1985), Langer (1968), U.K. Foreign and Commonwealth Office (1980), and U.S. Department of State (1981) Finally, these lists exclude ancient and medieval "republics," since none appears to fit Kant's commitment to liberal individualism (Holmes, 1979).

Liberalism and World Politics

1945–b
Switzerland
United States
Great Britain
Sweden
Canada
Australia
New Zealand
Finland
Ireland
Mexico
Uruguay, –1973
Chile, –1973
Lebanon, –1975
Costa Rica, –1948; –1953
Iceland, 1944–
France, 1945–
Denmark, 1945–
Norway, 1945–
Austria, 1945–
Brazil, 1945–1954; 1955–1964
Belgium, 1946
Luxemburg, 1946
Netherlands, 1946
Italy, 1946
Philippines, 1946–1972
India, 1947–1975; 1977–
Sri Lanka, 1948–1961;
    1963–1971; 1978–
Ecuador, 1948–1963; 1979–
Israel, 1949–
West Germany, 1949–
Greece, 1950–1967; 1975–
Peru 1950–1962; 1963–1968;
    1980–

El Salvador, 1950–1961
Turkey, 1950–1960; 1966–1971
Japan, 1951–
Bolivia, 1956–1969; 1982–
Colombia, 1958–
Venezuela, 1959–
Nigeria, 1961–1964;
    1979–1984
Jamaica, 1962–
Trinidad and Tobago, 1962–
Senegal, 1963–
Malaysia, 1963–
Botswana, 1966–
Singapore, 1965–
Portugal, 1976–
Spain, 1978–
Dominican Republic, 1978–
Honduras, 1981–
Papua New Guinea, 1982–
    Total = 50

a. There are domestic variations within these liberal regimes: Switzerland was liberal only in certain cantons; the United States was liberal only north of the Mason-Dixon line until 1865, when it became liberal throughout.

b. Selected list, excluding liberal regimes with populations less than one million. These include all states categorized as "free" by Gastil and those "partly free" (four-fifths or more free) states with a more pronounced capitalist orientation.

Michael W. Doyle

Appendix 2. International Wars Listed Chronologically

British-Maharattan (1817–1818)
Greek (1821–1828)
Franco-Spanish (1823)
First Anglo-Burmese (1823–1826)
Javanese (1825–1830)
Russo-Persian (1826–1828)
Russo-Turkish (1828–1829)
First Polish (1831)
First Syrian (1831–1832)
Texas (1835–1836)
First British-Afghan (1838–1842)
Second Syrian (1839–1840)
Franco-Algerian (1839 –1847)
Peruvian-Bolivian (1841)
First British-Sikh (1845–1846)
Mexican-American (1846–1848)
Austro-Sardinian (1848–1849)
First Schleswig-Holstein (1848–1849)
Hungarian (1848–1849)
Second British-Sikh (1848–1849)
Roman Republic (1849)
La Plata (1851–1852)

First Turco-Montenegran (1852–1853)
Crimean (1853–1856)
Anglo-Persian (1856–1857)
Sepoy (1857–1859)
Second Turco-Montenegran (1858–1859)
Italian Unification (1859)
Spanish-Moroccan (1859–1860)
Italo-Roman (1860)
Italo-Sicilian (1860–1861)
Franco-Mexican (1862–1867)
Ecuadorian-Colombian (1863)
Second Polish (1863–1864)
Spanish-Santo Dominican (1863–1865)
Second Schleswig-Holstein (1864)
Lopez (1864–1870)
Spanish-Chilean (1865–1866)
Seven Weeks (1866)
Ten Years (1868–1878)
Franco-Prussian (1870–1871)
Dutch-Achinese (1873–1878)
Balkan (1875–1877)
Russo-Turkish (1877–1878)

Note: This table is taken from Melvin Small and J. David Singer (1982, pp. 79–80). This is a partial list of international wars fought between 1816 and 1980. In Appendices A and B, Small and Singer identify a total of 575 wars during this period, but approximately 159 of them appear to be largely domestic, or civil wars.

This list excludes covert interventions, some of which have been directed by liberal regimes against other liberal regimes—for example, the United States' effort to destabilize the Chilean election and Allende's government. Nonetheless, it is significant that such interventions are not pursued publicly as acknowledged policy. The covert destabilization campaign against Chile is recounted by the Senate Select Committee to Study Governmental Operations with Respect to Intelligence Activities (1975, *Covert Action in Chile,* 1963–73).

Following the argument of this article, this list also excludes civil wars. Civil wars differ from international wars, not in the ferocity of combat, but in the issues that engender them. Two nations that could abide one another as independent neighbors separated by a border might well be the fiercest of enemies if forced to live together in one state, jointly deciding how to raise and spend taxes, choose leaders, and legislate fundamental questions of value. Notwithstanding these differences, no civil wars that I recall upset the argument of liberal pacification.

Liberalism and World Politics

Bosnian (1878)
Second British-Afghan (1878–1880)
Pacific (1879–1883)
British-Zulu (1879)
Franco-Indochinese (1882–1884)
Mahdist (1882–1885)
Sino-French (1884–1885)
Central American (1885)
Serbo-Bulgarian (1885)
Sino-Japanese (1894–1895)
Franco-Madagascan (1894–1895)
Cuban (1895–1898)
Italo-Ethiopian (1895–1896)
First Philippine (1896–1898)
Greco-Turkish (1897)
Spanish-American (1898)
Second Philippine (1899–1902)
Boer (1899–1902)
Boxer Rebellion (1900)
Ilinden (1903)
Russo-Japanese (1904–1905)
Central American (1906)
Central American (1907)
Spanish-Moroccan (1909–1910)
Italo-Turkish (1911–1912)
First Balkan (1912–1913)
Second Balkan (1913)
World War I (1914–1918)
Russian Nationalities (1917–1921)
Russo-Polish (1919–1920)
Hungarian-Allies (1919)
Greco-Turkish (1919–1922)
Riffian (1921–1926)
Druze (1925–1927)
Sino-Soviet (1929)
Manchurian (1931–1933)
Chaco (1932–1935)
Italo-Ethiopian (1935–1936)
Sino-Japanese (1937–1941)
Russo-Hungarian (1956)
Sinai (1956)
Tibetan (1956–1959)

Sino-Indian (1962)
Vietnamese (1965–1975)
Second Kashmir (1965)
Six Day (1967)
Israeli-Egyptian (1969–1970)
Football (1969)
Changkufeng (1938)
Nomohan (1939)
World War II (1939–1945)
Russo-Finnish (1939–1940)
Franco-Thai (1940–1941)
Indonesian (1945–1946)
Indochinese (1945–1954)
Madagascan (1947–1948)
First Kashmir (1947–1949)
Palestine (1948–1949)
Hyderabad (1948)
Korean (1950–1953)
Algerian (1954–1962)
Bangladesh (1971)
Philippine-MNLF (1972–)
Yom Kippur (1973)
Turco-Cypriot (1974)
Ethiopian-Eritrean (1974–)
Vietnamese-Cambodian (1975–)
Timor (1975–)
Saharan (1975–)
Ogaden (1976–)
Ugandan-Tanzanian (1978–1979)
Sino-Vietnamese (1979)
Russo-Afghan (1979–)
Iran-Iraqi (1980–)

Michael W. Doyle

Note

I would like to thank Marshall Cohen, Amy Gutmann, Ferdinand Hermens, Bonnie Honig, Paschalis Kitromilides, Klaus Knorr, Diana Meyers, Kenneth Oye, Jerome Schneewind, and Richard Ullman for their helpful suggestions. One version of this paper was presented at the American Section of the International Society for Social and Legal Philosophy, Notre Dame, Indiana, November 2-4, 1984, and will appear in *Realism and Morality,* edited by Kenneth Kipnis and Diana Meyers. Another version was presented on March 19, 1986, to the Avoiding Nuclear War Project, Center for Science and International Affairs, The John F. Kennedy School of Government, Harvard University. This essay draws on research assisted by a MacArthur Fellowship in International Security awarded by the Social Science Research Council.

References

Andreski, Stanislav. 1980. On the Peaceful Disposition of Military Dictatorships. *Journal of Strategic Studies*, 3:3–10.

Armstrong, A. C. 1931. Kant's Philosophy of Peace and War. *The Journal of Philosophy*, 28:197–204.

Aron, Raymond. 1966. *Peace and War: A Theory of International Relations.* Richard Howard and Annette Baker Fox, trans. Garden City, NY: Doubleday.

Aron, Raymond. 1974. *The Imperial Republic.* Frank Jellinek, trans. Englewood Cliffs, NJ: Prentice Hall.

Babst, Dean V. 1972. A Force for Peace. *Industrial Research.* 14 (April): 55–58.

Banks, Arthur, and William Overstreet, eds. 1983. *A Political Handbook of the World; 1982–1983.* New York: McGraw Hill.

Barnet, Richard. 1968. *Intervention and Revolution.* Cleveland: World Publishing Co.

Brzezinski, Zbigniew, and Samuel Huntington. 1963. *Political Power: USA/USSR.* New York: Viking Press.

Carnesale, Albert, Paul Doty, Stanley Hoffmann, Samuel Huntington, Joseph Nye, and Scott Sagan. 1983. *Living With Nuclear Weapons.* New York. Bantam.

Chan, Steve. 1984. Mirror, Mirror on the Wall . . . Are Freer Countries More Pacific? *Journal of Conflict Resolution,* 28:617–48.

Clemens, Walter C. 1982. The Superpowers and the Third World. In Charles Kegley and Pat McGowan, eds., *Foreign Policy; USA/USSR.* Beverly Hills: Sage. pp. 111–35

Doyle, Michael W. 1983a. Kant, Liberal Legacies, and Foreign Affairs: Part 1. *Philosophy and Public Affairs,* 12:205–35.

Doyle, Michael W. 1983b. Kant, Liberal Legacies, and Foreign Affairs: Part 2. *Philosophy and Public Affairs,* 12:323–53.

Doyle, Michael W. 1986. *Empires.* Ithaca: Cornell University Press.

The Europa Yearbook for 1985. 1985. 2 vols. London: Europa Publications.

Friedrich, Karl. 1948. *Inevitable Peace.* Cambridge, MA: Harvard University Press.

Gallie, W. B. 1978. *Philosophers of Peace and War*. Cambridge: Cambridge University Press.

Galston, William. 1975. *Kant and the Problem of History*. Chicago: Chicago University Press.

Gastil, Raymond. 1985. The Comparative Survey of Freedom 1985. *Freedom at Issue*, 82:3–16.

Haas, Michael. 1974. *International Conflict*. New York: Bobbs-Merrill.

Hassner, Pierre. 1972. Immanuel Kant. In Leo Strauss and Joseph Cropsey, eds., *History of Political Philosophy*. Chicago: Rand McNally. pp. 554–93.

Hermens, Ferdinand A. 1944. *The Tyrants' War and the People's Peace*. Chicago: University of Chicago Press.

Hinsley, F. H. 1967. *Power and the Pursuit of Peace*. Cambridge: Cambridge University Press.

Hoffmann, Stanley. 1965. Rousseau on War and Peace. In Stanley Hoffmann, ed. *The State of War*. New York: Praeger. pp. 45–87.

Holmes, Stephen. 1979. Aristippus in and out of Athens. *American Political Science Review*, 73:113 28.

Hulliung, Mark. 1983. *Citizen Machiavelli*. Princeton: Princeton University Press.

Hume, David. 1963. Of the Balance of Power. *Essays: Moral, Political, and Literary*. Oxford: Oxford University Press.

Kant, Immanuel. 1970. *Kant's Political Writings*, Hans Reiss, ed. H. B. Nisbet, trans. Cambridge: Cambridge University Press.

Kelly, George A. 1969. *Idealism, Politics, and History*. Cambridge: Cambridge University Press.

Keohane, Robert, and Joseph Nye. 1977. *Power and Interdependence*. Boston: Little Brown.

Langer, William L., ed. 1968. *The Encyclopedia of World History*. Boston: Houghton Mifflin.

Machiaveli, Niccolo. 1950. *The Prince and the Discourses*. Max Lerner, ed. Luigi Ricci and Christian Detmold, trans. New York: Modern Library.

Mansfield, Harvey C. 1970. Machievelli's New Regime. *Italian Quarterly*, 13:63–95.

Montesquieu, Charles de. 1949. *Spirit of the Laws*. New York: Hafner. (Originally published in 1748.)

Murphy, Jeffrie. 1970. *Kant: The Philosophy of Right*. New York: St. Martins.

Neustadt, Richard. 1970. *Alliance Politics*. New York: Columbia University Press.

Payne, James L. n.d. Marxism and Militarism. *Polity*. Forthcoming.

Pocock, J. G. A. 1975. *The Machiavellian Moment*. Princeton: Princeton University Press.

Polanyi, Karl. 1944. *The Great Transformation*. Boston: Beacon Press.

Posen, Barry, and Stephen VanEvera. 1980. Overarming and Underwhelming. *Foreign Policy*, 40:99–118.

Posen, Barry, and Stephen VanEvera. 1983. Reagan Administration Defense Policy. In Kenneth Oye, Robert Lieber, and Donald Rothchild, eds., *Eagle Defiant*. Boston: Little Brown. pp. 67–104.

Powell, G. Bingham. 1982. *Contemporary Democracies*. Cambridge, MA. Harvard University Press.

Reagan, Ronald. June 9, 1982. Address to Parliament. *New York Times*.

Riley, Patrick. 1983. *Kant's Political Philosophy*. Totowa, NJ: Rowman and Littlefield.

Rummel, Rudolph J. 1979. *Understanding Conflict and War*, 5 vols. Beverly Hills: Sage Publications.

Rummel, Rudolph J. 1983. Libertarianism and International Violence. *Journal of Conflict Resolution*, 27:27–71.

Russett, Bruce. 1985. The Mysterious Case of Vanishing Hegemony. *International Organization,* 39:207–31.

Schumpeter, Joseph. 1950. *Capitalism, Socialism, and Democracy.* New York: Harper Torchbooks.

Schumpeter, Joseph. 1955. The Sociology of Imperialism. In *Imperialism and Social Classes.* Cleveland: World Publishing Co. (Essay originally published in 1919.)

Schwarz, Wolfgang. 1962. Kant's Philosophy of Law and International Peace. *Philosophy and Phenomenonological Research,* 23:71-80.

Shell, Susan. 1980. The *Rights of Reason.* Toronto: University of Toronto Press.

Shklar, Judith. 1984. *Ordinary Vices.* Cambridge, MA.: Harvard University Press.

Skinner, Quentin. 1981. *Machiavelli.* New York: Hill and Wang.

Small, Melvin, and J. David Singer. 1976. The War-Proneness of Democratic Regimes. *The Jerusalem Journal of International Relations,* 1(4):50-69.

Small Melvin, and J. David Singer. 1982. *Resort to Arms.* Beverly Hills: Sage Publications.

Streit, Clarence. 1938. *Union Now: A Proposal for a Federal Union of the Leading Democracies.* New York: Harpers.

Thucydides. 1954. *The Peloponnesian War.* Rex Warner, ed. and trans. Baltimore: Penguin.

U.K. Foreign and Commonwealth Office. 1980. *A Yearbook of the Commonwealth 1980.* London: HMSO.

U.S. Congress. Senate. Select Committee to Study Governmental Operations with Respect to Intelligence Activities. 1975. *Covert Action in Chile, 1963–74.* 94th Cong., 1st sess., Washington, D.C.: U.S. Government Printing Office.

U.S. Department of State. 1981. *Country Reports on Human Rights Practices.* Washington, D.C.: U.S. Government Printing Office.

Waltz, Kenneth. 1962. Kant, Liberalism, and War. *American Political Science Review,* 56:331– 40.

Waltz, Kenneth. 1964. The Stability of a Bipolar World. *Daedalus,* 93:881–909.

Walzer, Michael. 1983. *Spheres of Justice.* New York: Basic Books.

Weede, Erich. 1984. Democracy and War Involvement. *Journal of Conflict Resolution,* 28:649–64.

Wilkenfeld, Jonathan. 1968. Domestic and Foreign Conflict Behavior of Nations. *Journal of Peace Research,* 5:56–69.

Williams, Howard. 1983. *Kant's Political Philosophy.* Oxford: Basil Blackwell.

Wright, Quincy. 1942. *A Study of History.* Chicago: Chicago University Press.

Yovel, Yirmiahu. 1980. *Kant and the Philosophy of History.* Princeton: Princeton University Press.

The Clash of Civilizations?

Samuel P. Huntington

THE NEXT PATTERN OF CONFLICT

WORLD POLITICS IS entering a new phase, and intellectuals have not hesitated to proliferate visions of what it will be—the end of history, the return of traditional rivalries between nation states, and the decline of the nation state from the conflicting pulls of tribalism and globalism, among others. Each of these visions catches aspects of the emerging reality. Yet they all miss a crucial, indeed a central, aspect of what global politics is likely to be in the coming years.

It is my hypothesis that the fundamental source of conflict in this new world will not be primarily ideological or primarily economic. The great divisions among humankind and the dominating source of conflict will be cultural. Nation states will remain the most powerful actors in world affairs, but the principal conflicts of global politics will occur between nations and groups of different civilizations. The clash of civilizations will dominate global politics. The fault lines between civilizations will be the battle lines of the future.

Conflict between civilizations will be the latest phase in the evolution of conflict in the modern world. For a century and a half after the emergence of the modern international system with the Peace of Westphalia, the conflicts of the Western world were largely among princes—emperors, absolute monarchs and constitutional monarchs attempting to expand their bureaucracies, their armies, their mercantilist economic

SAMUEL P. HUNTINGTON is Weatherland University Professor and Director of the John M. Olin Institute for Strategic Studies at Harvard University. This article is the product of the Olin Institute's project on "The Changing Security Environment and American National Interests." It appeared in the Summer 1993 issue of *Foreign Affairs*.

strength and, most important, the territory they ruled. In the process they created nation states, and beginning with the French Revolution the principal lines of conflict were between nations rather than princes. In 1793, as R. R. Palmer put it, "The wars of kings were over; the wars of peoples had begun." This nineteenth-century pattern lasted until the end of World War I. Then, as a result of the Russian Revolution and the reaction against it, the conflict of nations yielded to the conflict of ideologies, first among communism, fascism-Nazism and liberal democracy, and then between communism and liberal democracy. During the Cold War, this latter conflict became embodied in the struggle between the two superpowers, neither of which was a nation state in the classical European sense and each of which defined its identity in terms of its ideology.

These conflicts between princes, nation states and ideologies were primarily conflicts within Western civilization, "Western civil wars," as William Lind has labeled them. This was as true of the Cold War as it was of the world wars and the earlier wars of the seventeenth, eighteenth and nineteenth centuries. With the end of the Cold War, international politics moves out of its Western phase, and its centerpiece becomes the interaction between the West and non-Western civilizations and among non-Western civilizations. In the politics of civilizations, the peoples and governments of non-Western civilizations no longer remain the objects of history as targets of Western colonialism but join the West as movers and shapers of history.

THE NATURE OF CIVILIZATIONS

DURING THE COLD WAR the world was divided into the First, Second and Third Worlds. Those divisions are no longer relevant. It is far more meaningful now to group countries not in terms of their political or economic systems or in terms of their level of economic development but rather in terms of their culture and civilization.

What do we mean when we talk of a civilization? A civilization is a cultural entity. Villages, regions, ethnic groups, nationalities, religious groups, all have distinct cultures at different levels of cultural heterogeneity. The culture of a village in southern Italy may be different from that of a village in northern Italy, but both will share in a common Italian culture that distinguishes them from German villages. European communities, in turn, will share cultural features that distinguish them from Arab or Chinese communities. Arabs, Chinese and Westerners, however, are not part of any broader cultural entity. They constitute civilizations. A civilization is thus the highest cultural grouping of people and the broadest level of cultural identity people have short of that which distinguishes humans from other species. It is defined both by common objective elements, such as language, history, religion, customs, institutions, and by the subjective self-identification of people. People have levels of identity: a resident of Rome may define himself with varying degrees of intensity as a Roman, an Italian, a Catholic, a Christian, a European, a Westerner. The civilization to which he belongs is the broadest level of identification with which he intensely identifies. People can and do redefine their identities and, as a result, the composition and boundaries of civilizations change.

Civilizations may involve a large number of people, as with China ("a civilization pretending to be a state," as Lucian Pye put it), or a very small number of people, such as the Anglophone Caribbean. A civilization may include several nation states, as is the case with Western, Latin American and Arab civilizations, or only one, as is the case with Japanese civilization. Civilizations obviously blend and overlap, and may include subcivilizations. Western civilization has two major variants, European and North American, and Islam has its Arab, Turkic and Malay subdivisions. Civilizations are nonetheless meaningful entities, and while the lines between them are seldom sharp, they are real. Civilizations are dynamic; they rise and fall; they divide and merge. And, as any student of history knows, civilizations disappear and are buried in the sands of time.

Westerners tend to think of nation states as the principal actors in global affairs. They have been that, however, for only a few centuries. The broader reaches of human history have been the history of civilizations. In *A Study of History,* Arnold Toynbee identified 21 major civilizations; only six of them exist in the contemporary world.

WHY CIVILIZATIONS WILL CLASH

CIVILIZATION IDENTITY will be increasingly important in the future, and the world will be shaped in large measure by the interactions among seven or eight major civilizations. These include Western, Confucian, Japanese, Islamic, Hindu, Slavic-Orthodox, Latin American and possibly

Samuel P. Huntington

African civilization. The most important conflicts of the future will occur along the cultural fault lines separating these civilizations from one another.

Why will this be the case?

First, differences among civilizations are not only real; they are basic. Civilizations are differentiated from each other by history, language, culture, tradition and, most important, religion. The people of different civilizations have different views on the relations between God and man, the individual and the group, the citizen and the state, parents and children, husband and wife, as well as differing views of the relative importance of rights and responsibilities, liberty and authority, equality and hierarchy. These differences are the product of centuries. They will not soon disappear. They are far more fundamental than differences among political ideologies and political regimes. Differences do not necessarily mean conflict, and conflict does not necessarily mean violence. Over the centuries, however, differences among civilizations have generated the most prolonged and the most violent conflicts.

Second, the world is becoming a smaller place. The interactions between peoples of different civilizations are increasing; these increasing interactions intensify civilization consciousness and awareness of differences between civilizations and commonalities within civilizations. North African immigration to France generates hostility among Frenchmen and at the same time increased receptivity to immigration by "good" European Catholic Poles. Americans react far more negatively to Japanese investment than to larger investments from Canada and European countries. Similarly, as Donald Horowitz has pointed out, "An Ibo may be … an Owerri Ibo or an Onitsha Ibo in what was the Eastern region of Nigeria. In Lagos, he is simply an Ibo. In London, he is a Nigerian. In New York, he is an African." The interactions among peoples of different civilizations enhance the civilization-consciousness of people that, in turn, invigorates differences and animosities stretching or thought to stretch back deep into history.

Third, the processes of economic modernization and social change throughout the world are separating people from longstanding local identities. They also weaken the nation state as a source of identity. In much of the world religion has moved in to fill this gap, often in the form of movements that are labeled "fundamentalist." Such movements are found in Western Christianity, Judaism, Buddhism and Hinduism, as well as in Islam. In most countries and most religions the people active in fundamentalist movements are young, college-educated, middle-class technicians, professionals and business persons. The "unsecularization of the world," George Weigel has remarked, "is one of the dominant social facts of life in the late twentieth century." The revival of religion, "la revanche de Dieu," as Gilles Kepel labeled it, provides a basis for identity and commitment that transcends national boundaries and unites civilizations.

Fourth, the growth of civilization-consciousness is enhanced by the dual role of the West. On the one hand, the West is at a peak of power. At the same time, however, and perhaps as a result, a return to the roots phenomenon is occurring among non-Western civilizations. Increasingly one hears references to trends toward a turning inward and "Asianization" in Japan, the end of the Nehru legacy and the "Hinduization" of India, the failure of Western ideas of socialism and nationalism and hence "re-Islamization" of the Middle East, and now a debate over Westernization versus Russianization in Boris Yeltsin's country. A West at the peak of its power confronts non-Wests that increasingly have the desire, the will and the resources to shape the world in non-Western ways.

In the past, the elites of non-Western societies were usually the people who were most involved with the West, had been educated at Oxford, the Sorbonne or Sandhurst, and had absorbed Western attitudes and values. At the same time, the populace in non-Western countries often remained deeply imbued with the indigenous culture. Now, however, these relationships are being reversed. A de-Westernization and indigenization of elites is occurring in many non-Western countries at the same time that Western, usually American, cultures, styles and habits become more popular among the mass of the people.

Fifth, cultural characteristics and differences are less mutable and hence less easily compromised and resolved than political and economic ones. In the former Soviet Union, communists can become democrats, the rich can become poor and the poor rich, but Russians cannot become Estonians and Azeris cannot become Armenians. In class and ideological conflicts, the key question was "Which side are you on?" and people could and did choose sides and change sides. In conflicts between civilizations, the question is "What are you?" That is a given that cannot be changed. And as we know, from Bosnia to the Caucasus to the Sudan, the wrong answer to that question can mean a bullet in the head. Even more than ethnicity, religion discriminates

Samuel P. Huntington

sharply and exclusively among people. A person can be half-French and half-Arab and simultaneously even a citizen of two countries. It is more difficult to be half-Catholic and half-Muslim.

Finally, economic regionalism is increasing. The proportions of total trade that were intraregional rose between 1980 and 1989 from 51 percent to 59 percent in Europe, 33 percent to 37 percent in East Asia, and 32 percent to 36 percent in North America. The importance of regional economic blocs is likely to continue to increase in the future. On the one hand, successful economic regionalism will reinforce civilization-consciousness. On the other hand, economic regionalism may succeed only when it is rooted in a common civilization. The European Community rests on the shared foundation of European culture and Western Christianity. The success of the North American Free Trade Area depends on the convergence now underway of Mexican, Canadian and American cultures. Japan, in contrast, faces difficulties in creating a comparable economic entity in East Asia because Japan is a society and civilization unique to itself. However strong the trade and investment links Japan may develop with other East Asian countries, its cultural differences with those countries inhibit and perhaps preclude its promoting regional economic integration like that in Europe and North America.

Common culture, in contrast, is clearly facilitating the rapid expansion of the economic relations between the People's Republic of China and Hong Kong, Taiwan, Singapore and the overseas Chinese communities in other Asian countries. With the Cold War over, cultural commonalities increasingly overcome ideological differences, and mainland China and Taiwan move closer together. If cultural commonality is a prerequisite for economic integration, the principal East Asian economic bloc of the future is likely to be centered on China. This bloc is, in fact, already coming into existence. As Murray Weidenbaum has observed,

> Despite the current Japanese dominance of the region, the Chinese-based economy of Asia is rapidly emerging as a new epicenter for industry, commerce and finance. This strategic area contains substantial amounts of technology and manufacturing capability (Taiwan), outstanding entrepreneurial, marketing and services acumen (Hong Kong), a fine communications network (Singapore), a tremendous pool of financial capital (all three), and very large endowments of land, resources and labor (mainland China).... From Guangzhou to Singapore, from Kuala Lumpur to Manila, this influential network—often

The Clash of Civilizations?

based on extensions of the traditional clans—has been described as the backbone of the East Asian economy.[1]

Culture and religion also form the basis of the Economic Cooperation Organization, which brings together ten non-Arab Muslim countries: Iran, Pakistan, Turkey, Azerbaijan, Kazakhstan, Kyrgyzstan, Turkmenistan, Tadjikistan, Uzbekistan and Afghanistan. One impetus to the revival and expansion of this organization, founded originally in the 1960s by Turkey, Pakistan and Iran, is the realization by the leaders of several of these countries that they had no chance of admission to the European Community. Similarly, Caricom, the Central American Common Market and Mercosur rest on common cultural foundations. Efforts to build a broader Caribbean-Central American economic entity bridging the Anglo-Latin divide, however, have to date failed.

As people define their identity in ethnic and religious terms, they are likely to see an "us" versus "them" relation existing between themselves and people of different ethnicity or religion. The end of ideologically defined states in Eastern Europe and the former Soviet Union permits traditional ethnic identities and animosities to come to the fore. Differences in culture and religion create differences over policy issues, ranging from human rights to immigration to trade and commerce to the environment. Geographical propinquity gives rise to conflicting territorial claims from Bosnia to Mindanao. Most important, the efforts of the West to promote its values of democracy and liberalism as universal values, to maintain its military predominance and to advance its economic interests engender countering responses from other civilizations. Decreasingly able to mobilize support and form coalitions on the basis of ideology, governments and groups will increasingly attempt to mobilize support by appealing to common religion and civilization identity.

The clash of civilizations thus occurs at two levels. At the micro-level, adjacent groups along the fault lines between civilizations struggle, often violently, over the control of territory and each other. At the macro-level, states from different civilizations compete for relative military and economic power, struggle over the control of international in-

[1]Murray Weidenbaum, *Greater China: The Next Economic Superpower?*, St. Louis: Washington University Center for the Study of American Business, Contemporary Issues, Series 57, February 1993, pp. 2–3.

stitutions and third parties, and competitively promote their particular political and religious values.

THE FAULT LINES BETWEEN CIVILIZATIONS

THE FAULT LINES between civilizations are replacing the political and ideological boundaries of the Cold War as the flash points for crisis and bloodshed. The Cold War began when the Iron Curtain divided Europe politically and ideologically. The Cold War ended with the end of the Iron Curtain. As the ideological division of Europe has disappeared, the cultural division of Europe between Western Christianity, on the one hand, and Orthodox Christianity and Islam, on the other, has reemerged. The most significant dividing line in Europe, as William Wallace has suggested, may well be the eastern boundary of Western Christianity in the year 1500. This line runs along what are now the boundaries between Finland and Russia and between the Baltic states and Russia, cuts through Belarus and Ukraine separating the more Catholic western Ukraine from Orthodox eastern Ukraine, swings westward separating Transylvania from the rest of Romania, and then goes through Yugoslavia almost exactly along the line now separating Croatia and Slovenia from the rest of Yugoslavia. In the Balkans this line, of course, coincides with the historic boundary between the Hapsburg and Ottoman empires. The peoples to the north and west of this line are Protestant or Catholic; they shared the common experiences of European history—feudalism, the Renaissance, the Reformation, the Enlightenment, the French Revolution, the Industrial Revolution; they are generally economically better off than the peoples to the east; and they may now look forward to increasing involvement in a common European economy and to the consolidation of democratic political systems. The peoples to the east and south of this line are Orthodox or Muslim; they historically belonged to the Ottoman or Tsarist empires and were only lightly touched by the shaping events in the rest of Europe; they are generally less advanced economically; they seem much less likely to develop stable democratic political systems. The Velvet Curtain of culture has replaced the Iron Curtain of ideology as the most significant dividing line in Europe. As the events in Yugoslavia show, it is not only a line of difference; it is also at times a line of bloody conflict.

Conflict along the fault line between Western and Islamic civilizations has been going on for 1,300 years. After the founding of Islam, the Arab

The Clash of Civilizations?

and Moorish surge west and north only ended at Tours in 732. From the eleventh to the thirteenth century the Crusaders attempted with temporary success to bring Christianity and Christian rule to the Holy Land. From the fourteenth to the seventeenth century, the Ottoman Turks reversed the balance, extended their sway over the Middle East and the Balkans, captured Constantinople, and twice laid siege to Vienna. In the nineteenth and early twentieth centuries as Ottoman power declined Britain, France, and Italy established Western control over most of North Africa and the Middle East.

After World War II, the West, in turn, began to retreat; the colonial empires disappeared; first Arab nationalism and then Islamic fundamentalism manifested themselves; the West became heavily dependent on the Persian Gulf countries for its energy; the oil-rich Muslim countries became money-rich and, when they wished to, weapons-rich. Several wars occurred between Arabs and Israel (created by the West). France fought a bloody and ruthless war in Algeria for most of the 1950s; British and French forces invaded Egypt in 1956; American forces went into Lebanon in 1958; subsequently American forces returned to Lebanon, attacked Libya, and engaged in various military encounters with Iran; Arab and Islamic terrorists, supported by at least three Middle Eastern governments, employed the weapon of the weak and bombed Western planes and installations and seized Western hostages. This warfare between Arabs and the West culminated in 1990, when the United States sent a massive army to the Persian Gulf to defend some Arab countries against aggression by another. In its aftermath NATO planning is increasingly directed to potential threats and instability along its "southern tier."

This centuries-old military interaction between the West and Islam is unlikely to decline. It could become more virulent. The Gulf War left some Arabs feeling proud that Saddam Hussein had attacked Israel and stood up to the West. It also left many feeling humiliated and resentful of the West's military presence in the Persian Gulf, the West's overwhelming military dominance, and their apparent inability to shape their own destiny. Many Arab countries, in addition to the oil exporters, are reaching levels of economic and social development where autocratic forms of government become inappropriate and efforts to introduce democracy become stronger. Some openings in Arab political systems have already occurred. The principal beneficiaries of these openings have been Islamist movements. In the Arab world, in short,

Western democracy strengthens anti-Western political forces. This may be a passing phenomenon, but it surely complicates relations between Islamic countries and the West.

Those relations are also complicated by demography. The spectacular population growth in Arab countries, particularly in North Africa, has led to increased migration to Western Europe. The movement within Western Europe toward minimizing internal boundaries has sharpened political sensitivities with respect to this development. In Italy, France and Germany, racism is increasingly open, and political reactions and violence against Arab and Turkish migrants have become more intense and more widespread since 1990.

On both sides the interaction between Islam and the West is seen as a clash of civilizations. The West's "next confrontation," observes M. J. Akbar, an Indian Muslim author, "is definitely going to come from the Muslim world. It is in the sweep of the Islamic nations from the Maghreb to Pakistan that the struggle for a new world order will begin." Bernard Lewis comes to a similar conclusion:

> We are facing a mood and a movement far transcending the level of issues and policies and the governments that pursue them. This is no less than a clash of civilizations—the perhaps irrational but surely historic reaction of an ancient rival against our Judeo-Christian heritage, our secular present, and the worldwide expansion of both.[2]

Historically, the other great antagonistic interaction of Arab Islamic civilization has been with the pagan, animist, and now increasingly Christian black peoples to the south. In the past, this antagonism was epitomized in the image of Arab slave dealers and black slaves. It has been reflected in the on-going civil war in the Sudan between Arabs and blacks, the fighting in Chad between Libyan-supported insurgents and the government, the tensions between Orthodox Christians and Muslims in the Horn of Africa, and the political conflicts, recurring riots and communal violence between Muslims and Christians in Nigeria. The modernization of Africa and the spread of Christianity are likely to enhance the probability of violence along this fault line. Symptomatic of

---

[2]Bernard Lewis, "The Roots of Muslim Rage," *The Atlantic Monthly*, vol. 266, September 1990, p. 60; *Time*, June 15, 1992, pp. 24–28.

The Clash of Civilizations?

the intensification of this conflict was Pope John Paul II's speech in Khartoum in February 1993 attacking the actions of the Sudan's Islamist government against the Christian minority there.

On the northern border of Islam, conflict has increasingly erupted between Orthodox and Muslim peoples, including the carnage of Bosnia and Sarajevo, the simmering violence between Serb and Albanian, the tenuous relations between Bulgarians and their Turkish minority, the violence between Ossetians and Ingush, the unremitting slaughter of each other by Armenians and Azeris, the tense relations between Russians and Muslims in Central Asia, and the deployment of Russian troops to protect Russian interests in the Caucasus and Central Asia. Religion reinforces the revival of ethnic identities and restimulates Russian fears about the security of their southern borders. This concern is well captured by Archie Roosevelt:

> Much of Russian history concerns the struggle between the Slavs and the Turkic peoples on their borders, which dates back to the foundation of the Russian state more than a thousand years ago. In the Slavs' millennium-long confrontation with their eastern neighbors lies the key to an understanding not only of Russian history, but Russian character. To understand Russian realities today one has to have a concept of the great Turkic ethnic group that has preoccupied Russians through the centuries.[3]

The conflict of civilizations is deeply rooted elsewhere in Asia. The historic clash between Muslim and Hindu in the subcontinent manifests itself now not only in the rivalry between Pakistan and India but also in intensifying religious strife within India between increasingly militant Hindu groups and India's substantial Muslim minority. The destruction of the Ayodhya mosque in December 1992 brought to the fore the issue of whether India will remain a secular democratic state or become a Hindu one. In East Asia, China has outstanding territorial disputes with most of its neighbors. It has pursued a ruthless policy toward the Buddhist people of Tibet, and it is pursuing an increasingly ruthless policy toward its Turkic-Muslim minority. With the Cold War over, the underlying differences between China and the United States have reasserted themselves in areas

---

[3]Archie Roosevelt, *For Lust of Knowing*, Boston: Little, Brown, 1988, pp. 332–333.

such as human rights, trade and weapons proliferation. These differences are unlikely to moderate. A "new cold war," Deng Xaioping reportedly asserted in 1991, is under way between China and America.

The same phrase has been applied to the increasingly difficult relations between Japan and the United States. Here cultural difference exacerbates economic conflict. People on each side allege racism on the other, but at least on the American side the antipathies are not racial but cultural. The basic values, attitudes, behavioral patterns of the two societies could hardly be more different. The economic issues between the United States and Europe are no less serious than those between the United States and Japan, but they do not have the same political salience and emotional intensity because the differences between American culture and European culture are so much less than those between American civilization and Japanese civilization.

The interactions between civilizations vary greatly in the extent to which they are likely to be characterized by violence. Economic competition clearly predominates between the American and European sub-civilizations of the West and between both of them and Japan. On the Eurasian continent, however, the proliferation of ethnic conflict, epitomized at the extreme in "ethnic cleansing," has not been totally random. It has been most frequent and most violent between groups belonging to different civilizations. In Eurasia the great historic fault lines between civilizations are once more aflame. This is particularly true along the boundaries of the crescent-shaped Islamic bloc of nations from the bulge of Africa to central Asia. Violence also occurs between Muslims, on the one hand, and Orthodox Serbs in the Balkans, Jews in Israel, Hindus in India, Buddhists in Burma and Catholics in the Philippines. Islam has bloody borders.

CIVILIZATION RALLYING: THE KIN-COUNTRY SYNDROME

GROUPS OR STATES belonging to one civilization that become involved in war with people from a different civilization naturally try to rally support from other members of their own civilization. As the post-Cold War world evolves, civilization commonality, what H. D. S. Greenway has termed the "kin-country" syndrome, is replacing political ideology and traditional balance of power considerations as the principal basis for cooperation and coalitions. It can be seen gradually emerging in the post-

The Clash of Civilizations?

Cold War conflicts in the Persian Gulf, the Caucasus and Bosnia. None of these was a full-scale war between civilizations, but each involved some elements of civilizational rallying, which seemed to become more important as the conflict continued and which may provide a foretaste of the future.

First, in the Gulf War one Arab state invaded another and then fought a coalition of Arab, Western and other states. While only a few Muslim governments overtly supported Saddam Hussein, many Arab elites privately cheered him on, and he was highly popular among large sections of the Arab publics. Islamic fundamentalist movements universally supported Iraq rather than the Western-backed governments of Kuwait and Saudi Arabia. Forswearing Arab nationalism, Saddam Hussein explicitly invoked an Islamic appeal. He and his supporters attempted to define the war as a war between civilizations. "It is not the world against Iraq," as Safar Al-Hawali, dean of Islamic Studies at the Umm Al-Qura University in Mecca, put it in a widely circulated tape. "It is the West against Islam." Ignoring the rivalry between Iran and Iraq, the chief Iranian religious leader, Ayatollah Ali Khamenei, called for a holy war against the West: "The struggle against American aggression, greed, plans and policies will be counted as a jihad, and anybody who is killed on that path is a martyr." "This is a war," King Hussein of Jordan argued, "against all Arabs and all Muslims and not against Iraq alone."

The rallying of substantial sections of Arab elites and publics behind Saddam Hussein caused those Arab governments in the anti-Iraq coalition to moderate their activities and temper their public statements. Arab governments opposed or distanced themselves from subsequent Western efforts to apply pressure on Iraq, including enforcement of a no-fly zone in the summer of 1992 and the bombing of Iraq in January 1993. The Western-Soviet-Turkish-Arab anti-Iraq coalition of 1990 had by 1993 become a coalition of almost only the West and Kuwait against Iraq.

Muslims contrasted Western actions against Iraq with the West's failure to protect Bosnians against Serbs and to impose sanctions on Israel for violating U.N. resolutions. The West, they alleged, was using a double standard. A world of clashing civilizations, however, is inevitably a world of double standards: people apply one standard to their kin-countries and a different standard to others.

Second, the kin-country syndrome also appeared in conflicts in the former Soviet Union. Armenian military successes in 1992 and 1993 stimulated

Turkey to become increasingly supportive of its religious, ethnic and linguistic brethren in Azerbaijan. "We have a Turkish nation feeling the same sentiments as the Azerbaijanis," said one Turkish official in 1992. "We are under pressure. Our newspapers are full of the photos of atrocities and are asking us if we are still serious about pursuing our neutral policy. Maybe we should show Armenia that there's a big Turkey in the region." President Turgut Özal agreed, remarking that Turkey should at least "scare the Armenians a little bit." Turkey, Özal threatened again in 1993, would "show its fangs." Turkish Air Force jets flew reconnaissance flights along the Armenian border; Turkey suspended food shipments and air flights to Armenia; and Turkey and Iran announced they would not accept dismemberment of Azerbaijan. In the last years of its existence, the Soviet government supported Azerbaijan because its government was dominated by former communists. With the end of the Soviet Union, however, political considerations gave way to religious ones. Russian troops fought on the side of the Armenians, and Azerbaijan accused the "Russian government of turning 180 degrees" toward support for Christian Armenia.

Third, with respect to the fighting in the former Yugoslavia, Western publics manifested sympathy and support for the Bosnian Muslims and the horrors they suffered at the hands of the Serbs. Relatively little concern was expressed, however, over Croatian attacks on Muslims and participation in the dismemberment of Bosnia-Herzegovina. In the early stages of the Yugoslav breakup, Germany, in an unusual display of diplomatic initiative and muscle, induced the other 11 members of the European Community to follow its lead in recognizing Slovenia and Croatia. As a result of the pope's determination to provide strong backing to the two Catholic countries, the Vatican extended recognition even before the Community did. The United States followed the European lead. Thus the leading actors in Western civilization rallied behind their coreligionists. Subsequently Croatia was reported to be receiving substantial quantities of arms from Central European and other Western countries. Boris Yeltsin's government, on the other hand, attempted to pursue a middle course that would be sympathetic to the Orthodox Serbs but not alienate Russia from the West. Russian conservative and nationalist groups, however, including many legislators, attacked the government for not being more forthcoming in its support for the Serbs. By early 1993 several hundred Russians apparently were serving with the Serbian forces, and reports circulated of Russian arms being supplied to Serbia.

The Clash of Civilizations?

Islamic governments and groups, on the other hand, castigated the West for not coming to the defense of the Bosnians. Iranian leaders urged Muslims from all countries to provide help to Bosnia; in violation of the U.N. arms embargo, Iran supplied weapons and men for the Bosnians; Iranian-supported Lebanese groups sent guerrillas to train and organize the Bosnian forces. In 1993 up to 4,000 Muslims from over two dozen Islamic countries were reported to be fighting in Bosnia. The governments of Saudi Arabia and other countries felt under increasing pressure from fundamentalist groups in their own societies to provide more vigorous support for the Bosnians. By the end of 1992, Saudi Arabia had reportedly supplied substantial funding for weapons and supplies for the Bosnians, which significantly increased their military capabilities vis-à-vis the Serbs.

In the 1930s the Spanish Civil War provoked intervention from countries that politically were fascist, communist and democratic. In the 1990s the Yugoslav conflict is provoking intervention from countries that are Muslim, Orthodox and Western Christian. The parallel has not gone unnoticed. "The war in Bosnia-Herzegovina has become the emotional equivalent of the fight against fascism in the Spanish Civil War," one Saudi editor observed. "Those who died there are regarded as martyrs who tried to save their fellow Muslims."

Conflicts and violence will also occur between states and groups within the same civilization. Such conflicts, however, are likely to be less intense and less likely to expand than conflicts between civilizations. Common membership in a civilization reduces the probability of violence in situations where it might otherwise occur. In 1991 and 1992 many people were alarmed by the possibility of violent conflict between Russia and Ukraine over territory, particularly Crimea, the Black Sea fleet, nuclear weapons and economic issues. If civilization is what counts, however, the likelihood of violence between Ukrainians and Russians should be low. They are two Slavic, primarily Orthodox peoples who have had close relationships with each other for centuries. As of early 1993, despite all the reasons for conflict, the leaders of the two countries were effectively negotiating and defusing the issues between the two countries. While there has been serious fighting between Muslims and Christians elsewhere in the former Soviet Union and much tension and some fighting between Western and Orthodox Christians in the Baltic states, there has been virtually no violence between Russians and Ukrainians.

Samuel P. Huntington

Civilization rallying to date has been limited, but it has been growing, and it clearly has the potential to spread much further. As the conflicts in the Persian Gulf, the Caucasus and Bosnia continued, the positions of nations and the cleavages between them increasingly were along civilizational lines. Populist politicians, religious leaders and the media have found it a potent means of arousing mass support and of pressuring hesitant governments. In the coming years, the local conflicts most likely to escalate into major wars will be those, as in Bosnia and the Caucasus, along the fault lines between civilizations. The next world war, if there is one, will be a war between civilizations.

THE WEST VERSUS THE REST

THE WEST IS NOW at an extraordinary peak of power in relation to other civilizations. Its superpower opponent has disappeared from the map. Military conflict among Western states is unthinkable, and Western military power is unrivaled. Apart from Japan, the West faces no economic challenge. It dominates international political and security institutions and with Japan international economic institutions. Global political and security issues are effectively settled by a directorate of the United States, Britain and France, world economic issues by a directorate of the United States, Germany and Japan, all of which maintain extraordinarily close relations with each other to the exclusion of lesser and largely non-Western countries. Decisions made at the U.N. Security Council or in the International Monetary Fund that reflect the interests of the West are presented to the world as reflecting the desires of the world community. The very phrase "the world community" has become the euphemistic collective noun (replacing "the Free World") to give global legitimacy to actions reflecting the interests of the United States and other Western powers.4 Through the IMF and other international economic institutions, the West

---

4Almost invariably Western leaders claim they are acting on behalf of "the world community." One minor lapse occurred during the run-up to the Gulf War. In an interview on "Good Morning America," Dec. 21, 1990, British Prime Minister John Major referred to the actions "the West" was taking against Saddam Hussein. He quickly corrected himself and subsequently referred to "the world community." He was, however, right when he erred.

promotes its economic interests and imposes on other nations the economic policies it thinks appropriate. In any poll of non-Western peoples, the IMF undoubtedly would win the support of finance ministers and a few others, but get an overwhelmingly unfavorable rating from just about everyone else, who would agree with Georgy Arbatov's characterization of IMF officials as "neo-Bolsheviks who love expropriating other people's money, imposing undemocratic and alien rules of economic and political conduct and stifling economic freedom."

Western domination of the U.N. Security Council and its decisions, tempered only by occasional abstention by China, produced U.N. legitimation of the West's use of force to drive Iraq out of Kuwait and its elimination of Iraq's sophisticated weapons and capacity to produce such weapons. It also produced the quite unprecedented action by the United States, Britain and France in getting the Security Council to demand that Libya hand over the Pan Am 103 bombing suspects and then to impose sanctions when Libya refused. After defeating the largest Arab army, the West did not hesitate to throw its weight around in the Arab world. The West in effect is using international institutions, military power and economic resources to run the world in ways that will maintain Western predominance, protect Western interests and promote Western political and economic values.

That at least is the way in which non-Westerners see the new world, and there is a significant element of truth in their view. Differences in power and struggles for military, economic and institutional power are thus one source of conflict between the West and other civilizations. Differences in culture, that is basic values and beliefs, are a second source of conflict. V. S. Naipaul has argued that Western civilization is the "universal civilization" that "fits all men." At a superficial level much of Western culture has indeed permeated the rest of the world. At a more basic level, however, Western concepts differ fundamentally from those prevalent in other civilizations. Western ideas of individualism, liberalism, constitutionalism, human rights, equality, liberty, the rule of law, democracy, free markets, the separation of church and state, often have little resonance in Islamic, Confucian, Japanese, Hindu, Buddhist or Orthodox cultures. Western efforts to propagate such ideas produce instead a reaction against "human rights imperialism" and a reaffirmation of indigenous values, as can be seen in the support for religious fundamentalism by the younger generation in non-Western cultures. The very notion that there could be a "universal civilization" is a Western idea, directly at odds with the particularism of most Asian societies and their emphasis on what distinguishes one people from another. Indeed, the author of a review of 100 comparative studies of values in different societies concluded that "the values that are most important in the West are least important worldwide."[5] In the political realm, of course, these differences are most manifest in the efforts of the United States and other Western powers to induce other peoples to adopt Western ideas concerning democracy and human rights. Modern democratic government originated in the West. When it has developed in non-Western societies it has usually been the product of Western colonialism or imposition.

The central axis of world politics in the future is likely to be, in Kishore Mahbubani's phrase, the conflict between "the West and the Rest" and the responses of non-Western civilizations to Western power and values.[6] Those responses generally take one or a combination of three forms. At one extreme, non-Western states can, like Burma and North Korea, attempt to pursue a course of isolation, to insulate their societies from penetration or "corruption" by the West, and, in effect, to opt out of participation in the Western-dominated global community. The costs of this course, however, are high, and few states have pursued it exclusively. A second alternative, the equivalent of "band-wagoning" in international relations theory, is to attempt to join the West and accept its values and institutions. The third alternative is to attempt to "balance" the West by developing economic and military power and cooperating with other non-Western societies against the West, while preserving indigenous values and institutions; in short, to modernize but not to Westernize.

THE TORN COUNTRIES

IN THE FUTURE, as people differentiate themselves by civilization, countries with large numbers of peoples of different civilizations, such as the Soviet Union and Yugoslavia, are candidates for dismemberment. Some other countries have a fair degree of cultural homogeneity but are divided

---

[5]Harry C. Triandis, *The New York Times,* Dec. 25, 1990, p. 41, and "Cross-Cultural Studies of Individualism and Collectivism," Nebraska Symposium on Motivation, vol. 37, 1989, pp. 41–133.

[6]Kishore Mahbubani, "The West and the Rest," *The National Interest,* Summer 1992, pp. 3–13.

The Clash of Civilizations?

over whether their society belongs to one civilization or another. These are torn countries. Their leaders typically wish to pursue a bandwagoning strategy and to make their countries members of the West, but the history, culture and traditions of their countries are non-Western. The most obvious and prototypical torn country is Turkey. The late twentieth-century leaders of Turkey have followed in the Attatürk tradition and defined Turkey as a modern, secular, Western nation state. They allied Turkey with the West in NATO and in the Gulf War; they applied for membership in the European Community. At the same time, however, elements in Turkish society have supported an Islamic revival and have argued that Turkey is basically a Middle Eastern Muslim society. In addition, while the elite of Turkey has defined Turkey as a Western society, the elite of the West refuses to accept Turkey as such. Turkey will not become a member of the European Community, and the real reason, as President Özal said, "is that we are Muslim and they are Christian and they don't say that." Having rejected Mecca, and then being rejected by Brussels, where does Turkey look? Tashkent may be the answer. The end of the Soviet Union gives Turkey the opportunity to become the leader of a revived Turkic civilization involving seven countries from the borders of Greece to those of China. Encouraged by the West, Turkey is making strenuous efforts to carve out this new identity for itself.

During the past decade Mexico has assumed a position somewhat similar to that of Turkey. Just as Turkey abandoned its historic opposition to Europe and attempted to join Europe, Mexico has stopped defining itself by its opposition to the United States and is instead attempting to imitate the United States and to join it in the North American Free Trade Area. Mexican leaders are engaged in the great task of redefining Mexican identity and have introduced fundamental economic reforms that eventually will lead to fundamental political change. In 1991 a top adviser to President Carlos Salinas de Gortari described at length to me all the changes the Salinas government was making. When he finished, I remarked: "That's most impressive. It seems to me that basically you want to change Mexico from a Latin American country into a North American country." He looked at me with surprise and exclaimed: "Exactly! That's precisely what we are trying to do, but of course we could never say so publicly." As his remark indicates, in Mexico as in Turkey, significant elements in society resist the redefinition of their country's identity. In Turkey, European-oriented leaders have to make gestures to Islam (Özal's pilgrimage to Mecca); so also Mexico's North American-oriented leaders have to make gestures to those who hold Mexico to be a Latin American country (Salinas' Ibero-American Guadalajara summit).

Historically Turkey has been the most profoundly torn country. For the United States, Mexico is the most immediate torn country. Globally the most important torn country is Russia. The question of whether Russia is part of the West or the leader of a distinct Slavic-Orthodox civilization has been a recurring one in Russian history. That issue was obscured by the communist victory in Russia, which imported a Western ideology, adapted it to Russian conditions and then challenged the West in the name of that ideology. The dominance of communism shut off the historic debate over Westernization versus Russification. With communism discredited Russians once again face that question.

President Yeltsin is adopting Western principles and goals and seeking to make Russia a "normal" country and a part of the West. Yet both the Russian elite and the Russian public are divided on this issue. Among the more moderate dissenters, Sergei Stankevich argues that Russia should reject the "Atlanticist" course, which would lead it "to become European, to become a part of the world economy in rapid and organized fashion, to become the eighth member of the Seven, and to put particular emphasis on Germany and the United States as the two dominant members of the Atlantic alliance." While also rejecting an exclusively Eurasian policy, Stankevich nonetheless argues that Russia should give priority to the protection of Russians in other countries, emphasize its Turkic and Muslim connections, and promote "an appreciable redistribution of our resources, our options, our ties, and our interests in favor of Asia, of the eastern direction." People of this persuasion criticize Yeltsin for subordinating Russia's interests to those of the West, for reducing Russian military strength, for failing to support traditional friends such as Serbia, and for pushing economic and political reform in ways injurious to the Russian people. Indicative of this trend is the new popularity of the ideas of Petr Savitsky, who in the 1920s argued that Russia was a unique Eurasian civilization.[7] More extreme dissidents voice much more blatantly nationalist, anti-Western and anti-Semitic views, and urge Russia to redevelop its military strength and to es-

---

[7]Sergei Stankevich, "Russia in Search of Itself," *The National Interest,* Summer 1992, pp. 47–51; Daniel Schneider, "A Russian Movement Rejects Western Tilt," *Christian Science Monitor,* Feb. 5, 1993, pp. 5–7.

tablish closer ties with China and Muslim countries. The people of Russia are as divided as the elite. An opinion survey in European Russia in the spring of 1992 revealed that 40 percent of the public had positive attitudes toward the West and 36 percent had negative attitudes. As it has been for much of its history, Russia in the early 1990s is truly a torn country.

To redefine its civilization identity, a torn country must meet three requirements. First, its political and economic elite has to be generally supportive of and enthusiastic about this move. Second, its public has to be willing to acquiesce in the redefinition. Third, the dominant groups in the recipient civilization have to be willing to embrace the convert. All three requirements in large part exist with respect to Mexico. The first two in large part exist with respect to Turkey. It is not clear that any of them exist with respect to Russia's joining the West. The conflict between liberal democracy and Marxism-Leninism was between ideologies which, despite their major differences, ostensibly shared ultimate goals of freedom, equality and prosperity. A traditional, authoritarian, nationalist Russia could have quite different goals. A Western democrat could carry on an intellectual debate with a Soviet Marxist. It would be virtually impossible for him to do that with a Russian traditionalist. If, as the Russians stop behaving like Marxists, they reject liberal democracy and begin behaving like Russians but not like Westerners, the relations between Russia and the West could again become distant and conflictual.[8]

THE CONFUCIAN-ISLAMIC CONNECTION
THE OBSTACLES TO non-Western countries joining the West vary considerably. They are least for Latin American and East European countries. They are greater for the Orthodox countries of the former Soviet Union. They are still greater for Muslim, Confucian, Hindu and Buddhist soci-

---

[8]Owen Harries has pointed out that Australia is trying (unwisely in his view) to become a torn country in reverse. Although it has been a full member not only of the West but also of the ABCA military and intelligence core of the West, its current leaders are in effect proposing that it defect from the West, redefine itself as an Asian country and cultivate close ties with its neighbors. Australia's future, they argue, is with the dynamic economies of East Asia. But, as I have suggested, close economic cooperation normally requires a common cultural base. In addition, none of the three conditions necessary for a torn country to join another civilization is likely to exist in Australia's case.

eties. Japan has established a unique position for itself as an associate member of the West: it is in the West in some respects but clearly not of the West in important dimensions. Those countries that for reason of culture and power do not wish to, or cannot, join the West compete with the West by developing their own economic, military and political power. They do this by promoting their internal development and by cooperating with other non-Western countries. The most prominent form of this cooperation is the Confucian-Islamic connection that has emerged to challenge Western interests, values and power.

Almost without exception, Western countries are reducing their military power; under Yeltsin's leadership so also is Russia. China, North Korea and several Middle Eastern states, however, are significantly expanding their military capabilities. They are doing this by the import of arms from Western and non-Western sources and by the development of indigenous arms industries. One result is the emergence of what Charles Krauthammer has called "Weapon States," and the Weapon States are not Western states. Another result is the redefinition of arms control, which is a Western concept and a Western goal. During the Cold War the primary purpose of arms control was to establish a stable military balance between the United States and its allies and the Soviet Union and its allies. In the post-Cold War world the primary objective of arms control is to prevent the development by non-Western societies of military capabilities that could threaten Western interests. The West attempts to do this through international agreements, economic pressure and controls on the transfer of arms and weapons technologies.

The conflict between the West and the Confucian-Islamic states focuses largely, although not exclusively, on nuclear, chemical and biological weapons, ballistic missiles and other sophisticated means for delivering them, and the guidance, intelligence and other electronic capabilities for achieving that goal. The West promotes nonproliferation as a universal norm and nonproliferation treaties and inspections as means of realizing that norm. It also threatens a variety of sanctions against those who promote the spread of sophisticated weapons and proposes some benefits for those who do not. The attention of the West focuses, naturally, on nations that are actually or potentially hostile to the West.

The non-Western nations, on the other hand, assert their right to acquire and to deploy whatever weapons they think necessary for their security. They also have absorbed, to the full, the truth of the response of the Indian defense minister when asked what lesson he learned from the Gulf War: "Don't fight the United States unless you have nuclear weapons." Nuclear weapons, chemical weapons and missiles are viewed, probably erroneously, as the potential equalizer of superior Western conventional power. China, of course, already has nuclear weapons; Pakistan and India have the capability to deploy them. North Korea, Iran, Iraq, Libya and Algeria appear to be attempting to acquire them. A top Iranian official has declared that all Muslim states should acquire nuclear weapons, and in 1988 the president of Iran reportedly issued a directive calling for development of "offensive and defensive chemical, biological and radiological weapons."

Centrally important to the development of counter-West military capabilities is the sustained expansion of China's military power and its means to create military power. Buoyed by spectacular economic development, China is rapidly increasing its military spending and vigorously moving forward with the modernization of its armed forces. It is purchasing weapons from the former Soviet states; it is developing long-range missiles; in 1992 it tested a one-megaton nuclear device. It is developing power-projection capabilities, acquiring aerial refueling technology, and trying to purchase an aircraft carrier. Its military buildup and assertion of sovereignty over the South China Sea are provoking a multilateral regional arms race in East Asia. China is also a major exporter of arms and weapons technology. It has exported materials to Libya and Iraq that could be used to manufacture nuclear weapons and nerve gas. It has helped Algeria build a reactor suitable for nuclear weapons research and production. China has sold to Iran nuclear technology that American officials believe could only be used to create weapons and apparently has shipped components of 300-mile-range missiles to Pakistan. North Korea has had a nuclear weapons program under way for some while and has sold advanced missiles and missile technology to Syria and Iran. The flow of weapons and weapons technology is generally from East Asia to the Middle East. There is, however, some movement in the reverse direction; China has received Stinger missiles from Pakistan.

A Confucian-Islamic military connection has thus come into being, designed to promote acquisition by its members of the weapons and weapons technologies needed to counter the military power of the West. It may or may not last. At present, however, it is, as Dave McCurdy has said, "a renegades' mutual support pact, run by the proliferators and their backers." A new form of arms competition is thus occurring between Islamic-Confucian states and the West. In an old-fashioned arms race, each side developed its own arms to balance or to achieve superiority against the other side. In this new form of arms competition, one side is developing its arms and the other side is attempting not to balance but to limit and prevent that arms build-up while at the same time reducing its own military capabilities.

IMPLICATIONS FOR THE WEST

THIS ARTICLE DOES not argue that civilization identities will replace all other identities, that nation states will disappear, that each civilization will become a single coherent political entity, that groups within a civilization will not conflict with and even fight each other. This paper does set forth the hypotheses that differences between civilizations are real and important; civilization-consciousness is increasing; conflict between civilizations will supplant ideological and other forms of conflict as the dominant global form of conflict; international relations, historically a game played out within Western civilization, will increasingly be de-Westernized and become a game in which non-Western civilizations are actors and not simply objects; successful political, security and economic international institutions are more likely to develop within civilizations than across civilizations; conflicts between groups in different civilizations will be more frequent, more sustained and more violent than conflicts between groups in the same civilization; violent conflicts between groups in different civilizations are the most likely and most dangerous source of escalation that could lead to global wars; the paramount axis of world politics will be the relations between "the West and the Rest"; the elites in some torn non-Western countries will try to make their countries part of the West, but in most cases face major obstacles to accomplishing this; a central focus of conflict for the immediate future will be between the West and several Islamic-Confucian states.

This is not to advocate the desirability of conflicts between civilizations. It is to set forth descriptive hypotheses as to what the future may be like. If these are plausible hypotheses, however, it is necessary to consider their implications for Western policy. These implications should be divided between short-term advantage and long-term accommodation. In the short term it is clearly in the interest of the West to promote greater coop-eration and unity within its own civilization, particularly between its European and North American components; to incorporate into the West societies in Eastern Europe and Latin America whose cultures are close to those of the West; to promote and maintain cooperative relations with Russia and Japan; to prevent escalation of local inter-civilization conflicts into major inter-civilization wars; to limit the expansion of the military strength of Confucian and Islamic states; to moderate the reduction of Western military capabilities and maintain military superiority in East and Southwest Asia; to exploit differences and conflicts among Confucian and Islamic states; to support in other civilizations groups sympathetic to Western values and interests; to strengthen international institutions that reflect and legitimate Western interests and values and to promote the involvement of non-Western states in those institutions.

In the longer term other measures would be called for. Western civilization is both Western and modern. Non-Western civilizations have attempted to become modern without becoming Western. To date only Japan has fully succeeded in this quest. Non-Western civilizations will continue to attempt to acquire the wealth, technology, skills, machines and weapons that are part of being modern. They will also attempt to reconcile this modernity with their traditional culture and values. Their economic and military strength relative to the West will increase. Hence the West will increasingly have to accommodate these non-Western modern civilizations whose power approaches that of the West but whose values and interests differ significantly from those of the West. This will require the West to maintain the economic and military power necessary to protect its interests in relation to these civilizations. It will also, however, require the West to develop a more profound understanding of the basic religious and philosophical assumptions underlying other civilizations and the ways in which people in those civilizations see their interests. It will require an effort to identify elements of commonality between Western and other civilizations. For the relevant future, there will be no universal civilization, but instead a world of different civilizations, each of which will have to learn to coexist with the others. ☯

The Summoning

'But They Said, We Will Not Hearken.'

JEREMIAH 6:17

Fouad Ajami

IN JOSEPH CONRAD'S *Youth,* a novella published at the turn of the century, Marlowe, the narrator, remembers when he first encountered "the East":

> And then, before I could open my lips, the East spoke to me, but it was in a Western voice. A torrent of words was poured into the enigmatical, the fateful silence; outlandish, angry words mixed with words and even whole sentences of good English, less strange but even more surprising. The voice swore and cursed violently; it riddled the solemn peace of the bay by a volley of abuse. It began by calling me Pig, and from that went crescendo into unmentionable adjectives—in English.

The young Marlowe knew that even the most remote civilization had been made and remade by the West, and taught new ways.

Not so Samuel P. Huntington. In a curious essay, "The Clash of Civilizations," Huntington has found his civilizations whole and intact, watertight under an eternal sky. Buried alive, as it were, during the years of the Cold War, these civilizations (Islamic, Slavic-Orthodox, Western, Confucian, Japanese, Hindu, etc.) rose as soon as the stone was rolled off, dusted themselves off, and proceeded to claim the loyalty of their adherents. For this student of history and culture, civilizations have always seemed messy

FOUAD AJAMI is Majid Khadduri Professor of Middle Eastern Studies at the School of Advanced International Studies, The Johns Hopkins University. This article appeared in the September/October 1993 issue of *Foreign Affairs.*

creatures. Furrows run across whole civilizations, across individuals them-selves—that was modernity's verdict. But Huntington looks past all that. The crooked and meandering alleyways of the world are straightened out. With a sharp pencil and a steady hand Huntington marks out where one civilization ends and the wilderness of "the other" begins.

More surprising still is Huntington's attitude toward states, and their place in his scheme of things. From one of the most influential and bril-liant students of the state and its national interest there now comes an essay that misses the slyness of states, the unsentimental and cold-blooded nature of so much of what they do as they pick their way through chaos. Despite the obligatory passage that states will remain "the most powerful actors in world affairs," states are written off, their place given over to clashing civilizations. In Huntington's words, "The next world war, if there is one, will be a war between civilizations."

THE POWER OF MODERNITY

HUNTINGTON'S MEDITATION is occasioned by his concern about the state of the West, its power and the terms of its engagement with "the rest."[1] "He who gives, dominates," the great historian Fernand Braudel ob-served of the traffic of civilizations. In making itself over the centuries, the West helped make the others as well. We have come to the end of this trail, Huntington is sure. He is impressed by the "de-Westernization" of soci-eties, their "indigenization" and apparent willingness to go their own way. In his view of things such phenomena as the "Hinduization" of India and Islamic fundamentalism are ascendant. To these detours into "tradition" Huntington has assigned great force and power.

But Huntington is wrong. He has underestimated the tenacity of modernity and secularism in places that acquired these ways against great odds, always perilously close to the abyss, the darkness never far. India will not become a Hindu state. The inheritance of Indian secularism will hold. The vast middle class will defend it, keep the order intact to maintain

---

[1]The West itself is unexamined in Huntington's essay. No fissures run through it. No multiculturalists are heard from. It is orderly within its ram-parts. What doubts Huntington has about the will within the walls, he has kept within himself. He has assumed that his call to unity will be answered, for outside flutter the banners of the Saracens and the Confucians.

India's—and its own—place in the modern world of nations. There exists in that anarchic polity an instinctive dread of playing with fires that might consume it. Hindu chauvinism may coarsen the public life of the country, but the state and the middle class that sustains it know that a detour into religious fanaticism is a fling with ruin. A resourceful middle class partakes of global culture and norms. A century has passed since the Indian bourgeoisie, through its political vehicle the Indian National Congress, set out to claim for itself and India a place among nations. Out of that long struggle to overturn British rule and the parallel struggle against "communalism," the advocates of the national idea built a large and durable state. They will not cede all this for a political kingdom of Hindu purity.

We have been hearing from the traditionalists, but we should not exaggerate their power, for traditions are often most insistent and loud when they rupture, when people no longer really believe and when age-old customs lose their ability to keep men and women at home. The phenomenon we have dubbed as Islamic fundamentalism is less a sign of resurgence than of panic and bewilderment and guilt that the border with "the other" has been crossed. Those young urban poor, half-educated in the cities of the Arab world, and their Sorbonne-educated lay preachers, can they be evidence of a genuine return to tradition? They crash Europe's and America's gates in search of liberty and work, and they rail against the sins of the West. It is easy to understand Huntington's frustration with this kind of complexity, with the strange mixture of attraction and repulsion that the West breeds, and his need to simplify matters, to mark out the borders of civilizations.

Tradition-mongering is no proof, though, that these civilizations outside the West are intact, or that their thrashing about is an indication of their vitality, or that they present a conventional threat of arms. Even so thorough and far-reaching an attack against Western hegemony as Iran's theocratic revolution could yet fail to wean that society from the culture of the West. That country's cruel revolution was born of the realization of the "armed Imam" that his people were being seduced by America's ways. The gates had been thrown wide open in the 1970s, and the high walls Ayatollah Khomeini built around his polity were a response to that cultural seduction. Swamped, Iran was "rescued" by men claiming authenticity as their banner. One extreme led to another.

"We prayed for the rain of mercy and received floods," was the way Mehdi Bazargan, the decent modernist who was Khomeini's first prime minister, put it. But the millennium has been brought down to earth, and the dream of a pan-Islamic revolt in Iran's image has vanished into the wind. The terror and the shabbiness have caught up with the utopia. Sudan could emulate the Iranian "revolutionary example." But this will only mean the further pauperization and ruin of a desperate land. There is no rehabilitation of the Iranian example.

A battle rages in Algeria, a society of the Mediterranean, close to Europe—a wine-producing country for that matter—and in Egypt between the secular powers that be and an Islamic alternative. But we should not rush to print with obituaries of these states. In Algeria the nomenklatura of the National Liberation Front failed and triggered a revolt of the young, the underclass and the excluded. The revolt raised an Islamic banner. Caught between a regime they despised and a reign of virtue they feared, the professionals and the women and the modernists of the middle class threw their support to the forces of "order." They hailed the army's crackdown on the Islamicists; they allowed the interruption of a democratic process sure to bring the Islamicists to power; they accepted the "liberties" protected by the repression, the devil you know rather than the one you don't.

The Algerian themes repeat in the Egyptian case, although Egypt's dilemma over its Islamicist opposition is not as acute. The Islamicists continue to hound the state, but they cannot bring it down. There is no likelihood that the Egyptian state—now riddled with enough complacency and corruption to try the celebrated patience and good humor of the Egyptians—will go under. This is an old and skeptical country. It knows better than to trust its fate to enforcers of radical religious dogma. These are not deep and secure structures of order that the national middle classes have put in place. But they will not be blown away overnight.

Nor will Turkey lose its way, turn its back on Europe and chase after some imperial temptation in the scorched domains of Central Asia. Huntington sells that country's modernity and secularism short when he writes that the Turks—rejecting Mecca and rejected by Brussels—are likely to head to Tashkent in search of a Pan-Turkic role. There is no journey to that imperial past. Ataturk severed that link with fury, pointed his country westward, embraced the civilization of Europe and did it without qualms or second thoughts. It is on Frankfurt and Bonn—and Washington—not on Baku and Tashkent that the attention of the Turks is fixed. The inheritors of Ataturk's legacy are too shrewd to go chasing after imperial glory, gathering about them the scattered domains of the

Turkish peoples. After their European possessions were lost, the Turks clung to Thrace and to all that this link to Europe represents.

Huntington would have nations battle for civilizational ties and fidelities when they would rather scramble for their market shares, learn how to compete in a merciless world economy, provide jobs, move out of poverty. For their part, the "management gurus" and those who believe that the interests have vanquished the passions in today's world tell us that men want Sony, not soil.[2] There is a good deal of truth in what they say, a terrible exhaustion with utopias, a reluctance to set out on expeditions of principle or belief. It is hard to think of Russia, ravaged as it is by inflation, taking up the grand cause of a "second Byzantium," the bearer of the orthodox-Slavic torch.

And where is the Confucian world Huntington speaks of? In the busy and booming lands of the Pacific Rim, so much of politics and ideology has been sublimated into finance that the nations of East Asia have turned into veritable workshops. The civilization of Cathay is dead; the Indonesian archipelago is deaf to the call of the religious radicals in Tehran as it tries to catch up with Malaysia and Singapore. A different wind blows in the lands of the Pacific. In that world economics, not politics, is in command. The world is far less antiseptic than Lee Kuan Yew, the sage of Singapore, would want it to be. A nemesis could lie in wait for all the prosperity that the 1980s brought to the Pacific. But the lands of the Pacific Rim—protected, to be sure, by an American security umbrella—are not ready for a great falling out among the nations. And were troubles to visit that world they would erupt within its boundaries, not across civilizational lines.

The things and ways that the West took to "the rest"—those whole sentences of good English that Marlowe heard a century ago—have become the ways of the world. The secular idea, the state system and the balance of power, pop culture jumping tariff walls and barriers, the state as an instrument of welfare, all these have been internalized in the remotest places. We have stirred up the very storms into which we now ride.

THE WEAKNESS OF TRADITION

NATIONS "CHEAT": they juggle identities and interests. Their ways meander. One would think that the traffic of arms from North Korea and

---

[2]Kenichi Ohmae, "Global Consumers Want Sony, Not Soil," *New Perspectives Quarterly*, Fall 1991.

China to Libya and Iran and Syria shows this—that states will consort with any civilization, however alien, as long as the price is right and the goods are ready. Huntington turns this routine act of selfishness into a sinister "Confucian-Islamic connection." There are better explanations: the commerce of renegades, plain piracy, an "underground economy" that picks up the slack left by the great arms suppliers (the United States, Russia, Britain and France).

Contrast the way Huntington sees things with Braudel's depiction of the traffic between Christendom and Islam across the Mediterranean in the sixteenth century—and this was in a religious age, after the fall of Constantinople to the Turks and of Granada to the Spanish: "Men passed to and fro, indifferent to frontiers, states and creeds. They were more aware of the necessities for shipping and trade, the hazards of war and piracy, the opportunities for complicity or betrayal provided by circumstances."[3]

Those kinds of "complicities" and ambiguities are missing in Huntington's analysis. Civilizations are crammed into the nooks and crannies—and checkpoints—of the Balkans. Huntington goes where only the brave would venture, into that belt of mixed populations stretching from the Adriatic to the Baltic. Countless nationalisms make their home there, all aggrieved, all possessed of memories of a fabled past and equally ready for the demagogues vowing to straighten a messy map. In the thicket of these pan-movements he finds the line that marked "the eastern boundary of Western Christianity in the year 1500." The scramble for turf between Croatian nationalism and its Serbian counterpart, their "joint venture" in carving up Bosnia, are made into a fight of the inheritors of Rome, Byzantium and Islam.

But why should we fall for this kind of determinism? "An outsider who travels the highway between Zagreb and Belgrade is struck not by the decisive historical fault line which falls across the lush Slavonian plain but by the opposite. Serbs and Croats speak the same language, give or take a few hundred words, have shared the same village way of life for centuries."[4] The cruel genius of Slobodan Milosevic and Franjo Tudjman, men on horseback familiar in lands and situations of distress, was

---

3Ferdinand Braudel, *The Mediterranean and the Mediterranean World in the Age of Philip II*, Vol. II, New York: Harper & Row, 1976, p. 759.

4Michael Ignatieff, "The Balkan Tragedy," *New York Review of Books,* May 13, 1993.

Fouad Ajami

to make their bids for power into grand civilizational undertakings—the ramparts of the Enlightenment defended against Islam or, in Tudjman's case, against the heirs of the Slavic-Orthodox faith. Differences had to be magnified. Once Tito, an equal opportunity oppressor, had passed from the scene, the balancing act among the nationalities was bound to come apart. Serbia had had a measure of hegemony in the old system. But of the world that loomed over the horizon—privatization and economic reform—the Serbs were less confident. The citizens of Sarajevo and the Croats and the Slovenes had a head start on the rural Serbs. And so the Serbs hacked at the new order of things with desperate abandon.

Some Muslim volunteers came to Bosnia, driven by faith and zeal. Huntington sees in these few stragglers the sweeping power of "civilizational rallying," proof of the hold of what he calls the "kin-country syndrome." This is delusion. No Muslim cavalry was ever going to ride to the rescue. The Iranians may have railed about holy warfare, but the Chetniks went on with their work. The work of order and mercy would have had to be done by the United States if the cruel utopia of the Serbs was to be contested.

It should have taken no powers of prophecy to foretell where the fight in the Balkans would end. The abandonment of Bosnia was of a piece with the ways of the world. No one wanted to die for Srebrenica. The Europeans averted their gaze, as has been their habit. The Americans hesitated for a moment as the urge to stay out of the Balkans did battle with the scenes of horror. Then "prudence" won out. Milosevic and Tudjman may need civilizational legends, but there is no need to invest their projects of conquest with this kind of meaning.

In his urge to find that relentless war across Islam's "bloody borders," Huntington buys Saddam Hussein's interpretation of the Gulf War. It was, for Saddam and Huntington, a civilizational battle. But the Gulf War's verdict was entirely different. For if there was a campaign that laid bare the interests of states, the lengths to which they will go to restore a tolerable balance of power in a place that matters, this was it. A local despot had risen close to the wealth of the Persian Gulf, and a Great Power from afar had come to the rescue. The posse assembled by the Americans had Saudi, Turkish, Egyptian, Syrian, French, British and other riders.

True enough, when Saddam Hussein's dream of hegemony was shattered, the avowed secularist who had devastated the *ulama*, the men of religion in his country, fell back on Ayatollah Khomeini's language of fire and brimstone and borrowed the symbolism and battle cry of his old Iranian nemesis. But few, if any, were fooled by this sudden conversion to the faith. They knew the predator for what he was: he had a Christian foreign minister (Tariq Aziz); he had warred against the Iranian revolution for nearly a decade and had prided himself on the secularism of his regime. Prudent men of the social and political order, the *ulama* got out of the way and gave their state the room it needed to check the predator at the Saudi/Kuwaiti border.[5] They knew this was one of those moments when purity bows to necessity. Ten days after Saddam swept into Kuwait, Saudi Arabia's most authoritative religious body, the Council of Higher Ulama, issued a *fatwa*, or a ruling opinion, supporting the presence of Arab and Islamic and "other friendly forces." All means of defense, the ulama ruled, were legitimate to guarantee the people "the safety of their religion, their wealth, and their honor and their blood, to protect what they enjoy of safety and stability." At some remove, in Egypt, that country's leading religious figure, the Shaykh of Al Ashar, Shaykh Jadd al Haqq, denounced Saddam as a tyrant and brushed aside his Islamic pretensions as a cover for tyranny.

Nor can the chief Iranian religious leader Ayatollah Ali Khamenei's rhetoric against the Americans during the Gulf War be taken as evidence of Iran's disposition toward that campaign. Crafty men, Iran's rulers sat out that war. They stood to emerge as the principal beneficiaries of Iraq's defeat. The American-led campaign against Iraq held out the promise of tilting the regional balance in their favor. No tears were shed in Iran for what befell Saddam Hussein's regime.

It is the mixed gift of living in hard places that men and women know how to distinguish between what they hear and what there is: no illusions were thus entertained in vast stretches of the Arab Muslim world about Saddam, or about the campaign to thwart him for that matter. The fight in the gulf was seen for what it was: a bid for primacy met by an imperial expedition that laid it to waste. A circle was closed in the gulf: where once the order in the region "east of Suez" had been the work of the British, it was now provided by Pax Americana. The new power standing sentry in

5Huntington quotes one Safar al Hawali, a religious radical at Umm al Qura University in Mecca, to the effect that the campaign against Iraq was another Western campaign against Islam. But this can't do as evidence. Safar al Hawali was a crank. Among the *ulama* class and the religious scholars in Saudi Arabia he was, for all practical purposes, a loner.

the gulf belonged to the civilization of the West, as did the prior one. But the American presence had the anxious consent of the Arab lands of the Persian Gulf. The stranger coming in to check the kinsmen.

The world of Islam divides and sub-divides. The battle lines in the Caucasus, too, are not coextensive with civilizational fault lines. The lines follow the interests of states. Where Huntington sees a civilizational duel between Armenia and Azerbaijan, the Iranian state has cast religious zeal and fidelity to the wind. Indeed, in that battle the Iranians have tilted toward Christian Armenia.

THE WRIT OF STATES

WE HAVE BEEN delivered into a new world, to be sure. But it is not a world where the writ of civilizations runs. Civilizations and civilizational fidelities remain. There is to them an astonishing measure of permanence. But let us be clear: civilizations do not control states, states control civilizations. States avert their gaze from blood ties when they need to; they see brotherhood and faith and kin when it is in their interest to do so.

We remain in a world of self-help. The solitude of states continues; the disorder in the contemporary world has rendered that solitude more pronounced. No way has yet been found to reconcile France to Pax Americana's hegemony, or to convince it to trust its security or cede its judgment to the preeminent Western power. And no Azeri has come up with a way the lands of Islam could be rallied to the fight over Nagorno Karabakh. The sky has not fallen in Kuala Lumpur or in Tunis over the setbacks of Azerbaijan in its fight with Armenia.

The lesson bequeathed us by Thucydides in his celebrated dialogue between the Melians and the Athenians remains. The Melians, it will be recalled, were a colony of the Lacedaemonians. Besieged by Athens, they held out and were sure that the Lacedaemonians were "bound, if only for very shame, to come to the aid of their kindred." The Melians never wavered in their confidence in their "civilizational" allies: "Our common blood insures our fidelity."[6] We know what became of the Melians. Their allies did not turn up, their island was sacked, their world laid to waste. ☯

---

[6]Thucydides, *The Peloponnesian War,* New York: The Modern American Library, 1951, pp. 334–335.

Back to the Future

Instability in Europe After the Cold War

John J. Mearsheimer

THE PROFOUND changes now underway in Europe have been widely viewed as harbingers of a new age of peace. With the Cold War over, it is said, the threat of war that has hung over Europe for more than four decades is lifting. Swords can now be beaten into ploughshares; harmony can reign among the states and peoples of Europe. Central Europe, which long groaned under the massive forces of the two military blocs, can convert its military bases into industrial parks, playgrounds, and condominiums. Scholars of security affairs can stop their dreary quarrels over military doctrine and balance assessments, and turn their attention to finding ways to prevent global warming and preserve the ozone layer. European leaders can contemplate how to spend peace dividends. So goes the common view.

This article assesses this optimistic view by exploring in detail the consequences for Europe of an end to the Cold War. Specifically, I examine the effects of a scenario under which the Cold War comes to a complete end. The Soviet Union withdraws all of its forces from Eastern Europe, leaving the states in that region fully independent. Voices are thereupon raised in the United States, Britain, and Germany, arguing that American and British military forces in Germany have lost their principal *raison d'e-tre*, and these forces are withdrawn from the Continent. NATO and the Warsaw Pact then dissolve; they may persist on paper, but each ceases to

JOHN MEARSHEIMER is Professor of Political Science, University of Chicago. This article appeared in the Summer 1990 issue of *International Security*.

function as an alliance.[1] As a result, the bipolar structure that has characterized Europe since the end of World War II is replaced by a multipolar
structure. In essence, the Cold War we have known for almost half a century is over, and the postwar order in Europe is ended.[2]

How would such a fundamental change affect the prospects for peace
in Europe?[3] Would it raise or lower the risk of war?

I argue that the prospects for major crises and war in Europe are likely
to increase markedly if the Cold War ends and this scenario unfolds. The
next decades in a Europe without the superpowers would probably not
be as violent as the first 45 years of this century, but would probably be
substantially more prone to violence than the past 45 years.

This pessimistic conclusion rests on the argument that the distribution
and character of military power are the root causes of war and peace.
Specifically, the absence of war in Europe since 1945 has been a consequence

---

1. There is considerable support within NATO's higher circles, including the
Bush administration, for maintaining NATO beyond the Cold War. NATO leaders have not clearly articulated the concrete goals that NATO would serve in a
post-Cold War Europe, but they appear to conceive the future NATO as a means
for ensuring German security, thereby removing possible German motives for aggressive policies; and as a means to protect other NATO states against German
aggression. However, the Germans, who now provide the largest portion of the
Alliance's standing forces, are likely to resist such a role for NATO. A security
structure of this sort assumes that Germany cannot be trusted and that NATO
must be maintained to keep it in line. A united Germany is not likely to accept
for very long a structure that rests on this premise. Germans accepted NATO
throughout the Cold War because it secured Germany against the Soviet threat
that developed in the wake of World War II. Without that specific threat, which
now appears to be diminishing rapidly, Germany is likely to reject the continued
maintenance of NATO as we know it.

2. I am not arguing that a complete end to the Cold War is inevitable; also quite
likely is an intermediate outcome, under which the status quo is substantially
modified, but the main outlines of the current order remain in place. Specifically,
the Soviet Union may withdraw much of its force from Eastern Europe, but leave
significant forces behind. If so, NATO force levels would probably shrink
markedly, but NATO may continue to maintain significant forces in Germany.
Britain and the United States would withdraw some but not all of their troops from
the Continent. If this outcome develops, the basic bipolar military competition that
has defined the map of Europe throughout the Cold War will continue. I leave this
scenario unexamined, and instead explore what follows from a complete end to the
Cold War in Europe because this latter scenario is the less examined of the two, and
because the consequences, and therefore the desirability, of completely ending the
Cold War would still remain an issue if the intermediate outcome occurred.

of three factors: the bipolar distribution of military power on the Continent; the rough military equality between the two states comprising the two poles in Europe, the United States and the Soviet Union; and the fact that each superpower was armed with a large nuclear arsenal.[4] Domestic factors also affect the likelihood of war, and have helped cause the postwar peace. Most importantly, hyper-nationalism helped cause the two world wars, and the decline of nationalism in Europe since 1945 has contributed to the peacefulness of the postwar world. However, factors of military power have been most important in shaping past events, and will remain central in the future.

The departure of the superpowers from Central Europe would transform Europe from a bipolar to a multipolar system.[5] Germany, France, Britain, and perhaps Italy would assume major power status; the Soviet

---

3. The impact of such a change on human rights in Eastern Europe will not be considered directly in this article. Eastern Europeans have suffered great hardship as a result of the Soviet occupation. The Soviets have imposed oppressive political regimes on the region, denying Eastern Europeans basic freedoms. Soviet withdrawal from Eastern Europe will probably change that situation for the better, although the change is likely to be more of a mixed blessing than most realize. First, it is not clear that communism will be promptly replaced in all Eastern European countries with political systems that place a high premium on protecting minority rights and civil liberties. Second, the longstanding blood feuds among the nationalities in Eastern Europe are likely to re-emerge in a multipolar Europe, regardless of the existing political order. If wars break out in Eastern Europe, human rights are sure to suffer.

4. It is commonplace to characterize the polarity—bipolar or multipolar—of the international system at large, not a specific region. The focus in this article, however, is not on the global distribution of power, but on the distribution of power in Europe. Polarity arguments can be used to assess the prospects for stability in a particular region, provided the global and regional balances are distinguished from one another and the analysis is focused on the structure of power in the relevant region.

5. To qualify as a pole in a global or regional system, a state must have a reasonable prospect of defending itself against the leading state in the system by its own efforts. The United States and the Soviet Union have enjoyed clear military superiority over other European states, and all non-European states, throughout the Cold War; hence they have formed the two poles of both the global and European systems. What is happening to change this is that both the Soviet Union and the United States are moving forces out of Central Europe, which makes it more difficult for them to project power on the Continent and thus weakens their influence there; and reducing the size of those forces, leaving them less military power to project. Because of its proximity to Europe, the Soviet Union will remain a pole in the European system as long as it retains substantial military forces on its own territory. The United States can remain a pole in Europe only if it retains the capacity to project significant military power into Central Europe.

Union would decline from superpower status but would remain a major European power, giving rise to a system of five major powers and a number of lesser powers. The resulting system would suffer the problems common to multipolar systems, and would therefore be more prone to instability.[6] Power inequities could also appear; if so, stability would be undermined further.

The departure of the superpowers would also remove the large nuclear arsenals they now maintain in Central Europe. This would remove the pacifying effect that these weapons have had on European politics. Four principal scenarios are possible. Under the first scenario, Europe would become nuclear-free, thus eliminating a central pillar of order in the Cold War era. Under the second scenario, the European states do not expand their arsenals to compensate for the departure of the superpowers' weapons. In a third scenario, nuclear proliferation takes place, but is mismanaged; no steps are taken to dampen the many dangers inherent in the proliferation process. All three of these scenarios would raise serious risks of war.

In the fourth and least dangerous scenario, nuclear weapons proliferate in Europe, but the process is well-managed by the current nuclear powers. They take steps to deter preventive strikes on emerging nuclear powers, to set boundaries on the proliferation process by extending security umbrellas over the neighbors of emerging nuclear powers, to help emerging nuclear powers build secure deterrent forces, and to discourage them from deploying counterforce systems that threaten their neighbors' deterrents. This outcome probably provides the best hope for maintaining peace in Europe. However, it would still be more dangerous than the world of 1945-90. Moreover, it is not likely that proliferation would be well-managed.

Three counter-arguments might be advanced against this pessimistic set of predictions of Europe's future. The first argument holds that the peace will be preserved by the effects of the liberal international economic order that has evolved since World War II. The second rests on the observation that liberal democracies very seldom fight wars against each other, and holds that the past spread of democracy in Europe has bolstered peace, and that the ongoing democratization of Eastern Europe makes war still less likely. The third argument maintains that Europeans have learned from their disastrous experiences in this century that

6. Stability is simply defined as the absence of wars and major crises.

war, whether conventional or nuclear, is so costly that it is no longer a sensible option for states.

But the theories behind these arguments are flawed, as I explain; hence their prediction of peace in a multipolar Europe is flawed as well.

Three principal policy prescriptions follow from this analysis. First, the United States should encourage a process of limited nuclear proliferation in Europe. Specifically, Europe will be more stable if Germany acquires a secure nuclear deterrent, but proliferation does not go beyond that point. Second, the United States should not withdraw fully from Europe, even if the Soviet Union pulls its forces out of Eastern Europe. Third, the United States should take steps to forestall the re-emergence of hyper-nationalism in Europe.

METHODOLOGY:
HOW SHOULD WE THINK ABOUT EUROPE'S FUTURE?

PREDICTIONS ON the future risk of war and prescriptions about how best to maintain peace should rest on general theories about the causes of war and peace. This point is true for both academics and policymakers. The latter are seldom self-conscious in their uses of theory. Nevertheless, policymakers' views on the future of Europe are shaped by their implicit preference for one theory of international relations over another. Our task, then, is to decide which theories best explain the past, and will most directly apply to the future; and then to employ these theories to explore the consequences of probable scenarios.

Specifically, we should first survey the inventory of international relations theories that bear on the problem. What theories best explain the period of violence before the Cold War? What theories best explain the peace of the past 45 years? Are there other theories that explain little about pre-Cold War Europe, or Cold War Europe, but are well-suited for explaining what is likely to occur in a Europe without a Soviet and American military presence?

Next, we should ask what these theories predict about the nature of international politics in a post-Cold War multipolar Europe. Will the causes of the postwar peace persist, will the causes of the two world wars return, or will other causes arise?

We can then assess whether we should expect the next decades to be more peaceful, or at least as peaceful, as the past 45 years, or whether the future is more likely to resemble the first 45 years of the century. We can also ask what policy prescriptions these theories suggest.

John J. Mearsheimer

The study of international relations, like the other social sciences, does not yet resemble the hard sciences. Our stock of theories is spotty and often poorly tested. The conditions required for the operation of established theories are often poorly understood. Moreover, political phenomena are highly complex; hence precise political predictions are impossible without very powerful theoretical tools, superior to those we now possess. As a result, all political forecasting is bound to include some error. Those who venture to predict, as I do here, should therefore proceed with humility, take care not to claim unwarranted confidence, and admit that later hindsight will undoubtedly reveal surprises and mistakes.

Nevertheless, social science *should* offer predictions on the occurrence of momentous and fluid events like those now unfolding in Europe. Predictions can inform policy discourse. They help even those who disagree to frame their ideas, by clarifying points of disagreement. Moreover, predictions of events soon to unfold provide the best tests of social science theories, by making clear what it was that given theories have predicted about those events. In short, the world can be used as a laboratory to decide which theories best explain international politics. In this article I employ the body of theories that I find most persuasive to peer into the future. Time will reveal whether these theories in fact have much power to explain international politics.

The next section offers an explanation for the peacefulness of the post-World War II order. The section that follows argues that the end of the Cold War is likely to lead to a less stable Europe. Next comes an examination of the theories underlying claims that a multipolar Europe is likely to be as peaceful, if not more peaceful, than Cold War Europe. The concluding section suggests policy implications that follow from my analysis.

EXPLAINING THE "LONG PEACE"

The past 45 years represent the longest period of peace in European history.7 During these years Europe saw no major war, and only two minor

---

7. The term "long peace" was coined by John Lewis Gaddis, "The Long Peace: Elements of Stability in the Postwar International System," *International Security*, *Vol.* 10, No. 4 (Spring 1986), pp. 99-142.

conflicts (the 1956 Soviet intervention in Hungary and the 1974 Greco-Turkish war in Cyprus). Neither conflict threatened to widen to other countries. The early years of the Cold War (1945-63) were marked by a handful of major crises, although none brought Europe to the brink of war. Since 1963, however, there have been no East-West crises in Europe. It has been difficult—if not impossible—for the last two decades to find serious national security analysts who have seen a real chance that the Soviet Union would attack Western Europe.

The Cold War peace contrasts sharply with European politics during the first 45 years of this century, which saw two world wars, a handful of minor wars, and a number of crises that almost resulted in war. Some 50 million Europeans were killed in the two world wars; in contrast, probably no more than 15,000 died in the two post-1945 European conflicts.[8] Cold War Europe is far more peaceful than early twentieth-century Europe.

Both Europeans and Americans increasingly assume that peace and calm are the natural order of things in Europe and that the first 45 years of this century, not the most recent, were the aberration. This is understandable, since Europe has been free of war for so long that an ever-growing proportion of the Western public, born after World War II, has no direct experience with great-power war. However, this optimistic view is incorrect.

The European state system has been plagued with war since its inception. During much of the seventeenth and eighteenth centuries war was underway somewhere on the European Continent.[9] The nineteenth century held longer periods of peace, but also several major wars and crises. The first half of that century witnessed the protracted

---

7. The term "long peace" was coined by John Lewis Gaddis, "The Long Peace: Elements of Stability in the Postwar International System," *International Security*, *Vol.* 10, No. 4 (Spring 1986), pp. 99-142.

8. There were approximately 10,000 battle deaths in the Russo-Hungarian War of October-November 1956, and some 1500-5000 battle deaths in the July-August 1974 war in Cyprus. See Ruth Leger Sivard, *World Military and Social Expenditures 1989* (Washington, D.C.: World Priorities, 1989), p. 22; and Melvin Small and J. David Singer, *Resort to Arms: International and Civil Wars, 1816-1980* (Beverly Hills, Calif.: Sage, 1982). pp. 93-94.

9. For inventories of past wars, see Jack S. Levy, *War In the Modern Great Power System, 1945-1975* (Lexington: University Press of Kentucky, 1983); and Small and Singer, *Resort to Arms.*

and bloody Napoleonic Wars; later came the Crimean War, and the Italian and German wars of unification.[10] The wars of 1914-45 continued this long historical pattern. They represented a break from the events of previous centuries only in the enormous increase in their scale of destruction.

This era of warfare came to an abrupt end with the conclusion of World War II. A wholly new and remarkably peaceful order then developed on the Continent.

THE CAUSES OF THE LONG PEACE: MILITARY POWER AND STABILITY

What caused the era of violence before 1945? Why has the postwar era been so much more peaceful? The wars before 1945 each had their particular and unique causes, but the distribution of power in Europe—its multipolarity and the imbalances of power that often occurred among the major states in that multipolar system—was the crucial permissive condition that allowed these particular causes to operate. The peacefulness of the postwar era arose for three principal reasons: the bipolarity of the distribution of power on the Continent, the rough equality in military power between those two polar states, and the appearance of nuclear weapons, which vastly expanded the violence of war, making deterrence far more robust.[11]

These factors are aspects of the European state system—of the character of military power and its distribution among states—and not of the states themselves. Thus the keys to war and peace lie more

---

10. Europe saw no major war from 1815-1853 and from 1871-1914, two periods almost as long as the 45 years of the Cold War. There is a crucial distinction, however, between the Cold War and these earlier periods. Relations among the great powers deteriorated markedly in the closing years of the two earlier periods, leading in each case to a major war. On the other hand, the Cold War order has become increasingly stable with the passage of time and there is now no serious threat of war between NATO and the Warsaw Pact. Europe would surely remain at peace for the foreseeable future if the Cold War were to continue, a point that highlights the exceptional stability of the present European order.

11. The relative importance of these three factors cannot be stated precisely, but all three had substantial importance.

in the structure of the international system than in the nature of the individual states. Domestic factors—most notably hyper-nationalism—also helped cause the wars of the pre-1945 era, and the domestic structures of post-1945 European states have been more conducive to peace, but these domestic factors were less important than the character and distribution of military power between states. Moreover, hyper-nationalism was caused in large part by security competition among the European states, which compelled European elites to mobilize publics to support national defense efforts; hence even this important domestic factor was a more remote consequence of the international system.

Conflict is common among states because the international system creates powerful incentives for aggression.[12] The root cause of the problem is the anarchic nature of the international system. In anarchy there is no higher body or sovereign that protects states from one another. Hence each state living under anarchy faces the ever-present possibility that another state will use force to harm or conquer it. Offensive military action is always a threat to all states in the system.

Anarchy has two principal consequences. First, there is little room for trust among states because a state may be unable to recover if its trust is betrayed. Second, each state must guarantee its own survival since no other actor will provide its security. All other states are potential threats, and no international institution is capable of enforcing order or punishing powerful aggressors.

States seek to survive under anarchy by maximizing their power relative to other states, in order to maintain the means for self-defense. Relative power, not absolute levels of power, matters most to states. Thus, states seek opportunities to weaken potential adversaries and improve their relative power position. They sometimes see aggression as the best way to accumulate more power at the expense of rivals.

This competitive world is peaceful when it is obvious that the costs and risks of going to war are high, and the benefits of going to war are low. Two aspects of military power are at the heart of this incentive

---

12. The two classic works on this subject are Hans J. Morgenthau, *Politics Among Nations: The Struggle for Power and Peace,* 5th ed. (New York: Knopf, 1973); and Kenneth N. Waltz, *Theory of International Politics* (Reading, Mass.: Addison-Wesley, 1979).

structure: the distribution of power between states, and the nature of the military power available to them. The distribution of power between states tells us how well-positioned states are to commit aggression, and whether other states are able to check their aggression. This distribution is a function of the number of poles in the system, and their relative power. The nature of military power directly affects the costs, risks, and benefits of going to war. If the military weaponry available guarantees that warfare will be very destructive, states are more likely to be deterred by the cost of war.[13] If available weaponry favors the defense over the offense, aggressors are more likely to be deterred by the futility of aggression, and all states feel less need to commit aggression, since they enjoy greater security to begin with, and therefore feel less need to enhance their security by expansion.[14] If available weaponry tends to equalize the relative power of states, aggressors are discouraged from going to war. If military weaponry makes it easier to estimate the relative power of states, unwarranted optimism is discouraged and wars of miscalculation are less likely.

One can establish that peace in Europe during the Cold War has resulted from bipolarity, the approximate military balance between the superpowers, and the presence of large numbers of nuclear weapons on both sides in three ways: first, by showing that the general theories on which it rests are valid; second, by demonstrating that these theories can explain the conflicts of the pre-1945 era and the peace of the post-1945 era; and third, by showing that competing theories cannot account for the postwar peace.

---

13. The prospects for deterrence can also be affected by crisis stability calculations. See John J. Mearsheimer, "A Strategic Misstep: The Maritime Strategy and Deterrence in Europe," *International Security*, Vol. 11, No. 2 (Fall 1986), pp. 6-8.

14. See Robert Jervis, "Cooperation Under the Security Dilemma," *World Politics*, Vol. 30, No. 2 (January 1978), pp. 167-214; and Stephen Van Evera, "Causes of War" (unpub. PhD dissertation, University of California at Berkeley, 1984), chap. 3. As noted below, I believe that the distinction between offensive and defensive weapons and, more generally, the concept of an offense-defense balance, is relevant at the nuclear level. However, I do not believe those ideas are relevant at the conventional level. See John J. Mearsheimer, *Conventional Deterrence* (Ithaca: Cornell University Press, 1983), pp. 25-27.

Back to the Future

The Virtues of Bipolarity over Multipolarity

The two principal arrangements of power possible among states are bipolarity and multipolarity.[15] A bipolar system is more peaceful for three main reasons. First, the number of conflict dyads is fewer, leaving fewer possibilities for war. Second, deterrence is easier, because imbalances of power are fewer and more easily averted. Third, the prospects for deterrence are greater because miscalculations of relative power and of opponents' resolve are fewer and less likely.[16]

In a bipolar system two major powers dominate. The minor powers find it difficult to remain unattached to one of the major powers, because the major powers generally demand allegiance from lesser states. (This is especially true in core geographical areas, less so in peripheral areas.) Furthermore, lesser states have little opportunity to play the major powers off against each other, because when great powers are fewer in number, the system is more rigid. As a result, lesser states are hard-pressed to preserve their autonomy.

---

15. Hegemony represents a third possible distribution. Under a hegemony there is only one major power in the system. The rest are minor powers that cannot challenge the major power, but must act in accordance with the dictates of the major power. Every state would like to gain hegemony, because hegemony confers abundant security: no challenger poses a serious threat. Hegemony is rarely achieved, however, because power tends to be somewhat evenly distributed among states, because threatened states have strong incentives to join together to thwart an aspiring hegemon, and because the costs of expansion usually outrun the benefits before domination is achieved, causing extension to become overextension. Hegemony has never characterized the European state system at any point since it arose in the seventeenth century, and there is no prospect for hegemony in the foreseeable future; hence hegemony is not relevant to assessing the prospects for peace in Europe.

16. The key works on bipolarity and multipolarity include Thomas J. Christensen and Jack Snyder, "Chain Gangs and Passed Bucks: Predicting Alliance Patterns in Multipolarity," *International Organization,* Vol. 44, No. 2 (Spring 1990), pp. 137-168; Karl W. Deutsch and J. David Singer, "Multipolar Power Systems and International Stability," *World Politics,* Vol. 16, No. 3 (April 1964), pp. 390-406; Richard N. Rosecrance, "Bipolarity, Multipolarity, and the Future," *Journal of Conflict Resolution,* Vol. 10, No. 3 (September 1966), pp. 314-327; Kenneth N. Waltz, "The Stability of a Bipolar World," *Daedalus,* Vol. 93, No. 3 (Summer 1964), pp. 881-909; and Waltz, *Theory of International Politics,* chap. 8. My conclusions about bipolarity are similar to Waltz's, although there are important differences in our explanations, as will be seen below.

John J. Mearsheimer

In a multipolar system, by contrast, three or more major powers dominate. Minor powers in such a system have considerable flexibility regarding alliance partners and can opt to be free floaters. The exact form of a multipolar system can vary markedly, depending on the number of major and minor powers in the system, and their geographical arrangement.

A bipolar system has only one dyed across which war might break out: only two major powers contend with one another, and the minor powers are not likely to be in a position to attack each other. A multipolar system has many potential conflict situations. Major power dyads are more numerous, each posing the potential for conflict. Conflict could also erupt across dyads involving major and minor powers. Dyads between minor powers could also lead to war. Therefore, *ceteris paribus*, war is more likely in a multipolar system than a bipolar one.

Wars in a multipolar world involving just minor powers or only one major power are not likely to be as devastating as a conflict between two major powers. However, local wars tend to widen and escalate. Hence there is always a chance that a small war will trigger a general conflict.

Deterrence is more difficult in a multipolar world because power imbalances are commonplace, and when power is unbalanced, the strong become hard to deter.[17] Power imbalances can lead to conflict in two ways. First, two states can gang up to attack a third state. Second, a major power might simply bully a weaker power in a one-on-one encounter, using its superior strength to coerce or defeat the minor state.[18]

Balance of power dynamics can counter such power imbalances, but only if they operate efficiently.[19] No state can dominate another, either by ganging up or by bullying, if the others coalesce firmly against it, but prob-

---

17. Although a balance of power is more likely to produce deterrence than an imbalance of power, a balance of power between states does not guarantee that deterrence will obtain. States sometimes find innovative military strategies that allow them to win on the battlefield, even without marked advantage in the balance of raw military capabilities. Furthermore, the broader political forces that move a state towards war sometimes force leaders to pursue very risky military strategies, impelling states to challenge opponents of equal or even superior strength. See Mearsheimer, *Conventional Deterrence*, especially chap. 2.

18. This discussion of polarity assumes that the military strength of the major powers is roughly equal. The consequences of power asymmetries among great powers is discussed below.

19. See Stephen M. Walt, *The Origins of Alliances* (Ithaca: Cornell University Press, 1987); and Waltz, *Theory of International Politics*, pp. 123-128.

lems of geography or coordination often hinder the formation of such coalitions.[20] These hindrances may disappear in wartime, but are prevalent in peacetime, and can cause deterrence failure, even where an efficient coalition will eventually form to defeat the aggressor on the battlefield.

First, geography sometimes prevents balancing states from putting meaningful pressure on a potential aggressor. For example, a major power may not be able to put effective military pressure on a state threatening to cause trouble, because buffer states lie in between.

In addition, balancing in a multipolar world must also surmount difficult coordination problems. Four phenomena make coordination difficult. First, alliances provide collective goods, hence allies face the formidable dilemmas of collective action. Specifically, each state may try to shift alliance burdens onto the shoulders of its putative allies. Such "buck-passing" is a common feature of alliance politics [21] It is most common when the number of states required to form an effective blocking coalition is large. Second, a state faced with two potential adversaries might conclude that a protracted war between those adversaries would weaken both, even if one side triumphed; hence it may stay on the sidelines, hoping thereby to improve its power position relative to each of the combatants. (This strategy can fail, however, if one of the warring states quickly conquers the other and ends up more powerful, not less powerful, than before the war.) Third, some states may opt out of the balancing process because they believe that they will not be targeted by the aggressor, failing to recognize that they face danger until after the aggressor has won some initial victories. Fourth, diplomacy is an uncertain process, and thus it can take time to build a defensive coalition. A potential aggressor may conclude that it can succeed at aggression before the coalition is completed, and further may be prompted to exploit the window of opportunity that this situation presents before it closes.[22]

---

20. One exception bears mention: ganging up is still possible under multipolarity in the restricted case where there are only three powers in the system, and thus no allies available for the victim state.

21. See Mancur Olson and Richard Zeckhauser, "An Economic Theory of Alliances," *Review of Economics and Statistics,* Vol. 48, No. 3 (August 1966), pp. 266-279; and Barry R. Posen, *The Sources of Military Doctrine: France, Britain, and Germany between the World Wars* (Ithaca: Cornell University Press, 1984).

22. Domestic political considerations can also sometimes impede balancing behavior. For example, Britain and France were reluctant to ally with the Soviet Union in the 1930s because of their deep-seated antipathy to communism.

If these problems of geography and coordination are severe, states can lose faith in the balancing process. If so, they become more likely to bandwagon with the aggressor, since solitary resistance is futile.[23] Thus factors that weaken the balancing process can generate snowball effects that weaken the process still further.

The third major problem with multipolarity lies in its tendency to foster miscalculation of the resolve of opposing individual states, and of the strength of opposing coalitions.

War is more likely when a state underestimates the willingness of an opposing state to stand firm on issues of difference. It then may push the other state too far, expecting the other to concede, when in fact the opponent will choose to fight. Such miscalculation is more likely under multipolarity because the shape of the international order tends to remain fluid, due to the tendency of coalitions to shift. As a result, the international "rules of the road"—norms of state behavior, and agreed divisions of territorial rights and other privileges—tend to change constantly. No sooner are the rules of a given adversarial relationship worked out, than that relationship may become a friendship, a new adversarial relationship may emerge with a previous friend or neutral, and new rules must be established. Under these circumstances, one state may unwittingly push another too far, because ambiguities as to national rights and obligations leave a wider range of issues on which a state may miscalculate another's resolve. Norms of state behavior can come to be broadly understood and accepted by all states, even in multipolarity, just as basic norms of diplomatic conduct became generally accepted by the European powers during the eighteenth century. Nevertheless, a well-defined division of rights is generally more difficult when the number of states is large, and relations among them are in flux, as is the case with multipolarity.

War is also more likely when states underestimate the relative power of an opposing coalition, either because they underestimate the number of states who will oppose them, or because they exaggerate the number of allies who will fight on their own side.[24] Such errors are more likely in a system of many states, since states then must accurately

---

23. See Walt, *Origins of Alliances*, pp. 28-32, 173-178.

24. This point is the central theme of Waltz, "The Stability of a Bipolar World." Also see Geoffrey Blainey, *The Causes of War* (New York: Free Press, 1973), chap. 3.

predict the behavior of many states, not just one, in order to calculate the balance of power between coalitions.

A bipolar system is superior to a multipolar system on all of these dimensions. Bullying and ganging up are unknown, since only two actors compete. Hence the power asymmetries produced by bullying and ganging up are also unknown. When balancing is required, it is achieved efficiently. States can balance by either internal means—military buildup or external means— diplomacy and alliances. Under multipolarity states tend to balance by external means; under bipolarity they are compelled to use internal means. Internal means are more fully under state control, hence are more efficient, and are more certain to produce real balance.[25] The problems that attend efforts to balance by diplomatic methods—geographic complications and coordination difficulties—are bypassed. Finally, miscalculation is less likely than in a multipolar world. States are less likely to miscalculate others' resolve, because the rules of the road with the main opponent become settled over time, leading both parties to recognize the limits beyond which they cannot push the other. States also cannot miscalculate the membership of the opposing coalition, since each side faces only one main enemy. Simplicity breeds certainty; certainty bolsters peace.

There are no empirical studies that provide conclusive evidence of the effects of bipolarity and multipolarity on the likelihood of war. This undoubtedly reflects the difficulty of the task: from its beginning until 1945, the European state system was multipolar, leaving this history barren of comparisons that would reveal the differing effects of multipolarity and bipolarity. Earlier history does afford some apparent examples of bipolar systems, including some that were warlike—Athens and Sparta, Rome and Carthage— but this history is inconclusive, because it is sketchy and incomplete and therefore does not offer enough detail to validate the comparisons. Lacking a comprehensive survey of history, we cannot progress beyond offering examples pro and con, without knowing which set of examples best represents the universe of cases. As a result the case made here stops short of empirical demonstration, and rests chiefly on deduction. However, I believe that this deductive case provides a sound basis for accepting the argument that bipolarity is more peaceful than multipolarity; the deductive logic seems compelling, and there is no obvious historical ev-

---

25. Noting the greater efficiency of internal over external balancing is Waltz, *Theory of International Politics*, pp. 163, 168.

John J. Mearsheimer

idence that cuts against it. I show below that the ideas developed here apply to events in twentieth century Europe, both before and after 1945.

The Virtues of Equality of Power over Inequality

Power can be more or less equally distributed among the major powers of both bipolar and multipolar systems. Both systems are more peaceful when equality is greatest among the poles. Power inequalities invite war by increasing the potential for successful aggression; hence war is minimized when inequalities are least.[26]

How should the degree of equality in the distribution of power in a system be assessed? Under bipolarity, the overall equality of the system is simply a function of the balance of power between the two poles—an equal balance creates an equal system, a skewed balance produces an unequal system. Under multipolarity the focus is on the power balance between the two leading states in the system, but the power ratios across other potential conflict dyads also matter. The net system equality is an aggregate of the degree of equality among all of the poles. However, most general wars under multipolarity have arisen from wars of hegemony that have pitted the leading state—an aspiring hegemon—against the other major powers in the system. Such wars are most probable when a leading state emerges, and can hope to defeat each of the others if it can isolate them. This pattern characterized the wars that grew from the attempts at hegemony by Charles V, Philip II, Louis XIV, Revolutionary and Napoleonic France, Wilhelmine Germany, and Nazi Germany.[27] Hence the ratio between the

---

26. This discussion does not encompass the situation where power asymmetries are so great that one state emerges as a hegemon. See note 15.

27. This point is the central theme of Ludwig Dehio, *The Precarious Balance: Four Centuries of the European Power Struggle*, trans. Charles Fullman (New York: Knopf, 1962). Also see Randolph M. Siverson and Michael R. Tennefoss, "Power, Alliance, and the Escalation of International Conflict, 1815-1965," *American Political Science Review*, Vol. 78, No. 4 (December 1984), pp. 1057–1069. The two lengthy periods of peace in the nineteenth century (see note 10 above) were mainly caused by the equal distribution of power among the major European states. Specifically, there was no aspiring hegemon in Europe for most of these two periods. France, the most powerful state in Europe at the beginning of the nineteenth century, soon declined to a position of rough equality with its chief competitors, while Germany only emerged as a potential hegemon in the early twentieth century.

leader and its nearest competitor—in bipolarity or multipolarity—has more effect on the stability of the system than do other ratios, and is therefore the key ratio that describes the equality of the system. Close equality in this ratio lowers the risk of war.

The polarity of an international system and the degree of power equality of the system are related: bipolar systems tend more toward equality, because, as noted above, states are then compelled to balance by internal methods, and internal balancing is more efficient than external balancing. Specifically, the number-two state in a bipolar system can only hope to balance against the leader by mobilizing its own resources to reduce the gap between the two, since it has no potential major alliance partners. On the other hand, the second-strongest state in a multipolar system can seek security through alliances with others, and may be tempted to pass the buck to them, instead of building up its own strength. External balancing of this sort is especially attractive because it is cheap and fast. However, such behavior leaves intact the power gap between the two leading states, and thus leaves in place the dangers that such a power gap creates. Hence another source of stability under bipolarity lies in the greater tendency for its poles to be equal.

The Virtues of Nuclear Deterrence

Deterrence is most likely to hold when the costs and risks of going to war are obviously great. The more horrible the prospect of war, the less likely it is to occur. Deterrence is also most robust when conquest is most difficult. Aggressors then are more likely to be deterred by the futility of expansion, and all states feel less compelled to expand to increase their security, making them easier to deter because they are less compelled to commit aggression.

Nuclear weapons favor peace on both counts. They are weapons of mass destruction, and would produce horrendous devastation if used in any numbers. Moreover, if both sides' nuclear arsenals are secure from attack, creating a mutually assured retaliation capability (mutual assured destruction or MAD), nuclear weapons make conquest more difficult; international conflicts revert from tests of capability and will to purer tests of will, won by the side willing to run greater risks and pay greater costs. This gives defenders the advantage, because defenders usually value their freedom more than aggressors value new conquests. Thus nuclear weapons are a superb deterrent: they guarantee high costs, and are more useful for self-defense than for aggression.[28]

In addition, nuclear weapons affect the degree of equality in the system. Specifically, the situation created by MAD bolsters peace by moving power relations among states toward equality. States that possess nuclear deterrents can stand up to one another, even if their nuclear arsenals vary greatly in size, as long as both sides' nuclear arsenals are secure from attack. This situation of closer equality has the stabilizing effects noted above.

Finally, MAD also bolsters peace by clarifying the relative power of states and coalitions.[29] States can still miscalculate each other's will, but miscalculations of relative capability are less likely, since nuclear capabilities are not elastic to the specific size and characteristics of forces; once an assured destruction capability is achieved, further increments of nuclear power have little strategic importance. Hence errors in assessing these specific characteristics have little effect. Errors in predicting membership in war coalitions also have less effect, since unforeseen additions or subtractions from such coalitions will not influence war outcomes unless they produce a huge change in the nuclear balance enough to give one side meaningful nuclear superiority.

The Dangers of Hyper-Nationalism

Nationalism is best defined as a set of political beliefs which holds that a nation—a body of individuals with characteristics that purportedly distinguish them from other individuals—should have its own state.[30] Although nationalists often believe that their nation is unique or special,

---

28. Works developing the argument that nuclear weapons are essentially defensive in nature are Shai Feldman, *Israeli Nuclear Deterrence: A Strategy for the 1980s* (New York: Columbia University Press, 1982), pp. 45-49; Stephen Van Evera, "Why Europe Matters, Why the Third World Doesn't: American Grand Strategy after the Cold War," *Journal of Strategic Studies*, Vol. 13, No. 2 (June 1990,); and Van Evera, "Causes of War," chap. 13.

29. See Feldman, *Israeli Nuclear Deterrence*, pp. 5-52; and Van Evera, "Causes of War," pp. 697-699.

30. This definition is drawn from Ernest Gellner, *Nations and Nationalism* (Ithaca: Cornell University Press, 1983), which is an excellent study of the origins of nationalism. Nevertheless, Gellner pays little attention to how nationalism turns into a malevolent force that contributes to instability in the international system.

this conclusion does not necessarily mean that they think they are superior to other peoples, merely that they take pride in their own nation.

However, this benevolent nationalism frequently turns into ugly hypernationalism—the belief that other nations or nation-states are both inferior and threatening and must therefore be dealt with harshly. In the past, hypernationalism among European states has arisen largely because most European states are nation-states—states comprised of one principal nation—and these nation-states exist in an anarchic world, under constant threat from other states. In such a situation people who love their own nation and state can develop an attitude of contempt and loathing toward the nations who inhabit opposing states. The problem is exacerbated by the fact that political elites often feel compelled to portray adversary nations in the most negative way so as to mobilize public support for national security policies.

Malevolent nationalism is most likely to develop under military systems that require reliance on mass armies; the state may exploit nationalist appeals to mobilize its citizenry for the sacrifices required to sustain large standing armies. On the other hand, hyper-nationalism is least likely when states can rely on small professional armies, or on complex high-technology military organizations that do not require vast manpower. For this reason nuclear weapons work to dampen nationalism, since they shift the basis of military power away from pure reliance on mass armies, and toward greater reliance on smaller high-technology organizations.

In sum, hyper-nationalism is the most important domestic cause of war, although it is still a second-order force in world politics. Furthermore, its causes lie largely in the international system.

THE CAUSES OF THE LONG PEACE: EVIDENCE

The historical record shows a perfect correlation between bipolarity, equality of military power, and nuclear weapons, on the one hand, and the long peace, on the other hand. When an equal bipolarity arose and nuclear weapons appeared, peace broke out. This correlation suggests that the bipolarity theory, the equality theory, and the nuclear theory of the long peace are all valid. However, correlation alone does not prove causation. Other factors still may account for the long peace. One way to rule out this possibility is to enumerate what the three theories predict about both the pre-war and postwar eras, and then to ask if these predictions came true in detail during those different periods.

John J. Mearsheimer

Before the Cold War

The dangers of multipolarity are highlighted by events before both world wars. The existence of many dyads of potential conflict provided many possible ways to light the fuse to war in Europe. Diplomacy before World War I involved intense interactions among five major powers (Britain, France, Russia, Austria-Hungary, and Germany), and two minor powers (Serbia and Belgium). At least six significant adversarial relationships emerged: Germany versus Britain, France, Russia, and Belgium; and Austria-Hungary versus Serbia and Russia. Before World War II five major powers (Britain, France, the Soviet Union, Germany, and Italy) and seven minor powers (Belgium, Poland, Czechoslovakia, Austria, Hungary, Romania, and Finland) interacted. These relations produced some thirteen important conflicts: Germany versus Britain, France, the Soviet Union, Czechoslovakia, Poland, and Austria; Italy versus Britain and France; the Soviet Union versus Finland and Poland; Czechoslovakia versus Poland and Hungary; and Romania versus Hungary. This multiplicity of conflicts made the outbreak of war inherently more likely. Moreover, many of the state interests at issue in each of these conflicts were interconnected, raising the risk that any single conflict that turned violent would trigger a general war, as happened in both 1914 and 1939.

Before World War II Germany was able to gang up with others against some minor states, and to bully others into joining with it. In 1939 Germany bolstered its power by ganging up with Poland and Hungary to partition Czechoslovakia, and then ganged up with the Soviet Union against Poland. In 1938 Germany bullied the Czechs into surrendering the Sudetenland, and also bullied the Austrians into complete surrender.[31] By these successes Germany expanded its power, leaving it far stronger than its immediate neighbors, and thereby making deterrence much harder.

German power could have been countered before both world wars had the other European powers balanced efficiently against Germany. If so, Germany might have been deterred, and war prevented on both occasions. However, the other powers twice failed to do so. Before 1914 the scope of this failure was less pronounced; France and Russia balanced

---

31. Austria is not a pure case of bullying; there was also considerable pro-German support in Austria during the late 1930s.

forcefully against Germany, while only Britain failed to commit firmly against Germany before war began.[32]

Before 1939, failure to balance was far more widespread.[33] The Soviet Union failed to aid Czechoslovakia against Germany in 1938, partly for geographic reasons: they shared no common border, leaving the Soviets with no direct access to Czech territory. France failed to give effective aid to the Czechs and Poles, partly because French military doctrine was defensively oriented, but also because France had no direct access to Czech or Polish territory, and therefore could not easily deploy forces to bolster Czech and Polish defenses

Britain and France each passed the buck by transferring the cost of deterring Germany onto the other, thereby weakening their combined effort. The Soviet Union, with the Molotov-Ribbentrop Pact, sought to turn the German armies westward, hoping that they would become bogged down in a war of attrition similar to World War I on the Western Front. Some of the minor European powers, including Belgium, the Netherlands, Denmark, and the Scandinavian states, passed the buck to the major powers by standing on the sidelines during the crises of 1938 and 1939.

Britain and the United States failed to recognize that they were threatened by Germany until late in the game—1939 for Britain, 1940 for the United States—and they therefore failed to take an early stand. When they finally recognized the danger posed by Germany and resolved to respond, they lacked appropriate military forces. Britain could not pose a significant military threat to Germany until after it built up its own military forces and coordinated its plans and doctrine with its French and Pol-

---

32. Britain's failure to commit itself explicitly to a Continental war before the July Crisis was probably a mistake of great proportions. There is evidence that the German chancellor, Bethmann-Hollweg, tried to stop the slide towards war once it became apparent that Britain would fight with France and Russia against Germany, turning a Continental war into a world war. See Imanuel Geiss, ed., *July 1914: The Outbreak of the First World War* (New York: Norton, 1967), chap. 7. Had the Germans clearly understood British intentions before the crisis, they might have displayed much greater caution in the early stages of the crisis, when it was still possible to avoid war.

33. See Williamson Murray, *The Change in the European Balance of Power, 1938-1939: The Path to Ruin* (Princeton: Princeton University Press, 1984); Posen, *Sources of Military Doctrine;* and Arnold Wolfers, *Britain and France between Two Wars: Conflicting Strategies of Peace from Versailles to World War II* (New York: Norton, 1968); and Barry R. Posen, "Competing Images of the Soviet Union," *World Politics,* Vol. 39, No. 4 (July 1987), pp. 579-597.

ish allies. In the meantime deterrence failed. The United States did not launch a significant military buildup until after the war broke out.

Multipolarity also created conditions that permitted serious miscalculation before both world wars, which encouraged German aggression on both occasions. Before 1914, Germany was not certain of British opposition if it reached for continental hegemony, and Germany completely failed to foresee that the United States would eventually move to contain it. In 1939, Germany hoped that France and Britain would stand aside as it conquered Poland, and again failed to foresee eventual American entry into the war. As a result Germany exaggerated its prospects for success. This undermined deterrence by encouraging German adventurism.

In sum, the events leading up to the world wars amply illustrate the risks that arise in a multipolar world. Deterrence was undermined in both cases by phenomena that are more common under a multipolar rather than a bipolar distribution of power.[34]

Deterrence was also difficult before both wars because power was distributed asymmetrically among the major European powers. Specifically, Germany was markedly stronger than any of its immediate neighbors. In 1914 Germany clearly held military superiority over all of its European rivals; only together were they able to defeat it, and then only with American help. 1939 is a more ambiguous case. The results of the war reveal that the Soviet Union had the capacity to stand up to Germany, but this was not apparent at the beginning of the war. Hitler was confident that Germany would defeat the Soviet Union, and this confidence was key to his decision to attack in 1941.

Finally, the events leading up to both world wars also illustrate the risks that arise in a world of pure conventional deterrence in which weapons of mass destruction are absent. World War I broke out partly because all of the important states believed that the costs of war would be small, and that successful offense was feasible.[35] Before World War II

---

34. The problems associated with multipolarity were also common in Europe before 1900. Consider, for example, that inefficient balancing resulted in the collapse of the first four coalitions arrayed against Napoleonic France. See Steven T. Ross, *European Diplomatic History, 1789-1815: France Against Europe* (Garden City, N.Y.: Doubleday, 1969).

35. Stephen Van Evera, "The Cult of the Offensive and the Origins of the First World War," *International Security*, Vol. 9, No. 1 (Summer 1984), pp. 58-107. Also see Jack Snyder, *The Ideology of the Offensive: Military Decision-Making and the Disasters of 1914* (Ithaca: Cornell University Press, 1984).

these beliefs were less widespread, but had the same effect.[36] The lesser powers thought war would be costly and conquest difficult, but the leaders of the strongest state— Germany—saw the prospect of cheap victory, and this belief was enough to destroy deterrence and produce war. Had nuclear weapons existed, these beliefs would have been undercut, removing a key condition that permitted both wars.

What was the role of internal German politics in causing the world wars? So far I have focused on aspects of the international system surrounding Germany. This focus reflects my view that systemic factors were more important. But German domestic political and social developments also played a significant role, contributing to the aggressive character of German foreign policy. Specifically, German society was infected with a virulent nationalism between 1870 and 1945 that laid the basis for expansionist foreign policies.[37]

However, two points should be borne in mind. First, German hyper-nationalism was in part fueled by Germany's pronounced sense of insecurity, which reflected Germany's vulnerable location at the center of Europe, with relatively open borders on both sides. These geographic facts made German security problems especially acute; this situation gave German elites a uniquely strong motive to mobilize their public for war, which they did largely by fanning nationalism. Thus even German hyper-nationalism can be ascribed in part to the nature of the pre-1945 international system.

Second, the horror of Germany's murderous conduct during World War II should be distinguished from the scope of the aggressiveness of German foreign policy.[38] Germany was indeed aggressive, but not un-

---

36. Mearsheimer, *Conventional Deterrence*, chaps. 3-4.

37. See Ludwig Dehio, *Germany and World Politics in the Twentieth Century*, trans. Dieter Pevsner (New York: Norton, 1967); Fritz Fischer, *War of Illusions: German Policies from 1911 to 1914*, trans. Marian Jackson (New York: Norton, 1975); Paul M. Kennedy, *The Rise of the Anglo-German Antagonism*, 1860-1914 (London: Allen and Unwin, 1980), chap. 18; Hans Kohn, *The Mind of Germany: The Education of a Nation* (New York: Harper Torchbook, 1965), chaps. 7-12; and Louis L. Snyder, *German Nationalism: The Tragedy of a People* (Harrisburg, Pa.: Telegraph Press, 1952).

38. There is a voluminous literature on the German killing machine in World War II. Among the best overviews of the subject are Ian Kershaw, *The Nazi Dictatorship: Problems and Perspectives of Interpretation*, 2nd ed. (London: Arnold, 1989), chaps. 5, 8, 9; Henry L. Mason, "Imponderables of the Holocaust," *World Politics*, Vol. 34, No. 1 (October 1981), pp. 90-113; and Mason, "Implementing the Final Solution: The Ordinary Regulating of the Extraordinary," *World Politics*, Vol. 40, No. 4 (July 1988), pp. 542-569.

precedentedly so. Other states have aspired to hegemony in Europe, and sparked wars by their efforts; Germany was merely the latest to attempt to convert dominant into hegemonic power. What was unique about Germany's conduct was its policy of mass murder toward many of the peoples of Europe. The causes of this murderous policy should not be conflated with the causes of the two world wars. The policy of murder arose chiefly from domestic sources; the wars arose mainly from aspects of the distribution and character of power in Europe.

The Cold War Record

The European state system abruptly shifted from multipolar to bipolar after 1945. Three factors were responsible: the near-complete destruction of German power, the growth of Soviet power, and the permanent American commitment to the European Continent. The weakening of the German Reich was accomplished by allied occupation and dismemberment. Silesia, Pomerania, East Prussia, and parts of West Prussia and Brandenburg were given to other countries, the Sudetenland was returned to Czechoslovakia, and Austria was restored to independence. The rest of the German Reich was divided into two countries, East and West Germany, which became enemies. This reduction of German power, coupled with the physical presence of American and Soviet military might in the heart of Europe, eliminated the threat of German aggression.[39]

Meanwhile the Soviet Union extended its power westward, becoming the dominant power on the Continent and one of the two strongest powers in the world. There is no reason to think that the Soviets would not have reached for continental hegemony, as the Spanish, French, and Germans did earlier, had they believed they could win a hegemonic war. But the Soviets, unlike their predecessors, made no attempt to gain hegemony by force, leaving Europe in peace.

Bipolarity supplies part of the reason. Bipolarity made Europe a simpler place in which only one point of friction—the East-West conflict—had to be managed to avoid war. The two blocs encompassed most of Europe, leaving few unprotected weak states for the Soviets to conquer. As a result the Soviets have had few targets to bully. They have also been un-

---

39. See Anton W. DePorte, *Europe between the Superpowers: The Enduring Balance,* 2nd ed. (New Haven: Yale University Press, 1986).

able to gang up on the few states that are unprotected, because their West-bloc adversary has been their only potential ganging-up partner.

Bipolarity also left less room for miscalculation of both resolve and capability. During the first fifteen years of the Cold War, the rules of the road for the conflict were not yet established, giving rise to several serious crises. However, over time each side gained a clear sense of how far it could push the other, and what the other would not tolerate. A set of rules came to be agreed upon: an understanding on the division of rights in Austria, Berlin, and elsewhere in Europe; a proscription on secret unilateral re-deployment of large nuclear forces to areas contiguous to the opponent; mutual toleration of reconnaissance satellites; agreement on rules of peacetime engagement between naval forces; and so forth. The absence of serious crises during 1963-90 was due in part to the growth of such agreements on the rights of both sides, and the rules of conduct. These could develop in large part because the system was bipolar in character. Bipolarity meant that the same two states remained adversaries for a long period, giving them time to learn how to manage their conflict without war. By contrast, a multipolar world of shifting coalitions would repeatedly have forced adversaries to re-learn how their opponents defined interests, reach new accords on the division of rights, and establish new rules of competitive conduct.

Bipolarity also left less room to miscalculate the relative strength of the opposing coalitions. The composition of possible war coalitions has been clear because only two blocs have existed, each led by an overwhelmingly dominant power that could discipline its members. Either side could have miscalculated its relative military strength, but bipolarity removed ambiguity about relative strength of adversarial coalitions arising from diplomatic uncertainties.

The East-West military balance in Europe has been roughly equal throughout the Cold War, which has further bolstered stability. This approximate parity strengthened deterrence by ensuring that no state was tempted to use force to exploit a power advantage. Parity resulted partly from bipolarity: because the two blocs already encompassed all the states of Europe, both sides have balanced mainly by internal rather than external means. These more efficient means have produced a more nearly equal balance.

Nuclear weapons also played a key role in preventing war in post-World War II Europe.

Western elites on both sides of the Atlantic quickly recognized that nuclear weapons were vastly destructive and that their widespread use in Europe would cause unprecedented devastation. The famous *Carte Blanche* exercises conducted in Germany in 1955 made it manifestly clear that a nuclear war in Europe would involve far greater costs than another World War II.[40] Accordingly, Western policymakers rarely suggested that nuclear war could be "won," and instead emphasized the horrors that would attend nuclear war.

Moreover, they have understood that conventional war could well escalate to the nuclear level, and have in fact based NATO strategy on that reality.

Soviet leaders also recognized the horrendous results that a nuclear war would produce.[41] Some Soviet military officers have asserted that victory is possible in nuclear war, but even they have acknowledged that such a victory would be Pyrrhic. Soviet civilians have generally argued that victory is impossible. Furthermore, the Soviets long maintained that it was not possible to fight a purely conventional war in Europe, and that conventional victory would only prompt the loser to engage in nuclear escalation.[42] The Soviets later granted more possibility that a conventional war might be controlled, but still recognized that escalation is likely.[43] Under Gorbachev, Soviet military thinking has placed even greater emphasis on the need to avoid nuclear war and devoted more attention to the dangers of inadvertent nuclear war.[44]

---

40. See Hans Speier, *German Rearmament and Atomic War: The Views of German Military and Political Leaders* (Evanston, Ill.: Row, Peterson, 1957), chap. 10.

41. See Robert L. Arnett, "Soviet Attitudes Towards Nuclear War: Do They Really Think They Can Win?" *Journal of Strategic Studies,* Vol. 2, No. 2 (September 1979), pp. 172-191; and David Holloway, *The Soviet Union and the Arms Race* (New Haven: Yale University Press, 1983).

42. Thus Nikita Khrushchev explained, "Now that the big countries have thermonuclear weapons at their disposal, they are sure to resort to those weapons if they begin to lose a war fought with conventional means. If it ever comes down to a question of whether or not to face defeat, there is sure to be someone who will be in favor of pushing the button, and the missiles will begin to fly." Nikita Khrushchev, *Khrushchev Remembers: The Last Testament,* trans. and ed. by Strobe Talbott (New York: Bantam, 1976), pp. 603-604.

43. See James M. McConnell, "Shifts in Soviet Views on the Proper Focus of Military Development," *World Politics,* Vol. 37, No. 3 (April 1985), pp. 317-343.

44. See Stephen M. Meyer, "The Sources and Prospects of Gorbachev's New Political Thinking on Security," *International Security,* Vol. 13, No. 2 (Fall 1988), pp. 134-138.

Official rhetoric aside, policymakers on both sides have also behaved very cautiously in the presence of nuclear weapons. There is not a single case of a leader brandishing nuclear weapons during a crisis, or behaving as if nuclear war might be a viable option for solving important political problems. On the contrary, policymakers have never gone beyond nuclear threats of a very subtle sort, and have shown great caution when the possibility of nuclear confrontation has emerged.[45] This cautious conduct has lowered the risk of war.

Nuclear weapons also imposed an equality and clarity on the power relations between the superpowers. This equality and clarity represented a marked change from the earlier non-nuclear world, in which sharp power inequalities and miscalculations of relative power were common.[46]

During the Cold War, the United States and the Soviet Union have exhibited markedly less hyper-nationalism than did the European powers before 1945. After World War II, nationalism declined sharply within Europe, partly because the occupation forces took active steps to dampen it,[47] and also because the European states, no longer providing their own security, now lacked the incentive to purvey hyper-nationalism in order to bolster public support for national defense. More importantly, however, the locus of European politics shifted to the United States and the Soviet Union—two states that, each for its own reasons, had not exhibited nationalism of the virulent type found earlier in Eu-

---

45. See Hannes Adomeit, *Soviet Risk-taking and Crisis Behavior: A Theoretical and Empirical Analysis* (London: Allen and Unwin, 1982); Richard K. Betts, *Nuclear Blackmail and Nuclear Balance* (Washington, D.C.: Brookings, 1987), and McGeorge Bundy, *Danger and Survival: Choices about the Bomb in the First Fifty Years* (New York: Random House, 1988). Also see Joseph S. Nye, Jr., "Nuclear Learning and U.S.-Soviet Security Regimes," *International Organization,* Vol. 41, No. 3 (Summer 1987), pp. 371-402.

46. Some experts acknowledge that nuclear weapons had deterrent value in the early decades of the Cold War, but maintain that they had lost their deterrent value by the mid-1960s when the Soviets finally acquired the capability to retaliate massively against the American homeland. I reject this argument and have outlined my views in John J. Mearsheimer, "Nuclear Weapons and Deterrence in Europe," *International Security,* Vol. 9, No. 3 (Winter 1984/85), pp. 19-46.

47. See Paul M. Kennedy, "The Decline of Nationalistic History in the West, 1900-1970," *Journal of Contemporary History,* Vol. 8, No. 1 (January 1973), pp. 77-100; and E.H. Dance, *History the Betrayer* (London: Hutchinson, 1960).

rope. Nor has nationalism become virulent in either superpower during the Cold War. In part this reflects the greater stability of the postwar order, arising from bipolarity, military equality, and nuclear weapons; with less expectation of war, neither superpower has faced the need to mobilize its population for war. It also reflects a second effect of nuclear weapons: they have reduced the importance of mass armies for preserving sovereignty, thus diminishing the importance of maintaining a hyper-nationalized pool of manpower.

THE CAUSES OF THE LONG PEACE: COMPETING EXPLANATIONS

The claim that bipolarity, equality, and nuclear weapons have been largely responsible for the stability of the past 45 years is further strengthened by the absence of persuasive competing explanations. Two of the most popular theories of peace—*economic liberalism* and *peace-loving democracies*—are not relevant to the issue at hand.

Economic liberalism, which posits that a liberal economic order bolsters peace (discussed in more detail below), cannot explain the stability of postwar Europe, because there has been little economic exchange between the Soviet Union and the West over the past 45 years. Although economic flows between Eastern and Western Europe have been somewhat greater, in no sense has all of Europe been encompassed by a liberal economic order.

The peace-loving democracies theory (also discussed below) holds that democracies do not go to war against other democracies, but concedes that democracies are not especially pacific when facing authoritarian states. This theory cannot account for post-World War II stability because the Soviet Union and its allies in Eastern Europe have not been democratic over the past 45 years.

A third theory of peace, *obsolescence of war*, proposes that modern conventional war had become so deadly by the twentieth century that it was no longer possible to think of war as a sensible means to achieve national goals.[48] It took the two world wars to drive this point home,

---

48. This theory is most clearly articulated by John E. Mueller, *Retreat from Doomsday: The Obsolescence of Major War* (New York: Basic Books, 1989). See also Carl Kaysen, "Is War Obsolete? A Review Essay," *International Security*, Vol. 14, No. 4 (Spring 1990), pp. 42-64.

but by 1945 it was clear that large-scale conventional war had become irrational and morally unacceptable, like institutions such as slavery and dueling. Thus, even without nuclear weapons, statesmen in the Cold War would not seriously have countenanced war, which had become an anachronism. This theory, it should be emphasized, does not ascribe the absence of war to nuclear weapons, but instead points to the horrors of modern conventional war.

This argument probably provides the most persuasive alternative explanation for the stability of the Cold War, but it is not convincing on close inspection. The fact that World War II occurred casts serious doubt on this theory; if any war could have convinced Europeans to forswear conventional war, it should have been World War I, with its vast casualties. There is no doubt that conventional war among modern states could devastate the participants. Nevertheless, this explanation misses one crucial difference between nuclear and conventional war, a difference that explains why war is still a viable option for states. Proponents of this theory assume that all conventional wars are protracted and bloody wars of attrition, like World War I on the Western front. However, it is possible to score a quick and decisive victory in a conventional war and avoid the devastation that usually attends a protracted conventional war.[49] Conventional war can be won; nuclear war cannot be, since neither side can escape devastation by the other, regardless of the outcome on the battlefield. Thus, the incentives to avoid war are far greater in a nuclear than a conventional world, making nuclear deterrence much more robust than conventional deterrence.[50]

---

49. See Mearsheimer, *Conventional Deterrence*, chaps. 1-2.

50. German decision-making in the early years of World War II underscores this point. See Mearsheimer, *Conventional Deterrence*, chap. 4. The Germans were well aware from their experience in World War I that conventional war among major powers could have devastating consequences. Nevertheless, they decided three times to launch major land offensives: Poland (1939); France (1940); and the Soviet Union (1941). In each case, the Germans believed that they could win a quick and decisive victory and avoid a costly protracted war like World War I. Their calculations proved correct against Poland and France. They were wrong about the Soviets, who thwarted their blitzkrieg and eventually played the central role in bringing down the Third Reich. The Germans surely would have been deterred from attacking the Soviet Union if they had foreseen the consequences. However, the key point is that they saw some possibility of winning an easy and relatively cheap victory against the Red Army. That option is not available in a nuclear war.

John J. Mearsheimer

WHAT NEW order will emerge in Europe if the Soviets and Americans withdraw to their homelands and the Cold War order dissolves? What characteristics will it have? How dangerous will it be?

It is certain that bipolarity will disappear, and multipolarity will emerge in the new European order. The other two dimensions of the new order—the distribution of power among the major states, and the distribution of nuclear weapons among them—are not pre-determined, and several possible arrangements could develop. The probable stability of these arrangements would vary markedly. This section examines the scope of the dangers that each arrangement would present, and the likelihood that each will emerge.

The distribution and deployment patterns of nuclear weapons in the new Europe is the least certain, and probably the most important, element of the new order. Accordingly, this section proceeds by exploring the character of the four principal nuclear worlds that might develop: a denuclearized Europe, continuation of the current patterns of nuclear ownership, and nuclear proliferation either well-or ill-managed.

The best new order would incorporate the limited, managed proliferation of nuclear weapons. This would be more dangerous than the current order, but considerably safer than 1900-45. The worst order would be a non-nuclear Europe in which power inequities emerge between the principal poles of power. This order would be more dangerous than the current world, perhaps almost as dangerous as the world before 1945. Continuation of the current pattern, or mismanaged proliferation, would be worse than the world of today, but safer than the pre-1945 world.

EUROPE WITHOUT NUCLEAR WEAPONS

Some Europeans and Americans seek to eliminate nuclear weapons from Europe, and would replace the Cold War order with a wholly non-nuclear order. Constructing this nuclear-free Europe would require Britain, France and the Soviet Union to rid themselves of nuclear weapons. Proponents believe that a Europe without nuclear weapons would be the most peaceful possible arrangement; in fact, however, a nuclear-free Europe would be the most dangerous among possible post-Cold War orders. The pacifying effects of nuclear weapons—the security they provide, the caution they generate, the rough equality they impose, and the clarity of relative power they create— would be lost. Peace would then depend on the other dimensions of the new order—the number of poles, and the distribution of power among them. However, the new order will certainly be multipolar, and may be unequal; hence the system may be very prone to violence. The structure of power in Europe would look much like it did between the world wars, and it could well produce similar results.

The two most powerful states in post-Cold War Europe would probably be Germany and the Soviet Union. They would be physically separated by a band of small, independent states in Eastern Europe. Not much would change in Western Europe, although the states in that area would have to be concerned about a possible German threat on their eastern flank.

The potential for conflict in this system would be considerable. There would be many possible dyads across which war might break out. Power imbalances would be commonplace as a result of the opportunities this system would present for bullying and ganging up. There would be considerable opportunity for miscalculation. The problem of containing German power would emerge once again, but the configuration of power in Europe would make it difficult to form an effective counterbalancing coalition, for much the same reason that an effective counterbalancing coalition failed to form in the 1930s. Eventually the problem of containing the Soviet Union could also re-emerge. Finally, conflicts may erupt in Eastern Europe, providing the vortex that could pull others into a wider confrontation.

A reunified Germany would be surrounded by weaker states that would find it difficult to balance against German aggression. Without forces stationed in states adjacent to Germany, neither the Soviets nor the Americans would be in a good position to help them contain German power. Furthermore, those small states lying between Germany and the Soviet Union might fear the Soviets as much as the Germans, and hence may not be disposed to cooperate with the Soviets to deter German aggression. This problem in fact arose in the 1930s, and 45 years of Soviet occupation in the interim have done nothing to ease East European fears of a Soviet military presence. Thus, scenarios in which Germany uses military force against Poland, Czechoslovakia, or even Austria become possible.

The Soviet Union also might eventually threaten the new status quo. Soviet withdrawal from Eastern Europe does not mean that the Soviets will never feel compelled to return to Eastern Europe. The historical record provides abundant instances of Russian or Soviet involvement in Eastern Europe. Indeed, the Russian presence in Eastern Europe has surged and ebbed repeatedly over the past few centuries.[51] Thus, Soviet withdrawal now hardly guarantees a permanent exit.

Conflict between Eastern European states is also likely to produce instability in a multipolar Europe. There has been no war among the states in that region during the Cold War because the Soviets have tightly controlled them. This point is illustrated by the serious tensions that now exist between Hungary and Romania over Romanian treatment of the Hungarian minority in Transylvania, a region that previously belonged to Hungary and still has roughly 2 million Hungarians living within its borders. Were it not for the Soviet presence in Eastern Europe, this conflict could have brought Romania and Hungary to war by now, and it may bring them to war in the future.[52] This will not be the only danger spot within Eastern Europe if the Soviet empire crumbles.[53]

Warfare in Eastern Europe would cause great suffering to Eastern Europeans. It also might widen to include the major powers, because they would be drawn to compete for influence in that region, especially if disorder created fluid politics that offered opportunities for wider influence, or threatened defeat for friendly states. During the Cold War, both superpowers were drawn into Third World conflicts across the globe, often in distant areas of little strategic importance. Eastern Europe is directly adjacent to both the Soviet Union and Germany, and has considerable economic and strategic importance; thus trouble in Eastern

---

51. See, inter alia: Ivo J. Lederer, ea., *Russian Foreign Policy: Essays in Historical Perspective* (New Haven: Yale University Press, 1962); Andrei Lobanov-Rostovsky, *Russia and Europe, 1825-1878* (Ann Arbor, Mich.: George Wahr Publishing, 1954), and Marc Raeff, *Imperial Russia, 1682-1825: The Coming of Age of Modern Russia* (New York: Knopf, 1971), chap. 2.

52. To get a sense of the antipathy between Hungary and Romania over this issue, see *Witnesses to Cultural Genocide: First-Hand Reports on Romania's Minority Policies Today* (New York: American Transylvanian Federation and the Committee for Human Rights in Romania, 1979). The March 1990 clashes between ethnic Hungarians and Romanians in Tirgu Mures (Romanian Transylvania) indicate the potential for savage violence that is inherent in these ethnic conflicts.

53. See Zbigniew Brzezinski, "Post-Communist Nationalism," *Foreign Affairs*, Vol. 68, No. 5 (Winter 1989/1990), pp. 1-13; and Mark Kramer, "Beyond the Brezhnev Doctrine: A New Era in Soviet-East European Relations?" *International Security*, Vol. 14, No. 3 (Winter 1989/90), pp. 51-54.

Europe could offer even greater temptations to these powers than past conflicts in the Third World offered the superpowers. Furthermore, because the results of local conflicts will be largely determined by the relative success of each party in finding external allies, Eastern European states will have strong incentives to drag the major powers into their local conflicts.[54] Thus both push and pull considerations would operate to enmesh outside powers in local Eastern European wars.

Miscalculation is also likely to be a problem in a multipolar Europe. For example, the new order might well witness shifting patterns of conflict, leaving insufficient time for adversaries to develop agreed divisions of rights and agreed rules of interaction, or constantly forcing them to re-establish new agreements and rules as old antagonisms fade and new ones arise. It is not likely that circumstances would allow the development of a robust set of agreements of the sort that have stabilized the Cold War since 1963. Instead, Europe would resemble the pattern of the early Cold War, in which the absence of rules led to repeated crises. In addition, the multipolar character of the system is likely to give rise to miscalculation regarding the strength of the opposing coalitions.

It is difficult to predict the precise balance of conventional military power that would emerge between the two largest powers in post-Cold War Europe, especially since the future of Soviet power is now hard to forecast. The Soviet Union might recover its strength soon after withdrawing from Central Europe; if so, Soviet power would overmatch German power. Or centrifugal national forces may pull the Soviet Union apart, leaving no remnant state that is the equal of a united Germany.[55] What seems most likely is that Germany and the Soviet Union might emerge as powers of roughly equal strength. The first two scenarios, with their marked inequality between the two leading powers, would be especially worrisome, although there is cause for concern even if Soviet and German power are balanced.

---

54. The new prime minister of Hungary, Jozsef Antall, has already spoken of the need for a "European solution" to the problem of Romania's treatment of Hungarians in Transylvania. Celestine Bohlen, "Victor in Hungary Sees '45 as the Best of Times," *New York Times*, April 10, 1990, p. A8.

55. This article focuses on how changes in the strength of Soviet power and retraction of the Soviet empire would affect the prospects for stability in Europe. However, the dissolution of the Soviet Union, a scenario not explored here in any detail, would raise dangers that would be different from and in addition to those discussed here.

Resurgent hyper-nationalism will probably pose less danger than the problems described above, but some nationalism is likely to resurface in the absence of the Cold War and may provide additional incentives for war. A non-nuclear Europe is likely to be especially troubled by nationalism, since security in such an order will largely be provided by mass armies, which often cannot be maintained without infusing societies with hyper-nationalism. The problem is likely to be most acute in Eastern Europe, but there is also potential for trouble in Germany. The Germans have generally done an admirable job combatting nationalism over the past 45 years, and in remembering the dark side of their past. Nevertheless, worrisome portents are now visible; of greatest concern, some prominent Germans have lately advised a return to greater nationalism in historical education.[56] Moreover, nationalism will be exacerbated by the unresolved border disputes that will be uncovered by the retreat of American and Soviet power. Especially prominent is that of the border between Germany and Poland, which some Germans would change in Germany's favor.

However, it seems very unlikely that Europe will actually be denuclearized, despite the present strength of anti-nuclear feeling in Europe. For example, it is unlikely that the French, in the absence of America's protective cover and faced with a newly unified Germany, would get rid of their nuclear weapons. Also, the Soviets surely would remain concerned about balancing the American nuclear deterrent, and will therefore retain a deterrent of their own.

THE CURRENT OWNERSHIP PATTERN CONTINUES

A more plausible order for post-Cold War Europe is one in which Britain, France and the Soviet Union keep their nuclear weapons, but no new nuclear powers emerge in Europe. This scenario sees a nuclear-free zone in Central Europe, but leaves nuclear weapons on the European flanks.

This scenario, too, also seems unlikely, since the non-nuclear states will have substantial incentives to acquire their own nuclear weapons.

---

56. Aspects of this story are recounted in Richard J. Evans, *In Hitler's Shadow: West German Historians and the Attempt to Escape from the Nazi Past* (New York: Pantheon, 1989). A study of past German efforts to mischaracterize history is Holger H. Herwig, "Clio Deceived: Patriotic Self-Censorship in Germany After the Great War," *International Security*, Vol. 12, No. 2 (Fall 1987), pp. 5-44.

Germany would probably not need nuclear weapons to deter a conventional attack by its neighbors, since neither the French nor any of the Eastern European states would be capable of defeating a reunified Germany in a conventional war. The Soviet Union would be Germany's only legitimate conventional threat, but as long as the states of Eastern Europe remained independent, Soviet ground forces would be blocked from a direct attack. The Germans, however, might not be willing to rely on the Poles or the Czechs to provide a barrier and might instead see nuclear weapons as the best way to deter a Soviet conventional attack into Central Europe. The Germans might choose to go nuclear to protect themselves from blackmail by other nuclear powers. Finally, given that Germany would have greater economic strength than Britain or France, it might therefore seek nuclear weapons to raise its military status to a level commensurate with its economic status.

The minor powers of Eastern Europe would have strong incentives to acquire nuclear weapons. Without nuclear weapons, these Eastern European states would be open to nuclear blackmail from the Soviet Union and, if it acquired nuclear weapons, from Germany. No Eastern European state could match the conventional strength of Germany or the Soviet Union, which gives these minor powers a powerful incentive to acquire a nuclear deterrent, even if the major powers had none. In short, a continuation of the current pattern of ownership without proliferation seems unlikely.

How stable would this order be? The continued presence of nuclear weapons in Europe would have some pacifying effects. Nuclear weapons would induce greater caution in their owners, give the nuclear powers greater security, tend to equalize the relative power of states that possess them, and reduce the risk of miscalculation. However, these benefits would be limited if nuclear weapons did not proliferate beyond their current owners, for four main reasons.

First, the caution and the security that nuclear weapons impose would be missing from the vast center of Europe. The entire region between France and the Soviet Union, extending from the Arctic in the north to the Mediterranean in the south, and comprising some eighteen significant states, would become a large zone thereby made "safe" for conventional war. Second, asymmetrical power relations would be bound to develop, between nuclear and non-nuclear states and among non-nuclear states, raising the dangers that attend such asymmetries. Third, the risk of miscalculation would rise, reflecting the multipolar character of this system and the absence of nuclear weapons from a large portion of it. A durable agreed political order would be hard to build because political coalitions would tend to shift over time, causing miscalculations of resolve between adversaries. The relative strength of potential war coalitions would be hard to calculate because coalition strength would depend heavily on the vagaries of diplomacy. Such uncertainties about relative capabilities would be mitigated in conflicts that arose among nuclear powers: nuclear weapons tend to equalize power even among states or coalitions of widely disparate resources, and thus to diminish the importance of additions or defections from each coalition. However, uncertainty would still be acute among the many states that would remain non-nuclear. Fourth, the conventionally-armed states of Central Europe would depend for their security on mass armies, giving them an incentive to infuse their societies with dangerous nationalism in order to maintain public support for national defense efforts

NUCLEAR PROLIFERATION, WELL-MANAGED OR OTHERWISE

The most likely scenario in the wake of the Cold War is further nuclear proliferation in Europe. This outcome is laden with dangers, but also might provide the best hope for maintaining stability on the Continent. Its effects depend greatly on how it is managed. Mismanaged proliferation could produce disaster, while well-managed proliferation could produce an order nearly as stable as the current order. Unfortunately, however, any proliferation is likely to be mismanaged.

Four principal dangers could arise if proliferation is not properly managed. First, the proliferation process itself could give the existing nuclear powers strong incentives to use force to prevent their non-nuclear neighbors from gaining nuclear weapons, much as Israel used force to preempt Iraq from acquiring a nuclear capability.

Second, even after proliferation was completed, a stable nuclear competition might not emerge between the new nuclear states. The lesser European powers might lack the resources needed to make their nuclear forces survivable; if the emerging nuclear forces were vulnerable, this could create first-strike incentives and attendant crisis instability. Because their economies are far smaller, they would not be able to develop arsenals as large as those of the major powers; arsenals of small absolute size might thus be vulnerable. Furthermore, their lack of territorial expanse deprives them of possible basing modes, such as mobile missile basing, that would secure their deterrents. Several are landlocked, so they could not base nuclear weapons at sea, the most secure basing mode used by the superpowers. Moreover, their close proximity to one another deprives them of warning time, and thus of basing schemes that exploit warning to achieve invulnerability, such as by the quick launch of alert bombers. Finally, the emerging nuclear powers might also lack the resources required to develop secure command and control and adequate safety procedures for weapons management, thus raising the risk of accidental launch, or of terrorist seizure and use of nuclear weapons.

Third, the elites and publics of the emerging nuclear European states might not quickly develop doctrines and attitudes that reflect a grasp of the devastating consequences and basic unwinnability of nuclear war. There will probably be voices in post-Cold War Europe arguing that limited nuclear war is feasible, and that nuclear wars can be fought and won. These claims might be taken seriously in states that have not had much direct experience with the nuclear revolution.

Fourth, widespread proliferation would increase the number of fingers on the nuclear trigger, which in turn would increase the likelihood that nuclear weapons could be fired due to accident, unauthorized use, terrorist seizure, or irrational decision-making.

If these problems are not resolved, proliferation would present grave dangers. However, the existing nuclear powers can take steps to reduce these dangers. They can help deter preventive attack on emerging nuclear states by extending security guarantees. They can provide technical assistance to help newly nuclear-armed powers to secure their deterrents. And they can help socialize emerging nuclear societies to understand the nature of the forces they are acquiring. Proliferation managed in this manner can help bolster peace.

How broadly should nuclear weapons be permitted to spread? It would be best if proliferation were extended to Germany but not beyond.[57] Germany has a large economic base, and can therefore sustain a secure nuclear force. Moreover, Germany will feel insecure without

---

57. See David Garnham, "Extending Deterrence with German Nuclear Weapons," *International Security*, Vol. 10, No. 1 (Summer 1985), pp. 96-110.

nuclear weapons; and Germany's great conventional strength gives it significant capacity to disturb Europe if it feels insecure. Other states—especially in Eastern Europe—may also want nuclear weapons, but it would be best to prevent further proliferation. The reasons are, as noted above, that these states may be unable to secure their nuclear deterrents, and the unlimited spread of nuclear weapons raises the risk of terrorist seizure or possession by states led by irrational elites. However, if the broader spread of nuclear weapons proves impossible to prevent without taking extreme steps, the existing nuclear powers should let the process happen, while doing their best to channel it in safe directions.

However, even if proliferation were well-managed, significant dangers would remain. If all the major powers in Europe possessed nuclear weapons, history suggests that they would still compete for influence among the lesser powers and be drawn into lesser-power conflicts. The superpowers, despite the security that their huge nuclear arsenals provide, have competed intensely for influence in remote, strategically unimportant areas such as South Asia, Southeast Asia, and Central America. The European powers are likely to exhibit the same competitive conduct, especially in Eastern Europe, even if they possess secure nuclear deterrents.

The possibility of ganging up would remain: several nuclear states could join against a solitary nuclear state, perhaps aggregating enough strength to overwhelm its deterrent. Nuclear states also might bully their non-nuclear neighbors. This problem is mitigated if unbounded proliferation takes place, leaving few non-nuclear states subject to bullying by the nuclear states, but such widespread proliferation raises risks of its own, as noted above.

Well-managed proliferation would reduce the danger that states might miscalculate the relative strength of coalitions, since nuclear weapons clarify the relative power of all states, and diminish the importance of unforeseen additions and defections from alliances. However, the risk remains that resolve will be miscalculated, because patterns of conflict are likely to be somewhat fluid in a multipolar Europe, thus precluding the establishment of well-defined spheres of rights and rules of conduct.

Unbounded proliferation, even if it is well-managed, will raise the risks that appear when there are many fingers on the nuclear trigger—accident, unauthorized or irrational use, or terrorist seizure.

In any case, it is not likely that proliferation will be well-managed. The nuclear powers cannot easily work to manage proliferation while at the same time resisting it; there is a natural tension between the two goals. But they have several motives to resist. The established nuclear powers will be reluctant to give the new nuclear powers technical help in building secure deterrents, because it runs against the grain of state behavior to transfer military power to others, and because of the fear that sensitive military technology could be turned against the donor state if that technology were further transferred to its adversaries. The nuclear powers will also be reluctant to undermine the legitimacy of the 1968 Nuclear Non-Proliferation Treaty by allowing any signatories to acquire nuclear weapons, since this could open the floodgates to the wider proliferation that they seek to avoid, even if they would otherwise favor very limited proliferation. For these reasons the nuclear powers are more likely to spend their energy trying to thwart the process of proliferation, rather than managing it.

Proliferation can be more easily managed if it occurs during a period of relative international calm. Proliferation that occurred during a time of crisis would be especially dangerous, since states in conflict with the emerging nuclear powers would then have a strong incentive to interrupt the process by force. However, proliferation is likely not to begin until the outbreak of crisis, because there will be significant domestic opposition to proliferation within the potential nuclear powers, as well as significant external resistance from the established nuclear powers. Hence it may require a crisis to motivate the potential nuclear powers to pay the domestic and international costs of moving to build a nuclear force. Thus, proliferation is more likely to happen under disadvantageous international conditions than in a period of calm.

Finally, there are limits to the ability of the established nuclear powers to assist small emerging nuclear powers to build secure deterrents. For example, small landlocked powers cannot be given access to sea-based deterrents or land-mobile missile systems requiring vast expanses of land; these are geographic problems that technology cannot erase. Therefore even if the existing nuclear powers move to manage the proliferation process early and wisely, that process still may raise dangers that they cannot control.

John J. Mearsheimer

MANY STUDENTS of European politics will reject my pessimistic analysis of post–Cold War Europe and instead argue that a multipolar Europe is likely to be at least as peaceful as the present order. Three specific scenarios for a peaceful future have been advanced. Each rests on a well-known theory of international relations. However, each of these theories is flawed and thus cannot serve as the basis for reliable predictions of a peaceful order in a multipolar Europe; hence the hopeful scenarios they support lack plausibility.

Under the first optimistic scenario, even a non-nuclear Europe would remain peaceful because Europeans recognize that even a conventional war would be horrific. Sobered by history, national leaders will take great care to avoid war. This scenario rests on the "obsolescence of war" theory.

Although modern conventional war can certainly be very costly, there are several flaws in this argument. There is no systematic evidence demonstrating that Europeans believe war is obsolete. However, even if it were widely believed in Europe that war is no longer thinkable, attitudes could change. Public opinion on national security issues is notoriously fickle and responsive to elite manipulation and world events. Moreover, only one country need decide war is thinkable to make war possible again. Finally, it is possible that a conventional war could be fought and won without suffering grave losses, and elites who saw this possibility could believe war is a viable option.

Under the second optimistic scenario, the existing European Community (EC) grows stronger with time, a development heralded by the Single European Act, designed to create a unified Western European market by 1992. A strong EC then ensures that this economic order remains open and prosperous, and the open and prosperous character of the European economy keeps the states of Western Europe cooperating with each other. In this view, the present EC structure grows stronger, but not larger. Therefore, while conflict might emerge in Eastern Europe, the threat of an aggressive Germany would be removed by enmeshing the newly unified German state deeply in the EC. The theory underpinning this scenario is "economic liberalism."

A variant of this second scenario posits that the EC will spread to include Eastern Europe and possibly the Soviet Union, bringing prosperity and peace to these regions as well.[58] Some also maintain that the EC is likely to be so successful in the decade ahead that it will develop into a state apparatus: a unified Western European super-state would emerge and Germany would be subsumed in it. At some future point, the remainder of Europe would be incorporated into that super-state. Either way, suggest the proponents of this second scenario and its variants, peace will be bolstered.

Under the third scenario, war is avoided because many European states have become democratic since the early twentieth century, and liberal democracies simply do not fight against each other. At a minimum, the presence of liberal democracies in Western Europe renders that half of Europe free from armed conflict. At a maximum, as democracy spreads to Eastern Europe and the Soviet Union, it bolsters peace among these states, and between these states and Western Europe. This scenario is based on the theory that can be called "peace-loving democracies."

ECONOMIC LIBERALISM

The Logic of the Theory. Economic liberalism rejects the notion that the prospects for peace are tightly linked to calculations about military power, and posits instead that stability is mainly a function of international economic considerations. It assumes that modern states are primarily motivated by the desire to achieve prosperity, and that national leaders place the material welfare of their publics above all other considerations, including security. This is especially true of liberal democracies, where policymakers are under special pressure to ensure the economic well-being of their populations.[59] Thus, the key to achieving peace is establishment of an international economic system that fosters prosperity for all states.

The taproot of stability, according to this theory, is the creation and maintenance of a liberal economic order that allows free economic ex-

---

58. Jack Snyder, "Averting Anarchy in the New Europe," *International Security*, Vol. 14, No. 4 (Spring 1990), pp. 5–41.

59. This point about liberal democracies highlights the fact that economic liberalism and the theory of peace-loving democracies are often linked in the writings of international relations scholars. The basis of the linkage is what each theory has to say about peoples' motives. The claim that individuals mainly desire material prosperity, central to economic liberalism, meshes nicely with the belief that the citizenry are a powerful force against war, which, as discussed below, is central to the theory of peace-loving democracies.

change between states. Such an order works to dampen conflict and enhance political cooperation in three ways.[60]

First, it makes states more prosperous; this bolsters peace because prosperous states are more economically satisfied, and satisfied states are more peaceful. Many wars are waged to gain or preserve wealth, but states have less motive for such wars if they are already wealthy. Wealthy societies also stand to lose more if their societies are laid waste by war. For both reasons they avoid war.

Moreover, the prosperity spawned by economic liberalism feeds itself, by promoting international institutions that foster greater liberalism, which in turn promotes still greater prosperity. To function smoothly, a liberal economic order requires international regimes or institutions, such as the EC, the General Agreement on Tariffs and Trade (GATT), and the International Monetary Fund (IMF). These institutions perform two limited but important functions. First, they help states to verify that partners keep their cooperative commitments. Second, they provide resources to governments experiencing short-term problems arising from their exposure to international markets, and by doing so they allow states to eschew beggar-thy-neighbor policies that might otherwise undermine the existing economic

---

60. The three explanations discussed here rest on three of the most prominent theories advanced in the international political economy (IPE) literature. These three are usually treated as distinct theories and are given various labels. However, they share important common elements. Hence, for purposes of parsimony, I treat them as three strands of one general theory: economic liberalism. A caveat is in order. The IPE literature often fails to state its theories in a clear fashion, making them difficult to evaluate. Thus, I have construed these theories from sometimes opaque writings that might be open to contrary interpretations. My description of economic liberalism is drawn from the following works, which are among the best of the IPE genre: Richard N. Cooper, "Economic Interdependence and Foreign Policies in the Seventies," *World Politics*, Vol. 24, No. 2 (January 1972), pp. 158-181; Ernst B. Haas, "Technology, Pluralism, and the New Europe," in Joseph S. Nye, Jr., ed., *International Regionalism* (Boston: Little, Brown, 1968), pp. 149-176; Robert O. Keohane and Joseph S. Nye, Jr., *Power and Interdependence: World Politics in Transition* (Boston: Little, Brown, 1977); Robert O. Keohane, *After Hegemony: Cooperation and Discord in the World Political Economy* (Princeton: Princeton University Press, 1984); David Mitrany, *A Working Peace System* (Chicago: Quadrangle Press, 1966); Edward L. Morse, "The Transformation of Foreign Policies: Modernization, Interdependence, and Externalization," *World Politics*, Vol. 22, No. 3 (April 1970), pp. 371-392; and Richard N. Rosecrance, *The Rise of the Trading State: Commerce and Conquest in the Modern World* (New York: Basic Books, 1986).

order. Once in place, these institutions and regimes bolster economic cooperation, hence bolster prosperity. They also bolster themselves: once in existence they cause the expansion of their own size and influence, by proving their worth and selling themselves to states and publics. And as their power grows they become better able to promote cooperation, which promotes greater prosperity, which further bolsters their prestige and influence. In essence, a benevolent spiral-like relationship sets in between cooperation-promoting regimes and prosperity, in which each feeds the other.

Second, a liberal economic order fosters economic interdependence among states. Interdependence is defined as a situation in which two states are mutually vulnerable; each is a hostage of the other in the economic realm.[61] When interdependence is high, this theory holds, there is less temptation to cheat or behave aggressively towards other states because all states could retaliate. Interdependence allows states to compel each other to cooperate on economic matters, much as mutual assured destruction allows nuclear powers to compel each other to respect their security. All states are forced by the others to act as partners in the provision of material comfort for their home publics.

Third, some theorists argue that with ever-increasing political cooperation, international regimes will become so powerful that they will assume an independent life of their own, eventually growing into a super-state. This is a minority view; most economic liberals do not argue that regimes can become so powerful that they can coerce states to act against their own narrow interests. Instead most maintain that regimes essentially reflect the interests of the states that created and maintain them, and remain subordinate to other interests of these states. However, the "growth to super-statehood" view does represent an important strand of thought among economic liberals.

The main flaw in this theory is that the principal assumption underpinning it—that states are primarily motivated by the desire to achieve prosperity— is wrong. States are surely concerned about prosperity, and thus economic calculations are hardly trivial for them. However, states operate in both an international political environment and an international economic environment, and the former dominates the latter in cases where the two systems come into conflict. The reason is straightforward:

---

61. See Kenneth N. Waltz, "The Myth of National Interdependence," in Charles P. Kindelberger, ed., *The International Corporation* (Cambridge: MIT Press, 1970), pp. 205-223.

the international political system is anarchic, which means that each state must always be concerned to ensure its own survival. Since a state can have no higher goal than survival, when push comes to shove, international political considerations will be paramount in the minds of decision-makers.

Proponents of economic liberalism largely ignore the effects of anarchy on state behavior and concentrate instead on economic considerations. When this omission is corrected, however, their arguments collapse, for two reasons.

First, competition for security makes it very difficult for states to cooperate. When security is scarce, states become more concerned about relative gains than absolute gains.[62] They ask of an exchange not, "will both of us gain?" but instead, "who will gain more?"[63] When security is scarce, they reject even cooperation that would yield an absolute economic gain, if the other state would gain more of the yield, from fear that the other might convert its gain to military strength, and then use this strength to win by coercion in later rounds.[64] Cooperation is much easier to achieve if states worry only about absolute gains, as they are more likely to do when security is not so scarce. The goal then is simply to insure that the overall economic pie is expanding and each state is getting at least some part of the resulting benefits. However, anarchy guarantees that security will often be scarce; this heightens states' concerns about relative gains, which makes cooperation difficult unless gains can be finely sliced to reflect, and thus not disturb, the current balance of power.

In contrast to this view, economic liberals generally assume that states worry little about relative gains when designing cooperative agreements, but instead are concerned mainly about absolute gains. This assumption underlies their optimism over the prospects for international cooperation. However, it is not well-based: anarchy forces states to reject agreements that result in asymmetrical payoffs that shift the balance of power against them.

Second, interdependence is as likely to lead to conflict as cooperation, because states will struggle to escape the vulnerability that interdepen-

---

62. See Joseph M. Grieco, "Anarchy and the Limits of Cooperation: A Realist Critique of the Newest Liberal Institutionalism," *International Organization,* Vol. 42, No. 3 (Summer 1988) pp. 485-507; and Grieco, *Cooperation among Nations: Europe, America and Non-Tariff Barriers to Trade* (Ithaca: Cornell University Press, 1990).

63. Waltz, *Theory of International Politics,* p. 105.

64. It is important to emphasize that because military power is in good part a function of economic might, the consequences of economic dealings among states sometimes have important security implications.

dence creates, in order to bolster their national security. States that depend on others for critical economic supplies will fear cutoff or blackmail in time of crisis or war; they may try to extend political control to the source of supply, giving rise to conflict with the source or with its other customers. Interdependence, in other words, might very well lead to greater competition, not to cooperation.[65]

Several other considerations, independent of the consequences of anarchy, also raise doubts about the claims of economic liberals.

First, economic interactions between states often cause serious frictions, even if the overall consequences are positive. There will invariably be winners and losers within each state, and losers rarely accept defeat gracefully. In modern states, where leaders have to pay careful attention to their constituents, losers can cause considerable trouble. Even in cases where only winners are involved, there are sometimes squabbles over how the spoils are divided. In a sense, then, expanding the network of contacts among states increases the scope for international disagreements among them. They now have more to squabble about.

Second, there will be opportunities for blackmail and for brinkmanship in a highly dynamic economic system where states are dependent on each other. For example, although mutual vulnerabilities may arise among states, it is likely that the actual levels of dependence will not be equal. The less vulnerable states would probably have greater bargaining

---

65. There are numerous examples in the historical record of vulnerable states pursuing aggressive military policies for the purpose of achieving autarky. For example, this pattern of behavior was reflected in both Japan's and Germany's actions during the interwar period. On Japan, see Michael A. Barnhart, *Japan Prepares for Total War: The Search for Economic Security, 1919-1941* (Ithaca: Cornell University Press, 1987); and James B. Crowley, *Japan's Quest for Autonomy* (Princeton: Princeton University Press, 1966). On Germany, see William Carr, *Arms, Autarky and Aggression: A Study in German Foreign Policy, 1933-39* (New York: Norton, 1973). It is also worth noting that during the Arab oil embargo of the early 1970s, when it became apparent that the United States was vulnerable to OPEC pressure, there was much talk in America about using military force to seize Arab oil fields. See, for example, Robert W. Tucker, "Oil: The Issue of American Intervention," *Commentary*, January 1975, pp. 21-31; Miles Ignotus [said to be a pseudonym for Edward Luttwak], "Seizing Arab Oil," *Harpers*, March 1975, pp. 45-62; and U.S. Congress House Committee on International Relations, *Report on Oil Fields as Military Objectives: A Feasibility Study*, prepared by John M. Collins and Clyde R. Mark, 94th Cong., 1st sess. (Washington, D.C.: U.S. Government Printing Office [U.S. GPO], August 21, 1975).

power over the more dependent states and might attempt to coerce them into making extravagant concessions. Furthermore, different political systems, not to mention individual leaders, have different capacities for engaging in tough bargaining situations.

The Historical Record

During two periods in the twentieth century, Europe witnessed a liberal economic order with high levels of interdependence. Stability should have obtained during those periods, according to economic liberalism.

The first case clearly contradicts the theory. The years between 1890 and 1914 were probably the time of greatest economic interdependence in Europe's history. Yet World War I broke out following this period.[66]

The second case covers the Cold War years. During this period there has been much interdependence among the EC states, while relations among these states have been very peaceful. This case, not surprisingly, is the centerpiece of the economic liberals' argument.

The correlation in this second case does not mean, however, that interdependence has *caused* cooperation among the Western democracies. It is more likely that the prime cause was the Cold War, and that this was the main reason that intra-EC relations have flourished.[67] The Cold War caused these results in two different but mutually reinforcing ways.

First, old-fashioned balance of power logic mandated cooperation among the Western democracies. A powerful and potentially dangerous Soviet Union forced the Western democracies to band together to meet the common threat. Britain, Germany, and France no longer worried about each other, because all faced a greater menace from the Soviets. This Soviet threat muted concerns about relative gains arising from economic cooperation among the EC states by giving each Western democracy a vested interest in seeing its alliance partners grow powerful, since each additional

---

66. See Richard N. Rosecrance, et al., "Whither Interdependence?" *International Organization*, Vol. 31, No. 3 (Summer 1977), pp. 432-434.

67 This theme is reflected in Barry Buzan, "Economic Structure and International Security: The Limits of the Liberal Case," *International Organization*, Vol. 38, No. 4 (Autumn 1984), pp. 597–624; Robert Gilpin, U.S. *Power and the Multinational Corporation: The Political Economy of Foreign Direct Investment* (New York: Basic Books, 1975); and Robert A. Pollard, *Economic Security and the Origins of the Cold War*, 1945-1950 (New York: Columbia University Press, 1985).

increment of power helped deter the Soviets. The Soviet threat also muted relative-gains fears among Western European states by giving them all a powerful incentive to avoid conflict with each other while the Soviet Union loomed to the east, ready to harvest the gains of Western quarrels. This gave each Western state greater confidence that its Western partners would not turn their gains against it, as long as these partners behaved rationally.

Second, America's hegemonic position in NATO, the military counterpart to the EC, mitigated the effects of anarchy on the Western democracies and facilitated cooperation among them.[68] As emphasized, states do not trust each other in anarchy and they have incentives to commit aggression against each other. America, however, not only provided protection against the Soviet threat, but also guaranteed that no EC state would aggress against another. For example, France did not have to fear Germany as it rearmed, because the American presence in Germany meant that the Germans were not free to attack anyone. With the United States serving as night watchman, relative-gains concerns among the Western European states were mitigated and, moreover, those states were willing to allow their economies to become tightly interdependent.

In effect, relations among EC states were spared the effects of anarchy— fears about relative gains and an obsession with autonomy—because the United States served as the ultimate arbiter within the Alliance.

If the present Soviet threat to Western Europe is removed, and American forces depart for home, relations among the EC states will be fundamentally altered. Without a common Soviet threat and without the American night watchman, Western European states will begin viewing each other with greater fear and suspicion, as they did for centuries before the onset of the Cold War. Consequently, they will worry about the imbalances in gains as well as the loss of autonomy that results from cooperation.[69] Cooperation in this new order will be more difficult than it has been in the Cold War. Conflict will be more likely.

---

68. See Josef Joffe, "Europe's American Pacifier," *Foreign Policy*, No. 54 (Spring 1984), pp. 64-82.

69. Consider, for example, a situation where the European Community is successfully extended to include Eastern Europe and the Soviet Union, and that over time all states achieve greater prosperity. The Germans, however, do significantly better than all other states. Hence their relative power position, which is already quite strong, begins to improve markedly. It is likely that the French and the Soviets, just to name two states, would be deeply concerned by this situation.

John J. Mearsheimer

In sum, there are good reasons for looking with skepticism upon the claim that peace can be maintained in a multipolar Europe on the basis of a more powerful EC.

PEACE-LOVING DEMOCRACIES

The peace-loving democracies theory holds that domestic political factors, not calculations about military power or the international economic system, are the principal determinant of peace. Specifically, the argument is that the presence of liberal democracies in the international system will help to produce a stable order.[70] The claim is not that democracies go to war less often than authoritarian states. In fact, the historical record shows clearly that such is not the case.[71] Instead, the argument is that democracies do not go to war against other democracies. Thus, democracy must spread to Eastern Europe and the Soviet Union to insure peace in post-Cold War Europe.

It is not certain that democracy will take root among the states of Eastern Europe or in the Soviet Union. They lack a strong tradition of democracy; institutions that can accommodate the growth of democracy will have to be built from scratch. That task will probably prove to be difficult, especially in an unstable Europe. But whether democracy takes root in the East matters little for stability in Europe, since the theory of peace-loving democracies is unsound.

---

70. This theory has been recently articulated by Michael Doyle in three articles: "Liberalism and World Politics," [in this anthology]; "Kant, Liberal Legacies, and Foreign Affairs," *Philosophy and Public Affairs*, Vol. 12, No. 3 (Summer 1983), pp. 205-235; and "Kant, Liberal Legacies, and Foreign Affairs, Part 2," *Philosophy and Public Affairs*, Vol. 12, No. 4 (Fall 1983), pp. 323-353. Doyle draws heavily on Immanuel Kant's classic writings on the subject. This theory also provides the central argument in Francis Fukuyama's widely publicized essay on "The End of History?" [in this anthology]. For an excellent critique of the theory, see Samuel P. Huntington, "No Exit: The Errors of Endism," [in this anthology].

71. There is a good empirical literature on the relationship between democracy and war. See, for example, Steve Chan, "Mirror, Mirror on the Wall . . . Are the Freer Countries More Pacific?" *Journal of Conflict Resolution*, Vol. 28, No. 4 (December 1984), pp. 617-648; Erich Weede, "Democracy and War Involvement," in ibid., pp. 649-664; Bruce M. Russett and R. Joseph Monsen, "Bureaucracy and Polyarchy As Predictors of Performance," *Comparative Political Studies*, Vol. 8, No. 1 (April 1975), pp. 5-31; and Melvin Small and J. David Singer, "The War-Proneness of Democratic Regimes, 1816-1965," *The Jerusalem Journal of International Relations*, Vol. 1, No. 4 (Summer 1976), pp. 50-69.

Back to the Future

The Logic of the Theory

Two explanations are offered in support of the claim that democracies do not go to war against one another.

First, some claim that authoritarian leaders are more prone to go to war than leaders of democracies, because authoritarian leaders are not accountable to their publics, which carry the main burdens of war. In a democracy, by contrast, the citizenry that pays the price of war has greater say in the decision-making process. The people, so the argument goes, are more hesitant to start trouble because it is they who pay the blood price; hence the greater their power, the fewer wars.

The second argument rests on the claim that the citizens of liberal democracies respect popular democratic rights—those of their fellow countrymen, and those of individuals in other states. As a result they are reluctant to wage war against other democracies, because they view democratic governments as more legitimate than others, and are loath to impose a foreign regime on a democratic state by force. This would violate their own democratic principles and values. Thus an inhibition on war is introduced when two democracies face each other that is missing in other international relationships.

The first of these arguments is flawed because it is not possible to sustain the claim that the people in a democracy are especially sensitive to the costs of war and therefore less willing than authoritarian leaders to fight wars. In fact, the historical record shows that democracies are every bit as likely to fight wars as are authoritarian states.

Furthermore, mass publics, whether democratic or not, can become deeply imbued with nationalistic or religious fervor, making them prone to support aggression, regardless of costs. The widespread public support in post-revolutionary France for Napoleon's wars of aggression is just one example of this phenomenon. On the other hand, authoritarian leaders are just as likely as democratic publics to fear going to war, because war tends to unleash democratic forces that can undermine the regime.[72] War can impose high costs on authoritarian leaders as well as on their citizenries.

The second argument, which emphasizes the transnational respect for democratic rights among democracies, rests on a weaker factor that is usu-

---

72. See, for example, Stanislav Andreski, "On the Peaceful Disposition of Military Dictatorships," *Journal of Strategic Studies*, Vol. 3, No. 3 (December 1980), pp. 3-10.

ally overridden by other factors such as nationalism and religious fundamentalism. There is also another problem with the argument. The possibility always exists that a democracy will revert to an authoritarian state. This threat of backsliding means that one democratic state can never be sure that another democratic state will not change its stripes and turn on it sometime in the future. Liberal democracies must therefore worry about relative power among themselves, which is tantamount to saying that each has an incentive to consider aggression against the other to forestall future trouble. Lamentably, it is not possible for even liberal democracies to transcend anarchy.

The Historical Record

Problems with the deductive logic aside, the historical record seems to offer strong support for the theory of peace-loving democracies. There appears to have been no case where liberal democracies fought against each other. Although this evidence looks impressive at first glance, closer examination shows it to be indecisive. In fact, history provides no clear test of the theory. Four evidentiary problems leave the issue in doubt.

First, democracies have been few in number over the past two centuries, and thus there have not been many cases where two democracies were in a position to fight with each other. Only three prominent cases are usually cited: Britain and the United States (1832-present); Britain and France (1832–49, 1871-1940); and the Western democracies since 1945.

Second, there are other persuasive explanations for why war did not occur in those three cases, and these competing explanations must be ruled out before the peace-loving democracies theory can be accepted. While relations between the British and the Americans during the nineteenth century were hardly free of conflict,[73] their relations in the twentieth century were quite harmonious, and thus fit closely with how the theory would expect two democracies to behave towards each other. That harmony, however, can easily be explained by the presence of a common threat that forced Britain and the United

---

73. For a discussion of the hostile relations that existed between the United States and Britain during the nineteenth century, see H.C. Allen, *Great Britain and the United States: A History of Anglo-American Relations, 1783-1952* (London: Odhams, 1954).

States to work closely together.[74] Both faced a serious German threat in the first part of the century, and a Soviet threat later. The same basic argument applies to France and Britain. While Franco-British relations were not the best throughout most of the nineteenth century,[75] they improved significantly around the turn of the century with the rise of a common threat: Germany.[76] Finally, as noted above, the Soviet threat can explain the absence of war among the Western democracies since 1945.

Third, it bears mention that several democracies have come close to fighting one another, which suggests that the absence of war may be due simply to chance. France and Britain approached war during the Fashoda crisis of 1898. France and Weimar Germany might have come to blows over the Rhineland during the 1920s, had Germany possessed the military strength to challenge France. The United States has clashed with a number of elected governments in the Third World during the Cold War, including the Allende regime in Chile and the Arbenz regime in Guatemala.

Lastly, some would classify Wilhelmine Germany as a democracy, or at least a quasi-democracy; if so, World War I becomes a war among democracies.[77]

---

74. For a discussion of this rapprochement, see Stephen R. Rock, *Why Peace Breaks Out: Great Power Rapprochement in Historical Perspective* (Chapel Hill: University of North Carolina Press, 1989), chap. 2.

75. For a good discussion of Franco-British relations during the nineteenth century, see P.J.V. Rolo, *Entente Cordiale: The Origins and Negotiation of the Anglo-French Agreements of 8 April 1904* (New York: St. Martins, 1969), pp. 16-109.

76. Stephen Rock, who has examined the rapprochement between Britain and France, argues that the principal motivating force behind their improved relations derived from geopolitical considerations, not shared political beliefs. See Rock, *Why Peace Breaks Out*, chap. 4.

77. Doyle recognizes this problem and thus has a lengthy footnote that attempts to deal with it. See "Kant, Liberal Legacies, and Foreign Affairs [Part One]," pp. 216-217, n. 8. He argues that "Germany was a liberal state under republican law for domestic issues," but that the "emperor's active role in foreign affairs . . . made imperial Germany a state divorced from the control of its citizenry in foreign affairs." However, an examination of the decision-making process leading to World War I reveals that the emperor (Wilhelm II) was not a prime mover in foreign affairs and that he was no more bellicose than other members of the German elite including the leading civilian official, Chancellor Bethmann-Hollweg.

John J. Mearsheimer

CONCLUSION

THIS ARTICLE argues that bipolarity, an equal military balance, and nuclear weapons have fostered peace in Europe over the past 45 years. The Cold War confrontation produced these phenomena; thus the Cold War was principally responsible for transforming a historically violent region into a very peaceful place.

There is no doubt that the costs of the Cold War have been substantial. It inflicted oppressive political regimes on the peoples of Eastern Europe, who were denied basic human rights by their forced membership in the Soviet empire. It consumed national wealth, by giving rise to large and costly defense establishments in both East and West. It spawned bloody conflicts in the Third World; these produced modest casualties for the superpowers, but large casualties for the Third World nations. Nevertheless, the net human and economic cost of the Cold War order has been far less than the cost of the European order of 1900-45, with its vast violence and suffering.

A Cold War order without confrontation would have been preferable to the order that actually developed; then the peace that the Cold War order produced could have been enjoyed without its attendant costs. However, it was East-West enmity that gave rise to the Cold War order; there would have been no bipolarity, no equality, and no large Soviet and American nuclear forces in Europe without it. The costs of the Cold War arose from the same cause—East-West confrontation—as did its benefits. The good could not be had without the bad.

This article further argues that the demise of the Cold War order is likely to increase the chances that war and major crises will occur in Europe. Many observers now suggest that a new age of peace is dawning; in fact the opposite is true.

The implications of my analysis are straightforward, if paradoxical. The West has an interest in maintaining peace in Europe. It therefore has an interest in maintaining the Cold War order, and hence has an interest in the continuation of the Cold War confrontation; developments that threaten to end it are dangerous. The Cold War antagonism could be continued at lower levels of East-West tension than have prevailed in the past; hence the West is not injured by relaxing East-West tension, but a complete end to the Cold War would create more problems than it would solve.

The fate of the Cold War, however, is mainly in the hands of the Soviet Union. The Soviet Union is the only superpower that can seriously threaten to overrun Europe; it is the Soviet threat that provides the glue that holds NATO together. Take away that offensive threat and the United States is likely to abandon the Continent, whereupon the defensive alliance it has headed for forty years may disintegrate. This would bring to an end the bipolar order that has characterized Europe for the past 45 years.

The foregoing analysis suggests that the West paradoxically has an interest in the continued existence of a powerful Soviet Union with substantial military forces in Eastern Europe. Western interests are wholly reversed from those that Western leaders saw in the late 1940s: instead of seeking the retraction of Soviet power, as the West did then, the West now should hope that the Soviet Union retains at least some military forces in the Eastern European region.

There is little the Americans or the Western Europeans can or are likely to do to perpetuate the Cold War, for three reasons.

First, domestic political considerations preclude such an approach. Western leaders obviously cannot base national security policy on the need to maintain forces in Central Europe for the purpose simply of keeping the Soviets there. The idea of deploying large forces in order to bait the Soviets into an order-keeping competition would be dismissed as bizarre, and contrary to the general belief that ending the Cold War and removing the Soviet yoke from Eastern Europe would make the world safer and better.[78]

Second, the idea of propping up a declining rival runs counter to the basic behavior of states. States are principally concerned about their relative power position in the system; hence, they look for opportunities to take advantage of each other. If anything, they prefer to see adversaries decline, and thus will do whatever they can to speed up the process and maximize the distance of the fall. In other words, states do not ask which distribution of power best facilitates stability and then do everything possible

---

78. This point is illustrated by the 1976 controversy over the so-called "Sonnenfeldt Doctrine." Helmut Sonnenfeldt, an adviser to Secretary of State Henry Kissinger, was reported to have said in late 1975 that the United States should support Soviet domination of Eastern Europe. It was clear from the ensuing debate that whether or not Sonnenfeldt in fact made such a claim, no administration could publicly adopt that position. See U.S. Congress, House Committee on International Relations, *Hearings on United States National Security Policy Vis-à-Vis Eastern Europe (The "Sonnenfeldt Doctrine")*, 94th Cong., 2nd sess. (Washington, D.C.: U.S. GPO, April 12, 1976).

to build or maintain such an order. Instead, they each tend to pursue the more narrow aim of maximizing their power advantage over potential adversaries. The particular international order that results is simply a byproduct of that competition, as illustrated by the origins of the Cold War order in Europe. No state intended to create it. In fact, both the United States and the Soviet Union worked hard in the early years of the Cold War to undermine each other's position in Europe, which would have ended the bipolar order on the Continent. The remarkably stable system that emerged in Europe in the late 1940s was the unintended consequence of an intense competition between the superpowers.

Third, even if the Americans and the Western Europeans wanted to help the Soviets maintain their status as a superpower, it is not apparent that they could do so. The Soviet Union is leaving Eastern Europe and cutting its military forces largely because its economy is foundering. It is not clear that the Soviets themselves know how to fix their economy, and there is little that Western governments can do to help them solve their economic problems. The West can and should avoid doing malicious mischief to the Soviet economy, but at this juncture it is difficult to see how the West can have significant positive influence.[79]

The fact that the West cannot sustain the Cold War does not mean that the United States should abandon all attempts to preserve the current order. The United States should do what it can to direct events toward averting a complete mutual superpower withdrawal from Europe. For instance, the American negotiating position at the conventional arms control talks should aim toward large mutual force reductions, but should not contemplate complete mutual withdrawal. The Soviets may opt to withdraw all their forces unilaterally anyway; there is little the United States could do to prevent this.

POLICY RECOMMENDATIONS

If complete Soviet withdrawal from Eastern Europe proves unavoidable, the West faces the question of how to maintain peace in a multipolar Europe. Three policy prescriptions are in order.

---

79. For an optimistic assessment of how the West can enhance Gorbachev's prospects of succeeding, see Jack Snyder, "International Leverage on Soviet Domestic Change," *World Politics*, Vol. 42, No. 1 (October 1989), pp. 1-30.

First, the United States should encourage the limited and carefully managed proliferation of nuclear weapons in Europe. The best hope for avoiding war in post–Cold War Europe is nuclear deterrence; hence some nuclear proliferation is necessary to compensate for the withdrawal of the Soviet and American nuclear arsenals from Central Europe. Ideally, as I have argued, nuclear weapons would spread to Germany, but to no other state.

Second, Britain and the United States, as well as the Continental states, will have to balance actively and efficiently against any emerging aggressor to offset the ganging up and bullying problems that are sure to arise in post–Cold War Europe. Balancing in a multipolar system, however, is usually a problem-ridden enterprise, either because of geography or because of significant coordination problems. Nevertheless, two steps can be taken to maximize the prospects of efficient balancing.

The initial measure concerns Britain and the United States, the two prospective balancing states that, physically separated from the Continent, may thus conclude that they have little interest in what happens there. They would then be abandoning their responsibilities and, more importantly, their interests as off shore balancers. Both states' failure to balance against Germany before the two world wars made war more likely in each case. It is essential for peace in Europe that they not repeat their past mistakes, but instead remain actively involved in maintaining the balance of power in Europe.

Specifically, both states must maintain military forces that can be deployed to the Continent to balance against states that threaten to start a war. To do this they must also socialize their publics to support a policy of continued Continental commitment. Support for such a commitment will be more difficult to mobilize than in the past, because its principal purpose would be to preserve peace, rather than to prevent an imminent hegemony, and the latter is a simpler goal to explain publicly. Moreover, it is the basic nature of states to focus on maximizing relative power, not on bolstering stability, so this prescription asks them to take on an unaccustomed task. Nevertheless, the British and American stake in peace is real, especially since there is a sure risk that a European war might involve large-scale use of nuclear weapons. It should therefore be possible for both countries to lead their publics to recognize this interest and support policies that protect it.[80]

---

80. Advancing this argument is Van Evera, "Why Europe Matters, Why the Third World Doesn't."

The other measure concerns American attitudes and actions toward the Soviet Union. The Soviets may eventually return to their past expansionism and threaten to upset the status quo. If so, we are back to the Cold War; the West should respond as quickly and efficiently as it did the first time. However, if the Soviets adhere to status quo policies, Soviet power could play a key role in balancing against Germany and in maintaining order in Eastern Europe. It is important that, in those cases where the Soviets are acting in a balancing capacity, the United States recognize this, cooperate with its former adversary, and not let residual distrust from the Cold War interfere with the balancing process.

Third, a concerted effort should be made to keep hyper-nationalism at bay, especially in Eastern Europe. This powerful force has deep roots in Europe and has contributed to the outbreak of past European conflicts. Nationalism has been contained during the Cold War, but it is likely to reemerge once Soviet and American forces leave the heart of Europe.[81] It will be a force for trouble unless it is curbed. The teaching of honest national history is especially important, since the teaching of false chauvinist history is the main vehicle for spreading virulent nationalism. States that teach a dishonestly self-exculpating or self-glorifying history should be publicly criticized and sanctioned.[82]

On this count it is especially important that relations between Germany and its neighbors be handled carefully. Many Germans rightly feel that Germany has behaved very responsibly for 45 years, and has made an honest effort to remember and make amends for an ugly period of its past. Therefore, Germans quickly tire of lectures from foreigners demanding that they apologize once again for crimes committed before most of the current German population was born. On the other hand, peoples who have suffered at the hands of the Germans cannot forget their enormous suffering, and inevitably ask for repeated assurance that the past will not be repeated. This dialogue has the potential to spiral into mutual recriminations that could spark a renewed sense of persecution among Germans, and with it, a rebirth of German-nationalism. It is therefore incumbent on all parties in this discourse to proceed with un-

---

81. On the evolution of nationalistic history-teaching in Europe see Kennedy, "The Decline of Nationalistic History," and Dance, *History the Betrayer*.

82. My thinking on this matter has been influenced by conversations with Stephen Van Evera.

derstanding and respect for one another's feelings and experience. Specifically, others should not ask today's Germans to apologize for crimes they did not commit, but Germans must understand that others' ceaseless demands for reassurance have a legitimate basis in history, and should view these demands with patience and understanding.

None of these tasks will be easy to accomplish. In fact, I expect that the bulk of my prescriptions will not be followed; most run contrary to powerful strains of domestic American and European opinion, and to the basic nature of state behavior. Moreover, even if they are followed, this will not guarantee the peace in Europe. If the Cold War is truly behind us, the stability of the past 45 years is not likely to be seen again in the coming decades. ✪

Response to
"Back to the Future"

Robert O. Keohane

IN "BACK TO THE FUTURE: Instability in Europe After the Cold War," John Mearsheimer makes a number of arresting and controversial arguments about nuclear proliferation, the peacefulness of democratic states, and the impact on military conflict of economic interdependence and international institutions such as the European Community. I appreciate his willingness to make predictions while expressing humility about our theories, and I agree that the end of the Cold War allows us, within limits, to use the world "as a laboratory to decide which theories best explain international politics" (p. 9). But I think that he underestimates the impact of international institutions on world politics, particularly in contemporary Europe.

Professor Mearsheimer places great weight on the fact of "anarchy"—the absence of centralized enforcement powers on a global basis. However, on his own account, the Western European experience during the Cold War shows that anarchy does not necessarily prevent cooperation. Instead, although anarchy in this sense has been a constant throughout this century, cooperation among states has varied substantially. Thus Mearsheimer's statement that "anarchy guarantees that security will often be scarce" (p. 45) is unsatisfying, because it does not indicate the conditions under which a scarcity of security will occur. "Anarchy" is a disappointing analytical category because it is not a variable; we must look elsewhere to explain variations in the incidence of military conflict.

In a theory of state policy based on the assumption of rationality, as assumed by Professor Mearsheimer's form of realism, states seek to

ROBERT O. KEOHANE is Professor of Political Science at Duke University. This article appeared in the Fall 1990 issue of *International Security*.

maximize expected utility. Expected utility, as the label implies, depends on expectations about the consequences of alternative courses of action: that is, on judgments of probability. The rational judgments of leaders depend not simply on the absence of a centralized international government able to enforce its injunctions, but on their expectations about other states' likely actions.

Professor Mearsheimer agrees that expectations are important. He argues that where security is assured (as it has been among members of the European Community), states tend to seek absolute gains; but when security is scarce, they become more concerned about relative gains. Expectations, he argues, depend on domestic and international political structures. During the Cold War, bipolarity reduced the likelihood of conflict, and European states "lacked the incentive to purvey hyper-nationalism" (p. 29). Structural features of the European international system therefore created the conditions under which states rationally emphasized absolute gains and managed therefore to cooperate extensively with one another.

Without denying the importance of either of those variables, I suggest that the nature and strength of international institutions are also important determinants of expectations and therefore of state behavior. Insofar as states regularly follow the rules and standards of international institutions, they signal their willingness to continue patterns of cooperation, and therefore reinforce expectations of stability. Doing so does not mean eschewing either one's own interests or the search for influence: indeed, in contemporary Europe, Germany can best acquire both wealth and influence by building European institutions, thus reassuring its partners and preventing the formation of the balancing coalitions that Professor Mearsheimer describes: insofar as they assure states about their security, institutions allow governments to emphasize absolute rather than relative gains, and therefore maintain the conditions for their own existence. Conversely, when institutions collapse, they are particularly hard to reconstruct, since insecure states, seeking relative gains, find it extremely difficult to cooperate sufficiently to build significant international institutions.

It should be clear that the institutionalist argument made in the last paragraph does not depend on the assumptions that states are altruistic, that they always seek absolute gains, or that economic interdependence necessarily leads to cooperation. On the contrary, the view I put forward assumes that states are self-interested, that they may seek relative as well as absolute gains, and that interdependence can indeed lead to conflict. What distinguishes my argument from Professor Mearsheimer's is my claim that international institutions help to shape the expectations that both of us agree are crucial determinants of state behavior.

From a policy perspective, emphasizing institutions is particularly important, since they are more responsive to human action than either fundamental political tendencies such as hyper-nationalism, or the international political structures of bipolarity or multipolarity. In my view, avoiding military conflict in Europe after the Cold War depends greatly on whether the next decade is characterized by a continuous pattern of institutionalized cooperation. Will NATO and the Warsaw Pact be gradually transformed into non-antagonistic organizations? Will a powerful European Community increasingly attain political as well as economic union? Can broader institutions, such as the Conference on Security and Cooperation in Europe (CSCE), be strengthened in order to give states confidence in others' peaceful intentions toward them? Students of world politics could profitably spend more of their time asking how international institutions should be structured, both within Western and Central Europe and between Europe and other powerful states, in order to prevent the recurrence of a fear-driven slide toward military conflict that would be disastrous for our generation and those to follow.

Competitiveness:
A Dangerous Obsession

Paul Krugman

THE HYPOTHESIS IS WRONG

IN JUNE 1993, Jacques Delors made a special presentation to the leaders of the nations of the European Community, meeting in Copenhagen, on the growing problem of European unemployment. Economists who study the European situation were curious to see what Delors, president of the EC Commission, would say. Most of them share more or less the same diagnosis of the European problem: the taxes and regulations imposed by Europe's elaborate welfare states have made employers reluctant to create new jobs, while the relatively generous level of unemployment benefits has made workers unwilling to accept the kinds of low-wage jobs that help keep unemployment comparatively low in the United States. The monetary difficulties associated with preserving the European Monetary System in the face of the costs of German reunification have reinforced this structural problem.

It is a persuasive diagnosis, but a politically explosive one, and everyone wanted to see how Delors would handle it. Would he dare tell European leaders that their efforts to pursue economic justice have produced unemployment as an unintended by-product? Would he admit that the ems could be sustained only at the cost of a recession and face the implications of that admission for European monetary union?

Guess what? Delors didn't confront the problems of either the welfare state or the EMS. He explained that the root cause of European unemployment was a lack of competitiveness with the United States and

PAUL KRUGMAN is Professor of Economics at the Massachusetts Institute of Technology. His most recent book is *Pop Internationalism*. This article appeared in the March/April 1994 issue of *Foreign Affairs*.

Japan and that the solution was a program of investment in infrastructure and high technology.

It was a disappointing evasion, but not a surprising one. After all, the rhetoric of competitiveness—the view that, in the words of President Clinton, each nation is "like a big corporation competing in the global marketplace"—has become pervasive among opinion leaders throughout the world. People who believe themselves to be sophisticated about the subject take it for granted that the economic problem facing any modern nation is essentially one of competing on world markets—that the United States and Japan are competitors in the same sense that Coca-Cola competes with Pepsi—and are unaware that anyone might seriously question that proposition. Every few months a new best-seller warns the American public of the dire consequences of losing the "race" for the 21st century.[1] A whole industry of councils on competitiveness, "geo-economists" and managed trade theorists has sprung up in Washington. Many of these people, having diagnosed America's economic problems in much the same terms as Delors did Europe's, are now in the highest reaches of the Clinton administration formulating economic and trade policy for the United States. So Delors was using a language that was not only convenient but comfortable for him and a wide audience on both sides of the Atlantic.

---

[1]See, for just a few examples, Laura D'Andrea Tyson, *Who's Bashing Whom: Trade Conflict in High-Technology Industries*, Washington: Institute for International Economics, 1992; Lester C. Thurow, *Head to Head: The Coming Economic Battle among Japan, Europe, and America*, New York: Morrow, 1992; Ira C. Magaziner and Robert B. Reich, *Minding America's Business: The Decline and Rise of the American Economy*, New York: Vintage Books, 1983; Ira C. Magaziner and Mark Patinkin, *The Silent War: Inside the Global Business Battles Shaping America's Future*, New York: Vintage Books, 1990; Edward N. Luttwak, *The Endangered American Dream: How to Stop the United States from Becoming a Third World Country and How to Win the Geo-economic Struggle for Industrial Supremacy*, New York: Simon and Schuster, 1993; Kevin P. Phillips, *Staying on Top: The Business Case for a National Industrial Strategy*, New York: Random House, 1984; Clyde V. Prestowitz, Jr., *Trading Places: How We Allowed Japan to Take the Lead*, New York: Basic Books, 1988; William S. Dietrich, *In the Shadow of the Rising Sun: The Political Roots of American Economic Decline*, University Park: Pennsylvania State University Press, 1991; Jeffrey E. Garten, *A Cold Peace: America, Japan, Germany, and the Struggle for Supremacy*, New York: Times Books, 1992; and Wayne Sandholtz et al., *The Highest Stakes: The Economic Foundations of the Next Security System*, Berkeley Roundtable on the International Economy (BRIE), Oxford University Press, 1992.

Competitiveness: A Dangerous Obsession

Unfortunately, his diagnosis was deeply misleading as a guide to what ails Europe, and similar diagnoses in the United States are equally misleading. The idea that a country's economic fortunes are largely determined by its success on world markets is a hypothesis, not a necessary truth; and as a practical, empirical matter, that hypothesis is flatly wrong. That is, it is simply not the case that the world's leading nations are to any important degree in economic competition with each other, or that any of their major economic problems can be attributed to failures to compete on world markets. The growing obsession in most advanced nations with international competitiveness should be seen, not as a well-founded concern, but as a view held in the face of overwhelming contrary evidence. And yet it is clearly a view that people very much want to hold—a desire to believe that is reflected in a remarkable tendency of those who preach the doctrine of competitiveness to support their case with careless, flawed arithmetic.

This article makes three points. First, it argues that concerns about competitiveness are, as an empirical matter, almost completely unfounded. Second, it tries to explain why defining the economic problem as one of international competition is nonetheless so attractive to so many people. Finally, it argues that the obsession with competitiveness is not only wrong but dangerous, skewing domestic policies and threatening the international economic system. This last issue is, of course, the most consequential from the standpoint of public policy. Thinking in terms of competitiveness leads, directly and indirectly, to bad economic policies on a wide range of issues, domestic and foreign, whether it be in health care or trade.

MINDLESS COMPETITION

MOST PEOPLE who use the term "competitiveness" do so without a second thought. It seems obvious to them that the analogy between a country and a corporation is reasonable and that to ask whether the United States is competitive in the world market is no different in principle from asking whether General Motors is competitive in the North American minivan market.

In fact, however, trying to define the competitiveness of a nation is much more problematic than defining that of a corporation. The bottom line for a corporation is literally its bottom line: if a corporation cannot afford to pay its workers, suppliers, and bondholders, it will go out of business. So when we say that a corporation is uncompetitive, we mean that its market position is unsustainable—that unless it improves its performance, it will cease to exist. Countries, on the other hand, do not go out of business. They may be happy or unhappy with their economic performance, but they have no well-defined bottom line. As a result, the concept of national competitiveness is elusive.

One might suppose, naively, that the bottom line of a national economy is simply its trade balance, that competitiveness can be measured by the ability of a country to sell more abroad than it buys. But in both theory and practice a trade surplus may be a sign of national weakness, a deficit a sign of strength. For example, Mexico was forced to run huge trade surpluses in the 1980s in order to pay the interest on its foreign debt since international investors refused to lend it any more money; it began to run large trade deficits after 1990 as foreign investors recovered confidence and began to pour in new funds. Would anyone want to describe Mexico as a highly competitive nation during the debt crisis era or describe what has happened since 1990 as a loss in competitiveness?

Most writers who worry about the issue at all have therefore tried to define competitiveness as the combination of favorable trade performance and something else. In particular, the most popular definition of competitiveness nowadays runs along the lines of the one given in Council of Economic Advisors Chairman Laura D'Andrea Tyson's *Who's Bashing Whom?:* competitiveness is "our ability to produce goods and services that meet the test of international competition while our citizens enjoy a standard of living that is both rising and sustainable." This sounds reasonable. If you think about it, however, and test your thoughts against the facts, you will find out that there is much less to this definition than meets the eye.

Consider, for a moment, what the definition would mean for an economy that conducted very little international trade, like the United States in the 1950s. For such an economy, the ability to balance its trade is mostly a matter of getting the exchange rate right. But because trade is such a small factor in the economy, the level of the exchange rate is a minor influence on the standard of living. So in an economy with very little international trade, the growth in living standards—and thus "competitiveness" according to Tyson's definition— would be determined almost entirely by domestic factors, primarily the rate of productivity growth. That's domestic productivity growth, period—not productivity growth relative to other countries. In other words, for an economy with very little international trade, "competitiveness" would turn out to be a funny way of saying "productivity" and would have nothing to do with international competition.

Competitiveness: A Dangerous Obsession

But surely this changes when trade becomes more important, as indeed it has for all major economies? It certainly could change. Suppose that a country finds that although its productivity is steadily rising, it can succeed in exporting only if it repeatedly devalues its currency, selling its exports ever more cheaply on world markets. Then its standard of living, which depends on its purchasing power over imports as well as domestically produced goods, might actually decline. In the jargon of economists, domestic growth might be outweighed by deteriorating terms of trade.[2] So "competitiveness" could turn out really to be about international competition after all.

There is no reason, however, to leave this as a pure speculation; it can easily be checked against the data. Have deteriorating terms of trade in fact been a major drag on the U.S. standard of living? Or has the rate of growth of U.S. real income continued essentially to equal the rate of domestic productivity growth, even though trade is a larger share of income than it used to be?

To answer this question, one need only look at the national income accounts data the Commerce Department publishes regularly in the *Survey of Current Business*. The standard measure of economic growth in the United States is, of course, real GNP—a measure that divides the value of goods and services produced in the United States by appropriate price indexes to come up with an estimate of real national output. The Commerce Department also, however, publishes something called "command GNP." This is similar to real GNP except that it divides U.S. exports not by the export price index, but by the price index for U.S. imports. That is, exports are valued by what Americans can buy with the money exports

---

[2]An example may be helpful here. Suppose that a country spends 20 percent of its income on imports, and that the prices of its imports are set not in domestic but in foreign currency. Then if the country is forced to devalue its currency—reduce its value in foreign currency—by 10 percent, this will raise the price of 20 percent of the country's spending basket by 10 percent, thus raising the overall price index by 2 percent. Even if domestic *output* has not changed, the country's real *income* will therefore have fallen by 2 percent. If the country must repeatedly devalue in the face of competitive pressure, growth in real income will persistently lag behind growth in real output.

It's important to notice, however, that the size of this lag depends not only on the amount of devaluation but on the share of imports in spending. A 10 percent devaluation of the dollar against the yen does not reduce U.S. real income by 10 percent—in fact, it reduces U.S. real income by only about 0.2 percent because only about 2 percent of U.S. income is spent on goods produced in Japan.

bring. Command GNP therefore measures the volume of goods and services the U.S. economy can "command"—the nation's purchasing power—rather than the volume it produces.[3] And as we have just seen, "competitiveness" means something different from "productivity" if and only if purchasing power grows significantly more slowly than output.

Well, here are the numbers. Over the period 1959-73, a period of vigorous growth in U.S. living standards and few concerns about international competition, real GNP per worker-hour grew 1.85 percent annually, while command GNP per hour grew a bit faster, 1.87 percent. From 1973 to 1990, a period of stagnating living standards, command GNP growth per hour slowed to 0.65 percent. Almost all (91 percent) of that slowdown, however, was explained by a decline in domestic productivity growth: real GNP per hour grew only 0.73 percent.

Similar calculations for the European Community and Japan yield similar results. In each case, the growth rate of living standards essentially equals the growth rate of domestic productivity—not productivity relative to competitors, but simply domestic productivity. Even though world trade is larger than ever before, national living standards are overwhelmingly determined by domestic factors rather than by some competition for world markets.

How can this be in our interdependent world? Part of the answer is that the world is not as interdependent as you might think: countries are nothing at all like corporations. Even today, U.S. exports are only 10 percent of the value-added in the economy (which is equal to GNP). That is, the United States is still almost 90 percent an economy that produces goods and services for its own use. By contrast, even the largest corporation sells hardly any of its output to its own workers; the "exports" of General Motors—its sales to people who do not work there—are virtually all of its sales, which are more than 2.5 times the corporation's value-added.

Moreover, countries do not compete with each other the way corporations do. Coke and Pepsi are almost purely rivals: only a negligible fraction of Coca-Cola's sales go to Pepsi workers, only a negligible fraction of the goods Coca-Cola workers buy are Pepsi products. So if

---

[3]In the example in the previous footnote, the devaluation would have no effect on real GNP, but command GNP would have fallen by two percent. The finding that in practice command GNP has grown almost as fast as real GNP therefore amounts to saying that events like the hypothetical case in footnote one are unimportant in practice.

Competitiveness: A Dangerous Obsession

Pepsi is successful, it tends to be at Coke's expense. But the major industrial countries, while they sell products that compete with each other, are also each other's main export markets and each other's main suppliers of useful imports. If the European economy does well, it need not be at U.S. expense; indeed, if anything a successful European economy is likely to help the U.S. economy by providing it with larger markets and selling it goods of superior quality at lower prices.

International trade, then, is not a zero-sum game. When productivity rises in Japan, the main result is a rise in Japanese real wages; American or European wages are in principle at least as likely to rise as to fall, and in practice seem to be virtually unaffected.

It would be possible to belabor the point, but the moral is clear: while competitive problems could arise in principle, as a practical, empirical matter the major nations of the world are not to any significant degree in economic competition with each other. Of course, there is always a rivalry for status and power—countries that grow faster will see their political rank rise. So it is always interesting to *compare* countries. But asserting that Japanese growth diminishes U.S. status is very different from saying that it reduces the U.S. standard of living—and it is the latter that the rhetoric of competitiveness asserts.

One can, of course, take the position that words mean what we want them to mean, that all are free, if they wish, to use the term "competitiveness" as a poetic way of saying productivity, without actually implying that international competition has anything to do with it. But few writers on competitiveness would accept this view. They believe that the facts tell a very different story, that we live, as Lester Thurow put it in his best-selling book, *Head to Head*, in a world of "win-lose" competition between the leading economies. How is this belief possible?

CARELESS ARITHMETIC

ONE OF THE remarkable, startling features of the vast literature on competitiveness is the repeated tendency of highly intelligent authors to engage in what may perhaps most tactfully be described as "careless arithmetic." Assertions are made that sound like quantifiable pronouncements about measurable magnitudes, but the writers do not actually present any data on these magnitudes and thus fail to notice that the actual numbers contradict their assertions. Or data are presented that are supposed to support an assertion, but the writer fails to notice that his own numbers imply that what he is saying cannot be true. Over and over again one finds books and articles on competitiveness that seem to the unwary reader to be full of convincing evidence but that strike anyone familiar with the data as strangely, almost eerily inept in their handling of the numbers. Some examples can best illustrate this point. Here are three cases of careless arithmetic, each of some interest in its own right.

Trade Deficits and the Loss of Good Jobs. In a recent article published in Japan, Lester Thurow explained to his audience the importance of reducing the Japanese trade surplus with the United States. U.S. real wages, he pointed out, had fallen six percent during the Reagan and Bush years, and the reason was that trade deficits in manufactured goods had forced workers out of high-paying manufacturing jobs into much lower-paying service jobs.

This is not an original view; it is very widely held. But Thurow was more concrete than most people, giving actual numbers for the job and wage loss. A million manufacturing jobs have been lost because of the deficit, he asserted, and manufacturing jobs pay 30 percent more than service jobs.

Both numbers are dubious. The million-job number is too high, and the 30 percent wage differential between manufacturing and services is primarily due to a difference in the length of the workweek, not a difference in the hourly wage rate. But let's grant Thurow his numbers. Do they tell the story he suggests?

The key point is that total U.S. employment is well over 100 million workers. Suppose that a million workers were forced from manufacturing into services and as a result lost the 30 percent manufacturing wage premium. Since these workers are less than 1 percent of the U.S. labor force, this would reduce the average U.S. wage rate by less than 1/100 of 30 percent—that is, by less than 0.3 percent.

This is too small to explain the 6 percent real wage decline *by a factor of 20*. Or to look at it another way, the annual wage loss from deficit-induced deindustrialization, which Thurow clearly implies is at the heart of U.S. economic difficulties, is on the basis of his own numbers roughly equal to what the U.S. spends on health care every week.

Something puzzling is going on here. How could someone as intelligent as Thurow, in writing an article that purports to offer hard quantitative evidence of the importance of international competition to the U.S. economy, fail to realize that the evidence he offers clearly shows that the channel of harm that he identifies was not the culprit?

Competitiveness: A Dangerous Obsession

High Value-added Sectors. Ira Magaziner and Robert Reich, both now influential figures in the Clinton Administration, first reached a broad audience with their 1982 book, *Minding America's Business.* The book advocated a U.S. industrial policy, and in the introduction the authors offered a seemingly concrete quantitative basis for such a policy: "Our standard of living can only rise if (i) capital and labor increasingly flow to industries with high value-added per worker and (ii) we maintain a position in those industries that is superior to that of our competitors."

Economists were skeptical of this idea on principle. If targeting the right industries was simply a matter of moving into sectors with high value-added, why weren't private markets already doing the job?[4] But one might dismiss this as simply the usual boundless faith of economists in the market; didn't Magaziner and Reich back their case with a great deal of real-world evidence?

Well, *Minding America's Business* contains a lot of facts. One thing it never does, however, is actually justify the criteria set out in the introduction. The choice of industries to cover clearly implied a belief among the authors that high value-added is more or less synonymous with high technology, but nowhere in the book do any numbers compare actual value-added per worker in different industries.

Such numbers are not hard to find. Indeed, every public library in America has a copy of the *Statistical Abstract of the United States,* which each year contains a table presenting value-added and employment by industry in U.S. manufacturing. All one needs to do, then, is spend a few minutes in the library with a calculator to come up with a table that ranks U.S. industries by value-added per worker.

The table on page 170 shows selected entries from pages 740-744 of the 1991 *Statistical Abstract.* It turns out that the U.S. industries with really high value-added per worker are in sectors with very high ratios of capital to labor, like cigarettes and petroleum refining. (This was predictable: because capital-intensive industries must earn a normal return on large investments, they must charge prices that are a larger markup

---

[4]"Value-added" has a precise, standard meaning in national income accounting: the value added of a firm is the dollar value of its sales, minus the dollar value of the inputs it purchases from other firms, and as such it is easily measured. Some people who use the term, however, may be unaware of this definition and simply use "high value-added" as a synonym for "desirable."

over labor costs than labor-intensive industries, which means that they have high value-added per worker). Among large industries, value-added per worker tends to be high in traditional heavy manufacturing sectors like steel and autos. High-technology sectors like aerospace and electronics turn out to be only roughly average.

This result does not surprise conventional economists. High value-added per worker occurs in sectors that are highly capital-intensive, that is, sectors in which an additional dollar of capital buys little extra value-added. In other words, there is no free lunch.

But let's leave on one side what the table says about the way the economy works, and simply note the strangeness of the lapse by Magaziner and Reich. Surely they were not calling for an industrial policy that would funnel capital and labor into the steel and auto industries in preference to high-tech. How, then, could they write a whole book dedicated to the proposition that we should target high value-added industries without ever checking to see which industries they meant?

Value Added Per Worker, 1988
(in thousands of dollars)

CIGARETTES	488
PETROLEUM REFINING	283
AUTOS	99
STEEL	97
AIRCRAFT	68
ELECTRONICS	64
ALL MANUFACTURING	66

Labor Costs. In his own presentation at the Copenhagen summit, British Prime Minister John Major showed a chart indicating that European unit labor costs have risen more rapidly than those in the United States and Japan. Thus he argued that European workers have been pricing themselves out of world markets.

But a few weeks later Sam Brittan of the *Financial Times* pointed out a strange thing about Major's calculations: the labor costs were not adjusted for exchange rates. In international competition, of course, what matters for a U.S. firm are the costs of its overseas rivals measured in dollars, not marks or yen. So international comparisons of labor costs, like the tables the Bank of England routinely publishes, always convert them into a common currency. The numbers presented by Major, however, did not make this standard adjustment. And it was a good thing for his presentation that they didn't. As Brittan pointed out, European labor costs have not risen in relative terms when the exchange rate adjustment is made.

If anything, this lapse is even odder than those of Thurow or Magaziner and Reich. How could John Major, with the sophisticated statistical resources of the U.K. Treasury behind him, present an analysis that failed to make the most standard of adjustments?

These examples of strangely careless arithmetic, chosen from among dozens of similar cases, by people who surely had both the cleverness and the resources to get it right, cry out for an explanation. The best working hypothesis is that in each case the author or speaker wanted to believe in the competitive hypothesis so much that he felt no urge to question it; if data were used at all, it was only to lend credibility to a predetermined belief, not to test it. But why are people apparently so anxious to define economic problems as issues of international competition?

THE THRILL OF COMPETITION

THE COMPETITIVE metaphor—the image of countries competing with each other in world markets in the same way that corporations do—derives much of its attractiveness from its seeming comprehensibility. Tell a group of businessmen that a country is like a corporation writ large, and you give them the comfort of feeling that they already understand the basics. Try to tell them about economic concepts like comparative advantage, and you are asking them to learn something new. It should not be surprising if many prefer a doctrine that offers the gain of apparent sophistication without the pain of hard thinking. The rhetoric of competitiveness has become so widespread, however, for three deeper reasons.

First, competitive images are exciting, and thrills sell tickets. The subtitle of Lester Thurow's huge best-seller, *Head to Head*, is "The Coming Economic Battle among Japan, Europe, and America"; the jacket proclaims that "the decisive war of the century has begun . . . and America may already have decided to lose." Suppose that the subtitle had described the real situation: "The coming struggle in which each big economy will succeed or fail based on its own efforts, pretty much independently of how well the others do." Would Thurow have sold a tenth as many books?

Second, the idea that U.S. economic difficulties hinge crucially on our failures in international competition somewhat paradoxically makes those difficulties seem easier to solve. The productivity of the average American worker is determined by a complex array of factors, most of them unreachable by any likely government policy. So if you accept the reality that our "competitive" problem is really a domestic productivity problem pure and simple, you are unlikely to be optimistic about any dramatic turnaround. But if you can convince yourself that the problem is really one of failures in international competition—that imports are pushing workers out of high-wage jobs, or subsidized foreign competition is driving the United States out of the high value-added sectors—then the answers to economic malaise may seem to you to involve simple things like subsidizing high technology and being tough on Japan.

Finally, many of the world's leaders have found the competitive metaphor extremely useful as a political device. The rhetoric of competitiveness turns out to provide a good way either to justify hard choices or to avoid them. The example of Delors in Copenhagen shows the usefulness of competitive metaphors as an evasion. Delors had to say something at the EC summit; yet to say anything that addressed the real roots of European unemployment would have involved huge political risks. By turning the discussion to essentially irrelevant but plausible-sounding questions of competitiveness, he bought himself some time to come up with a better answer (which to some extent he provided in December's white paper on the European economy—a paper that still, however, retained "competitiveness" in its title).

By contrast, the well-received presentation of Bill Clinton's initial economic program in February 1993 showed the usefulness of competitive rhetoric as a motivation for tough policies. Clinton proposed a set of painful spending cuts and tax increases to reduce the Federal deficit. Why? The real reasons for cutting the deficit are disappointingly undramatic: the deficit siphons off funds that might otherwise have been productively invested, and thereby exerts a steady if small drag on U.S. economic growth. But Clinton was able instead to offer a stirring patriotic appeal, calling on the nation to act now in order to make the economy competitive in the global market—with the implication that dire economic consequences would follow if the United States does not.

Many people who know that "competitiveness" is a largely meaningless concept have been willing to indulge competitive rhetoric precisely because they believe they can harness it in the service of good policies. An overblown fear of the Soviet Union was used in the 1950s to justify the building of the interstate highway system and the expansion of math and science education. Cannot the unjustified fears about foreign competition similarly be turned to good, used to justify serious efforts to reduce the budget deficit, rebuild infrastructure, and so on?

Competitiveness: A Dangerous Obsession

A few years ago this was a reasonable hope. At this point, however, the obsession with competitiveness has reached the point where it has already begun dangerously to distort economic policies.

THE DANGERS OF OBSESSION

THINKING AND speaking in terms of competitiveness poses three real dangers. First, it could result in the wasteful spending of government money supposedly to enhance U.S. competitiveness. Second, it could lead to protectionism and trade wars. Finally, and most important, it could result in bad public policy on a spectrum of important issues.

During the 1950s, fear of the Soviet Union induced the U.S. government to spend money on useful things like highways and science education. It also, however, led to considerable spending on more doubtful items like bomb shelters. The most obvious if least worrisome danger of the growing obsession with competitiveness is that it might lead to a similar misallocation of resources. To take an example, recent guidelines for government research funding have stressed the importance of supporting research that can improve U.S. international competitiveness. This exerts at least some bias toward inventions that can help manufacturing firms, which generally compete on international markets, rather than service producers, which generally do not. Yet most of our employment and value-added is now in services, and lagging productivity in services rather than manufactures has been the single most important factor in the stagnation of U.S. living standards.

A much more serious risk is that the obsession with competitiveness will lead to trade conflict, perhaps even to a world trade war. Most of those who have preached the doctrine of competitiveness have not been old-fashioned protectionists. They want their countries to win the global trade game, not drop out. But what if, despite its best efforts, a country does not seem to be winning, or lacks confidence that it can? Then the competitive diagnosis inevitably suggests that to close the borders is better than to risk having foreigners take away high-wage jobs and high-value sectors. At the very least, the focus on the supposedly competitive nature of international economic relations greases the rails for those who want confrontational if not frankly protectionist policies.

We can already see this process at work, in both the United States and Europe. In the United States, it was remarkable how quickly the sophis-

Paul Krugman

ticated interventionist arguments advanced by Laura Tyson in her published work gave way to the simple-minded claim by U.S. Trade Representative Mickey Kantor that Japan's bilateral trade surplus was costing the United States millions of jobs. And the trade rhetoric of President Clinton, who stresses the supposed creation of high-wage jobs rather than the gains from specialization, left his administration in a weak position when it tried to argue with the claims of NAFTA foes that competition from cheap Mexican labor will destroy the U.S. manufacturing base.

Perhaps the most serious risk from the obsession with competitiveness, however, is its subtle indirect effect on the quality of economic discussion and policymaking. If top government officials are strongly committed to a particular economic doctrine, their commitment inevitably sets the tone for policy-making on all issues, even those which may seem to have nothing to do with that doctrine. And if an economic doctrine is flatly, completely and demonstrably wrong, the insistence that discussion adhere to that doctrine inevitably blurs the focus and diminishes the quality of policy discussion across a broad range of issues, including some that are very far from trade policy per se.

Consider, for example, the issue of health care reform, undoubtedly the most important economic initiative of the Clinton administration, almost surely an order of magnitude more important to U.S. living standards than anything that might be done about trade policy (unless the United States provokes a full-blown trade war). Since health care is an issue with few direct international linkages, one might have expected it to be largely insulated from any distortions of policy resulting from misguided concerns about competitiveness.

But the administration placed the development of the health care plan in the hands of Ira Magaziner, the same Magaziner who so conspicuously failed to do his homework in arguing for government promotion of high value-added industries. Magaziner's prior writings and consulting on economic policy focused almost entirely on the issue of international competition, his views on which may be summarized by the title of his 1990 book, *The Silent War.* His appointment reflected many factors, of course, not least his long personal friendship with the first couple. Still, it was not irrelevant that in an administration committed to the ideology of competitiveness Magaziner, who has consistently recommended that national industrial policies be based on the corporate strategy concepts he learned during his years at the Boston Consulting Group, was regarded as an economic policy expert.

We might also note the unusual process by which the health care reform was developed. In spite of the huge size of the task force, recognized experts in the health care field were almost completely absent, notably though not exclusively economists specializing in health care, including economists with impeccable liberal credentials like Henry Aaron of the Brookings Institution. Again, this may have reflected a number of factors, but it is probably not irrelevant that anyone who, like Magaziner, is strongly committed to the ideology of competitiveness is bound to have found professional economists notably unsympathetic in the past—and to be unwilling to deal with them on any other issue.

To make a harsh but not entirely unjustified analogy, a government wedded to the ideology of competitiveness is as unlikely to make good economic policy as a government committed to creationism is to make good science policy, even in areas that have no direct relationship to the theory of evolution.

ADVISERS WITH NO CLOTHES

IF THE OBSESSION with competitiveness is as misguided and damaging as this article claims, why aren't more voices saying so? The answer is, a mixture of hope and fear.

On the side of hope, many sensible people have imagined that they can appropriate the rhetoric of competitiveness on behalf of desirable economic policies. Suppose that you believe that the United States needs to raise its savings rate and improve its educational system in order to raise its productivity. Even if you know that the benefits of higher productivity have nothing to do with international competition, why not describe this as a policy to enhance competitiveness if you think that it can widen your audience? It's tempting to pander to popular prejudices on behalf of a good cause, and I have myself succumbed to that temptation.

As for fear, it takes either a very courageous or very reckless economist to say publicly that a doctrine that many, perhaps most, of the world's opinion leaders have embraced is flatly wrong. The insult is all the greater when many of those men and women think that by using the rhetoric of competitiveness they are demonstrating their sophistication about economics. This article may influence people, but it will not make many friends.

Unfortunately, those economists who have hoped to appropriate the rhetoric of competitiveness for good economic policies have instead had their own credibility appropriated on behalf of bad ideas. And somebody has to point out when the emperor's intellectual wardrobe isn't all he thinks it is.

So let's start telling the truth: competitiveness is a meaningless word when applied to national economies. And the obsession with competitiveness is both wrong and dangerous.✆

From Geopolitics to Geo-Economics

Logic of Conflict, Grammar of Commerce

Edward N. Luttwak

EXCEPT FOR those unfortunate parts of the world where armed confrontations or civil strife persist for purely regional or internal reasons, the waning of the Cold War is steadily reducing the importance of military power in world affairs.

True, in the central strategic arena, where Soviet power finally encountered the *de facto* coalition of Americans, Europeans, Japanese, and Chinese, existing military forces have diminished very little so far. Nevertheless, as a Soviet-Western war becomes ever more implausible, the ability to threaten or reassure is equally devalued (and by the same token, of course, there is no longer a unifying threat to sustain the coalition against all divisive impulses). Either way, the deference that armed strength could evoke in the dealings of governments over all matters—notably including economic questions—has greatly declined, and seems set to decline further.

Everyone, it appears, now agrees that the methods of commerce are displacing military methods—with disposable capital in lieu of firepower, civilian innovation in lieu of military-technical advancement, and market penetration in lieu of garrisons and bases. But these are all tools, not purposes; what purposes will they serve?

If the players left in the field by the waning importance of military power were purely economic entities—labor-sellers, entrepreneurs, corporations—then only the logic of commerce would govern world affairs. Instead of World Politics, the intersecting web of power relationships on

EDWARD N. LUTTWAK holds the Burke Chair in Strategy at the Center for Strategic and International Studies, Washington, D.C. This article appeared in the Summer 1990 issue of *The National Interest*. © 1990 by National Affairs, Inc.

the international scene, we would simply have World Business, a myriad of economic interactions spanning the globe. In some cases, the logic of commerce would result in fierce competition. In others, the same logic would lead to alliances between economic entities in any location to capitalize ventures, vertically integrate, horizontally co-develop, co-produce, or co-market goods and services. But competitively or cooperatively, *the action on all sides would always unfold without regard to frontiers.* If that were to happen, not only military methods but the logic of conflict itself—which is adversarial, zero-sum, and paradoxical—would be displaced. This, or something very much like it, is in fact what many seem to have in mind when they speak of a new global interdependence and its beneficial consequences.[1]

LOGIC AND GRAMMAR

BUT THINGS are not quite that simple. The international scene is still primarily occupied by states and blocs of states that extract revenues, regulate economic as well as other activities for various purposes, pay out

---

[1] The logic of conflict is "zero-sum" since the gain of one side is the loss of the other, and vice versa. That is so in war, in geopolitical confrontations short of war, and in oligopolistic competition (as the market share of one oligopolist can only increase at the expense of another's); but not in a many-sided ("perfect") competition, wherein any two sides can both gain (or lose) market shares concurrently. The logic of conflict is paradoxical (i.e., governed by apparent contradictions and the coincidence of opposites) because all actions unfold in the presence of an adversary that reacts against whatever is being done. That is why—to give a static example—the worst of approach roads for an attack may be the best, if it confers the advantage of surprise (making the bad road paradoxically good and the good road paradoxically bad). Or, to give a dynamic example-involving the coincidence of opposites-why victorious armies that advance too far advance to their own defeat by overextension, just as weapons that are too effective are the most likely to be made ineffectual by the enemy countermeasures that their very effectiveness evokes. This same dynamic evolution toward the coincidence of opposites is operative at every level of strategy: thus the Soviet Union's accumulation of power eventually resulted in its impotence, as other states were frightened into forming a coalition against Moscow. In all dynamic manifestations of the logic of conflict there is such a culminating point, beyond which actions evolve into their opposite. In the linear logic of everyday life (and economic competition), by contrast, good is good and bad is bad, and success can facilitate further success without any necessary culminating point. For a systematic comparison, see my *Strategy: The Logic of War and Peace* (Cambridge: Harvard University Press, 1987).

benefits, offer services, provide infrastructures, and—of increasing importance—finance or otherwise sponsor the development of new technologies and new products. As territorial entities, spatially rather than functionally defined, states cannot follow a commercial logic that would ignore their own boundaries.

What logic then do they follow?

- Do they seek to collect as much in revenues as their fiscal codes prescribe—or are they content to let other states or blocs of states tax away what they themselves could obtain? Since the former is the reality (that is, a zero-sum situation in which the gain of one is the loss of another), here the ruling logic is the logic of conflict.

- Do they regulate economic activities to achieve disinterestedly trans-national purposes—or do they seek to maximize outcomes within their own boundaries, even if this means that the outcomes are suboptimal elsewhere? Since the latter is the predominant, if not exclusive, reality, economic regulation is as much a tool of statecraft as military defenses ever were. Hence, insofar as external repercussions are considered, the logic of state regulation is in part the logic of conflict. As such, its attributes include the typically warlike use of secrecy and deception for the sake of surprise (as, for example, when product standards are first defined in secret consultations with domestic producers, long before their public enunciation).

- Do states and blocs of states pay out benefits and offer services transnationally—or (fractional aid allocations apart) do they strive to restrict such advantages to their own residents? Likewise, do they design infrastructures to maximize their transnational utility—or do they aim for domestically optimal and appropriately competitive configurations, regardless of how others are affected? Since the latter is the reality, the logic of state action is again in part the logic of conflict. (The competitive building of huge international airports in adjacent, minuscule, Persian Gulf sheikhdoms is an extreme example of such behavior, but such conduct is not uncommon in milder forms.)

- Finally, do states and blocs of states promote technological innovation for its own sake—or do they seek thereby to maximize benefits within their own boundaries? Since the latter is the reality, the logic of conflict applies. (Three obvious examples are the obstacles that long delayed the introduction of Concorde flights into U.S. airports, Japanese barriers against U.S. supercomputers and telecommunications, and the development of rival High Definition Television formats.)

As this is how things are, it follows that—even if we leave aside the persistence of armed confrontations in unfortunate parts of the world and wholly disregard what remains of the Cold War—World Politics is still not about to give way to World Business, i.e., the free interaction of commerce governed only by its own nonterritorial logic.

Instead, what is going to happen—and what we are already witnessing—is a much less complete transformation of state action represented by the emergence of "Geo-economics." This neologism is the best term I can think of to describe the admixture of the logic of conflict with the methods of commerce—or, as Clausewitz would have written, the logic of war in the grammar of commerce.

THE NATURE OF THE BEAST

WITH STATES and blocs of states still in existence, it could not be otherwise. As spatial entities structured to jealously delimit their own territories, to assert their exclusive control within them, and variously to attempt to influence events beyond their borders, states are inherently inclined to strive for relative advantage against like entities on the international scene, even if only by means other than force.

Moreover, states are subject to the internal impulses of their own bureaucracies, whose officials compete to achieve whatever goals define bureaucratic success, including goals in the international economic arena that may as easily be conflictual as competitive or cooperative. Actually much more than that is happening: *As bureaucracies writ large, states are themselves impelled by the bureaucratic urges of role-preservation and role-enhancement to acquire a "geo-economic" substitute for their decaying geopolitical role.*

There is also a far more familiar phenomenon at work: the instrumentalization of the state by economic interest groups that seek to manipulate its activities on the international scene for their own purposes, often by requiring adversarial "geo-economic" stances. No sphere of state action is immune: fiscal policy can be profitably used so as to place imports at a disadvantage; regulations, benefits, services, and infrastructures can all be configured to favor domestic interests in various ways; and, of course, the provision of state funds for domestic technological development is inherently discriminatory against unassisted foreign competitors.

The incidence of both adversarial bureaucratic impulses and adversarial manipulations of the state by interest groups will vary greatly from country to country. But fundamentally, states will tend to act "geo-economically" simply because of what they are: spatially-defined entities structured to outdo each other on the world scene. For all the other functions that states have acquired as providers of individual benefits, assorted services, and varied infrastructures, their *raison d'etre* and the ethos that sustains them still derive from their chronologically first function: to provide security from foes without (as well as outlaws within).

Relatively few states have had to fight to exist, but all states exist to fight—or at least they are structured as if that were their dominant function. Even though most of the existing 160-odd independent states have never fought any external wars, and most of those that have fought have not done so for generations, the governing structures of the modern state are still heavily marked by conflictual priorities, the need to prepare for, or to wage, interstate conflict. In how many major countries does the Minister for Telecommunications, or Energy, or Trade outrank the Defense Minister? Only—appropriately enough—in Japan, where Defense (*Boecho*) is a *Cho* or lesser department (translated as agency), as opposed to a *Sho* or ministry, as in *Tsusansho,* the Ministry of Trade. The *Boecho's* head, while a minister, does not hold cabinet rank.

It is true, of course, that, under whatever name, "geo-economics" has always been an important aspect of international life. In the past, however, the outdoing of others in the realm of commerce was overshadowed by strategic priorities and strategic modalities. Externally, if the logic of conflict dictated the necessity for cooperation against a common enemy while, in contrast, the logic of commerce dictated competition, the preservation of the alliance was almost always given priority. (That indeed is how all the commercial quarrels between the United States and Western Europe—over frozen chickens, microchips, beef, and the rest—and between the United States and Japan—from textiles in the 1960s to supercomputers in the 1980s—were so easily contained during the past decades of acute Soviet-Western confrontation. As soon as commercial quarrels became noisy enough to attract the attention of political leaders on both sides, they were promptly suppressed by those leaders—often by paying off all parties—before they could damage political relations and thus threaten the imperative of strategic cooperation.) Internally, insofar as national cohesion was sustained against divisive social and economic tensions by the unifying urgencies of external antagonisms, it was armed conflict or the threat of it—not commercial animosities—that best served to unite nations.

Now, however, as the relevance of military threats and military alliances wanes, geo-economic priorities and modalities are becoming dominant in state action. Trade quarrels may still be contained by the fear of the economic consequences of an action-reaction cycle of punitive measures, but they will no longer simply be suppressed by political interventions on both sides, urgently motivated by the strategic imperative of preserving alliance cooperation against a common enemy. And if internal cohesion has to be preserved by a unifying threat, that threat must now be economic. Such a reordering of modalities is already fully manifest in the expressed attitudes of other Europeans to the new undivided Germany, and even more so in American attitudes toward Japan. Gorbachev's redirection of Soviet foreign policy had barely started when Japan began to be promoted to the role of the internally unifying Chief Enemy, judging by the evidence of opinion polls, media treatments, advertisements, and congressional pronouncements.

Should we conclude from all this that the world is regressing to a new age of mercantilism? Is that what "geo-economics" identifies, quite redundantly? Not so. The goal of mercantilism was to maximize gold stocks, whereas the goal of geo-economics (aggrandizement of the state aside) could only be to provide the best possible employment for the largest proportion of the population. In the past, moreover, when commercial quarrels evolved into political quarrels, they could become military confrontations almost automatically; and in turn military confrontations could readily lead to war.

In other words, mercantilism was a *subordinated modality*, limited and governed by the ever-present possibility that the loser in the mercantilist (or simply commercial) competition would switch to the grammar of war. Spain might decree that all trade to and from its American colonies could only travel in Spanish bottoms through Spanish ports, but British and Dutch armed merchantmen could still convey profitable cargoes to disloyal colonists in defiance of Spanish sloops; and, with war declared, privateers could seize outright the even more profitable cargoes bound for Spain. Likewise, the Dutch sent their frigates into the Thames to reply to the mercantilist legislation of the British Parliament that prohibited their cabotage, just as much earlier the Portuguese had sunk Arab ships with which they could not compete in the India trade.

"Geo-economics," on the other hand, is emerging in a world where there is *no superior modality.* Import-restricted supercomputers cannot be forcibly delivered by airborne assault to banks or universities in need of them, nor can competition in the world automobile market be assisted by the sinking of export car ferries on the high seas. That force has lost the role it once had in the age of mercantilism—as an *admissible* adjunct to economic competition—is obvious enough. But of course the decay of the military grammar of geopolitics is far more pervasive than this, even if it is by no means universal.[2]

Students of international relations may still be taught to admire the classic forms of *realpolitik,* with its structure of anticipatory calculations premised on the feasibility of war. But for some decades now the dominant elites of the greatest powers have ceased to consider war as a practical solution for military confrontations between them, because non-nuclear fighting would only be inconclusively interrupted by the fear of nuclear war, while the latter is self-inhibiting. (In accordance with the always paradoxical logic of conflict, the application of the fusion technique meant that nuclear weapons exceeded the culminating point of utility, becoming less useful as they became more efficient.)

For exactly the same reason, military confrontations were themselves still considered very much worth pursuing—and rightly so, for war was thereby precluded throughout the decades of Soviet-Western antagonism. More recently, however, the dominant elites of the greatest powers appear to have concluded that military confrontations between them are

---

[2]In the train of history, the last wagons, such as the fragile states of sub-Saharan Africa, are still prebellic: they cannot yet wage war on each other, because regimes sustained only by the direct force of their armies cannot send those armies away to remote frontiers. The wagons at the head of the train by contrast are now postbellic because their ruling elites have become convinced that they cannot usefully fight one another. Only the wagons in the middle—countries such as India, Israel, Iran, Iraq, and a few others—are still capable of war with each other. But of course the train of history can not only stop but reverse its direction: in the second century B.C. the Romans already categorized prebellic societies (tribes too loosely organized to resist them) and advanced postbellic societies (of the Hellenized east) for which war could not be profitable. Things changed.

only dissuasive of threats that are themselves most implausible. It is that new belief that has caused the decisive devaluation of military strength as an instrument of statecraft in the direct relations of the greatest powers.

Hence, while the methods of mercantilism could always be dominated by the methods of war, in the new "geo-economic" era not only the *causes* but also the *instruments* of conflict must be economic. If commercial quarrels do lead to political clashes, as they are now much more likely to do with the waning of the imperatives of geopolitics, those political clashes must be fought out with the weapons of commerce: the more or less disguised restriction of imports, the more or less concealed subsidization of exports, the funding of competitive technology projects, the support of selected forms of education, the provision of competitive infrastructures, and more.

PLAYING THE NEW GAME

THE DISCUSSION so far has focused on the actual and prospective role of states and, by implication, of blocs of states engaged in "geo-economic" conduct. But what happens on the world economic scene will not of course be defined by such conduct; indeed the role of "geo-economics" in the doings and undoings of the world economy should be far smaller than the role of geopolitics in world politics as a whole.

First, the propensity of states to act geo-economically will vary greatly, even more than their propensity to act geopolitically. For reasons historical and institutional, or doctrinal and political, some states will maintain a strictly *laissez faire* attitude, simply refusing to act "geo-economically." Both the very prosperous and the very poor might be in that category, just as both Switzerland and Burma have long been geopolitically inactive. In other cases, the desirable scope of geo-economic activism by the state is already becoming a focal point of political debate and partisan controversy: witness the current Democratic-Republican dispute on "industrial policy" in the United States. In still other cases, such as that of France, the dominant elites that long insisted on a very ambitious degree of geopolitical activism (ambitious, that is, in terms of the resources available) are now easily shifting their emphasis to demand much more geo-economic activism from the French state. And then, of course, there are the states—Japan most notably—whose geoeconomic propensities are not in question.

Second, there is the much more important limitation that states and blocs of states acting "geo-economically" must do so within an arena that is not exclusively theirs, in which they coexist with private economic operators large and small, from individuals to the largest multinational corporations. While states occupy virtually all of the world's political space, they occupy only a fraction of the total economic space, and global political-economic trends such as privatization are reducing that fraction even further. (On the other hand, the role of states is increasing precisely in the economic sectors whose importance is itself increasing, sectors defined by the commercial application of the most advanced technologies.)

Of the different forms of coexistence between geo-economically active states and private economic operators, there is no end. Coexistence can be passive and disregarded, as in the relationship (or lack of it) between the state and the myriad of small, localized service businesses. With neither wanting anything from the other—except for the taxes that the fiscal authorities demand—the two can simply coexist without interacting or communicating.

At the opposite extreme, there is the intense positive interaction between politically weighty businesses in need of state support on the world economic scene, and the bureaucracies or politicians that they seek to manipulate for their own purposes. Or, going the other way, there is the equally intense and equally positive interaction that occurs when states seek to guide large companies for their own geo-economic purposes, or even select them as their "chosen instrument" (a specialized form of coexistence that dates back at least to the seventeenth-century East India companies, Dutch and Danish as well as, most famously, British).

Even more common, no doubt, are the cases of reciprocal manipulation, most notably in the remarkably uniform dealings of the largest international oil companies—whether American, British, or French—with their respective (and otherwise very different) state authorities. In each case, the state has been both user and used, and the companies both instruments and instrumentalizers.

Negative state–private sector interactions are not likely to be common, but they could be very important when they do occur. Geoeconomically active states that oppose rival foreign states will also obviously oppose private foreign companies that are the chosen instruments of those rivals, as well as private foreign companies that simply have the misfortune to stand in the way. An era of intense "geo-economic" activity might thus become an era of unprecedented risk for important private companies in important sectors. If they invest Y million of their funds to develop X technology, they may find themselves irremediably overtaken by the X project of country Z, funded by the taxpayer in the amount of 2Y million, or 20Y million for that matter. Or private companies may find themselves competing with foreign undercutters determined to drive them out of business, and amply funded for that purpose by their state authorities. As public funding for such purposes is likely to be concealed, a victim-company may enter a market quite unaware of its fatal disadvantage. In such diverse ways the international economy will be pervasively affected by that fraction of its life that is geo-economic rather than simply economic in character (just as in the past the geopolitical activity of the few greatest powers decisively conditioned the politics of the many).

Perhaps the pan-Western trade accords of the era of armed confrontation with the Soviet Union—based on the original General Agreement on Tariffs and Trade—may survive without the original impulse that created them, and may serve to inhibit the overt use of tariffs and quotas as the geo-economic equivalent of fortified lines. And that inheritance of imposed amity may also dissuade the hostile use of all other "geo-economic" weapons, from deliberate regulatory impediments to customs-house conspiracies aimed at rejecting imports covertly—the commercial equivalents of the ambushes of war. But that still leaves room for far more important weapons: the competitive development of commercially important new technologies, the predatory financing of their sales during their embryonic stage, and the manipulation of the standards that condition their use—the geoeconomic equivalents of the offensive campaigns of war.

Today, there is a palpably increasing tension between the inherently conflictual nature of states (and blocs of states) and the intellectual recognition of many of their leaders and citizens that while war is a zero-sum encounter by nature, commercial relations need not be and indeed rarely have been. The outcome of that tension within the principal countries and blocs will determine the degree to which we will live in a geo-economic world.☯

Workers and the World Economy

Ethan B. Kapstein

BREAKING THE POSTWAR BARGAIN

THE GLOBAL economy is leaving millions of disaffected workers in its train. Inequality, unemployment, and endemic poverty have become its handmaidens. Rapid technological change and heightening international competition are fraying the job markets of the major industrialized countries. At the same time systemic pressures are curtailing every government's ability to respond with new spending. Just when working people most need the nation-state as a buffer from the world economy, it is abandoning them.

This is not how things were supposed to work. The failure of today's advanced global capitalism to keep spreading the wealth poses a challenge not just to policymakers but to modern economic "science" as well. For generations, students were taught that increasing trade and investment, coupled with technological change, would drive national productivity and create wealth. Yet over the past decade, despite a continuing boom in international trade and finance, productivity has faltered, and inequality in the United States and unemployment in Europe have worsened.

President Bill Clinton may have been right to proclaim that "the era of big government is over," and perhaps the American people will ultimately decide that those who need assistance should look elsewhere for help. But if the post–World War II social contract with workers—of full employment and comprehensive social welfare—is to be broken, politi-

ETHAN B. KAPSTEIN is the Harold Stassen Professor of International Political Economy at the University of Manchester. His most recent book is *Governing the Global Economy: International Finance and the State.* This article appeared in the May/June 1996 issue of *Foreign Affairs.*

cal support for the burgeoning global economy could easily collapse. For international economic integration is not some uncontrollable fact of life, but has deepened because of a series of policy decisions taken by the major industrial powers over the last 45 years. It is time to recognize that those decisions, while benefiting the world economy as a whole, have begun to have widespread negative consequences. The forces acting on today's workers inhere in the structure of today's global economy, with its open and increasingly fierce competition on the one hand and fiscally conservative units—states—on the other. Countermeasures, therefore, must also be deep, sustained, and widespread. Easing pressures on the "losers" of the new open economy must now be the focus of economic policy if the process of globalization is to be sustained.

It is hardly sensationalist to claim that in the absence of broad-based policies and programs designed to help working people, the political debate in the United States and many other countries will soon turn sour. Populists and demagogues of various stripes will find "solutions" to contemporary economic problems in protectionism and xenophobia. Indeed, in every industrialized nation, such figures are on the campaign trail. Growing income inequality, job insecurity, and unemployment are widely seen as the flip side of globalization. That perception must be changed if Western leaders wish to maintain the international system their predecessors created. After all, the fate of the global economy ultimately rests on domestic politics in its constituent states.

The spread of the dogma of restrictive fiscal policy is undermining the bargain struck with workers in every industrial country. States are basically telling their workers that they can no longer afford the postwar deal and must minimize their obligations. The current obsession with balanced budgets in the United States and the Maastricht criteria in Europe must be replaced by an equally vigilant focus on growth and equity. National responses to this global problem are likely to fail, as any state that deviates from "responsible" economic policies will be punished by currency markets and bondholders. States must now reorient their economic policies toward growth, but it should be done as part of a coordinated international effort. Calling for such economic policy coordination might seem utopian in the current political environment, but it has been done before.

The world may be moving inexorably toward one of those tragic moments that will lead future historians to ask, why was nothing done in time? Were the economic and policy elites unaware of the profound disruption that economic and technological change were causing working men and women? What prevented them from taking the steps necessary to prevent a global social crisis?

THE GREAT TRANSFORMATION

THE CURRENT predicament is hardly unprecedented. Writing in *Progress and Poverty* in 1879, the reformer Henry George observed that "at the beginning of this marvelous era it was natural to expect, and it was expected, that laborsaving inventions would lighten the toil and improve the condition of the laborer; that the enormous increase in the power of producing wealth would make real poverty a thing of the past." George chronicled the many technologies, such as the steam engine and telegraph, that had been introduced in his lifetime, and the great explosion in commerce and trade that followed.

But far from heralding an era of prosperity, "disappointment has followed disappointment. From all parts of the civilized world come complaints of industrial depression . . . of want and suffering and anxiety among the working classes." George observed that the massive investment in technology had only resulted in increasing returns to capital and falling wages for working people. Thus "the mere laborer has no more interest in the general advance of productive power than the Cuban slave has . . . in the price of sugar."

During the nineteenth century, the world enjoyed a secular increase in trade and investment under the aegis of a liberal Great Britain, while the adoption of the international gold standard created the illusion of domestic financial stability. But profound social dislocation accompanied this process of globalization and would eventually contribute to its undoing.

Britain's decision in 1846 to lift the Corn Laws, which had long protected domestic agriculture, is the classic example of a policy consciously designed to globalize the economy in favor of specific interests. With industrialization, the Manchester factory owners needed more labor. The simple solution was to get farm hands off the land and pay them low wages. The most efficient way to achieve this goal was to introduce foreign competition in agricultural products, forcing down prices and ensuring that farmers and tenants could no longer earn their livelihood. Labor flooded into the cities, and these workers were paid relatively low wages because the price of food—their major expenditure—was falling.

Ethan B. Kapstein

Throughout the Industrial Revolution various regulations that had long governed economic life—many dating back to the Middle Ages—were dismantled, and rural laborers found their traditional ways of life torn asunder. Workers became commodities like grain and coal, with demand for and supply of their services a function of market requirements. Such a laissez-faire approach to labor markets was inherently unstable, as the philosopher Karl Polanyi later explained in *The Great Transformation*. He described the process by which landless working people throughout Europe entered a world of urban poverty, creating a political cauldron. During periods of prolonged depression these laborers became easy prey for extremist political forces. Polanyi argued that it was the complete unraveling of economic and labor market regulations and traditions in the nineteenth century that caused such tremendous social and political upheaval in the early twentieth, culminating in the collapse of the world economy and the outbreak of the First and Second World Wars.

The Great Transformation was published in 1944, the year that the Bretton Woods conference to restructure the international economy was held. And it was Polanyi's version of history that the postwar policymakers brought with them. As Treasury Secretary Henry Morgenthau said, "All of us have seen the great economic tragedy of our time. We saw the worldwide depression of the 1930s. We saw currency disorders develop and spread from land to land, destroying the basis for international trade and international investment and even international faith. In their wake, we saw unemployment and wretchedness. . . . We saw their victims fall prey . . . to demagogues and dictators. We saw bewilderment and bitterness become the breeders of fascism, and finally, of war." The post–World War II global economy resulted from a series of conscious policy decisions, reached in the belief that increased economic exchange could be a force for world peace and prosperity.

The postwar leaders were committed to rebuilding the world economy, but this time with a significant difference. In globalization's previous incarnation, governments had done little to protect working people from its malign effects, and their mistake exacted a price in revolutions and war. Having learned from that experience, statesmen now designed a liberal world economy that maintained an active domestic role for the state in order to ensure that equity and growth went hand in hand.

Thus the new global economy would include both domestic and international components. Of greatest significance, the state would supervise most aspects of economic life. In the United States, for example, the Truman administration passed the Employment Act, which set as its objective full employment, and the G.I. Bill, which provided veterans with education and housing benefits. Across Europe, ambitious social welfare policies were enacted. In every industrial country, labor was not to be treated as a commodity, subject to the free market's destructive whims, and the organization of workers into labor unions was actively encouraged. The implicit agreement struck between states and their societies—what John G. Ruggie has termed the bargain of "embedded liberalism"—ensured that the gains from economic globalization would be used to compensate the losers in the interests of political stability.[1]

Western leaders constructed international regimes for money and trade that by charter were to be responsive to domestic political and economic concerns. When they launched the General Agreement on Tariffs and Trade (GATT) to liberalize and expand commerce among the member states, they also established safeguards to protect workers from unfair trade practices and to assist those who were displaced. When they created an international monetary system to avoid ceaseless rounds of competitive currency devaluation, they also established the International Monetary Fund (IMF) as a lender of last resort for balance-of-payments emergencies. When they formed a European Common Market to promote regional trade and investment, they also permitted states to retain considerable autonomy in social policy.

But the Bretton Woods order would prove unsustainable. It was very generous to workers and capitalists, but it required high levels of economic growth. The oil crises of 1973-74 and 1978-79 hammered the industrial countries, prompting stagflation, that insidious mixture of stagnation and inflation. Furthermore, increasing foreign trade meant greater competition for national firms, while financial deregulation permitted capital to become more footloose. These developments, in turn, led to widespread corporate restructuring and a glut of unskilled labor, which translated into higher unemployment, less tax revenue, and greater pressure on state resources. The crisis of the welfare state had begun.

---

[1]John G. Ruggie, "International Regimes, Transactions, and Change: Embedded Liberalism in the Postwar Economic Order," *International Organization*, Spring 1982, pp. 195-231.

Faced with the exploding costs of cradle-to-grave support for increasingly idle populations, Western states in the 1980s began to adopt stringent monetary and fiscal policies. Workers, of course, have had little say in this process. Indeed, what governments are really trying to do is break their postwar deal with workers while maintaining their commitment to an open economy. They cannot have it both ways, and instead the policy focus should be on negotiating a package that helps workers adjust to ongoing economic changes.

WORKERS OF THE WORLD

NOBODY DISPUTES that the past two decades have been cruel to unskilled workers in the industrial countries. Growing income inequality has given rise to millions of working poor in the United States, and this sorry condition is now becoming apparent in Western Europe. Between 1973 and 1993 the real hourly wage of Americans without a high school diploma fell from $11.85 an hour to $8.64 an hour. In the early 1970s households in the top 5 percent of the income bracket earned 10 times more than those in the bottom 5 percent; today they make almost 15 times more. Similar trends are evident in Britain and even that most egalitarian country, Sweden.

Workers have been further squeezed by the decline in manufacturing employment. Manufacturing employment in the United States fell by 1.4 million between 1978 and 1990. Those who lost their jobs were, in general, the unskilled, and when they found new work it was usually at lower pay. The experience has now become familiar to middle managers as well, as evidenced by the recent spate of major corporate layoffs. The failure of the industrial sector to generate new jobs has been a major cause of labor's economic problems, and perhaps some of America's social problems more generally. Fully two percent of all working-age American men are behind bars.

In Western Europe, the unemployment figures are frightening. In France, average unemployment between 1969 and 1973 was 2.6 percent; today it is over 11 percent. In Germany the rate was below 1 percent; today it is approaching 10 percent. In Belgium, the unemployment rate has quadrupled over the past 20 years. The Europeans have created a lost generation of workers and are now suffering for it in terms of increased crime, drug abuse, violence against immigrants, and the increasing popularity of extremist political groups. In this context, it is sobering to realize that Germany's current level of four million unemployed is the highest it has been since the early 1930s.

At the same time, there has been a dramatic decline in unionized labor in both the United States and Europe. The unionized portion of the U.S. labor force has dropped by more than one-third—from 25 to 16 percent—since the 1970s, and organized labor is also declining in Austria, France, Germany, Italy, the Netherlands, Switzerland, and the United Kingdom.[2] Labor is losing its political voice, and the consequences of its demise—lower wages and benefits for unskilled workers, greater job insecurity, and less political interest in the economic losers—should not be dismissed.

Further, it should be recalled that organized labor in the north has been a prime mover behind unionization and the promotion of human rights in the developing countries of the south. International activism by unions has been a help to workers in Latin America and other countries struggling to win the right to collective bargaining, as well as better health and safety standards. Now that all industrial workers—unionized or not—could benefit from this type of activism in such countries as China and India, and other non- or anti-union regions of the world, organized labor is no longer vigorous enough to play this role. To be sure, unions are hardly perfect; they too form entrenched interests that hinder labor market flexibility and job creation. But their historical role in economic development and social equity has been forgotten.

THE BATTLE OF THE CAUSES

SOLUTIONS TO these bleak trends need not await some consensus among economists about their causes. Policymakers debating these issues are like firefighters idly wondering what started the blaze while the house burns to the ground. The two traditional culprits that have once again emerged from the economics literature are trade and technology. A third, cited by few economists but by some journalists and politicians, is immigration.

---

[2]Melvin Reder and Lloyd Ulman, "Unionism and Unification," in *Labor and an Integrated Europe*, ed. Lloyd Ulman, Barry Eichengreen, and William T. Dickens, Washington: The Brookings Institution, 1993, p. 24.

Economists who focus on the effects of trade, such as Adrian Wood, have argued that the contemporary problems of unskilled workers in the north are linked to a strong increase in trade between north and south and a change in its composition.[3] Historically, the developing countries provided the industrial world with agricultural goods and raw materials in exchange for manufactured goods. The gains from such trade have been analyzed and extolled by economists since David Ricardo, sustaining the free trade movement.

Such trade is rightly celebrated, since it makes nations wealthier than they would otherwise be. More recently, however, the south has moved into the business of manufacturing, from clothing to consumer electronics. Today such goods account for over 50 percent of the south's exports and surpass its commodity exports in value. As is well known, workers in these developing countries are generally paid peanuts for their labor— less than a dollar an hour in such countries as China, India, and Pakistan—and in many countries, including China, they are prevented by law from forming unions or otherwise bargaining collectively.

According to a theory proposed by Paul A. Samuelson and Wolfgang Stolper in 1941, two countries that practice free trade and have the same technology should eventually see their wages equalize. In effect, wages in the First World are forced down by competition from developing countries in similar industries. Ironically, even though falling wages would seem to confirm Stolper-Samuelson, some economists are now claiming that its assumptions are wrong.[4]

In Western Europe wages are less skewed than in the United States, but the continent has paid for relative equality with higher unemployment. Economic theory also helps to explain why this is so. If Germany begins importing Polish goods produced with unskilled labor, and regulations and other rigidities prevent wages from falling to Polish levels, unemployment among unskilled German workers will rise in the absence of new job creation.

---

[3]Adrian Wood, *North-South Trade, Employment and Inequality: Changing Futures in a Skill-driven World,* New York: Oxford University Press, 1994.

[4]See, for instance, Jagdish Bhagwati and Vivek H. Dehejia, "Freer Trade and Wages of the Unskilled—Is Marx Striking Again?" in *Trade and Wages: Leveling Wages Down?* ed. Jagdish Bhagwati and Marvin H. Kosters, Washington: AEI Press, 1994, pp. 36-75.

Many American economists, such as Paul Krugman and Robert Z. Lawrence, contest these explanations. They point out that foreign trade remains too small a share of economic activity in most industrial nations to be responsible for such large and pervasive phenomena as unemployment and income inequality, and they assert that technology must be responsible for these changes. According to this school of thought, the introduction of new technology—say, computers—creates a surplus of unskilled labor. At the same time, the new technology increases the demand for the skilled workers who know how to run it, raising their wages. As a result, income inequality widens because of the good old-fashioned law of supply and demand. The evidence for this line of reasoning is the heavy investment in new technology by manufacturing during the 1980s, when growing wage inequality became apparent in the United States.

But economists are wrong to treat trade and technology as competing explanations. A significant share of new technology, for example, has been induced by foreign competition. Indeed, when one looks at those industries that have suffered great job losses on the one hand and enjoyed significant investment in new technology on the other, they are concentrated in sectors, like steel and automobiles, that have faced tremendous pressure from imports. Still, the widespread introduction of technology across many sectors suggests that domestic competition spurred much of this investment.

As a general explanation, technology is unsatisfactory. It is never clearly distinguished from other kinds of capital, and there is no reason that its introduction must in principle reduce the wages of the unskilled. Technology is for economists the residual that accounts for everything their theories cannot.

Yet a final explanation for labor's lament is immigration. During the 1980s the United States had the largest immigration boom in its postwar history. Between 1980 and 1989 more than six million legal immigrants alone came to its shores. In 1994 more than three million arrived illegally. The net effect of legal migration has been positive. The new arrivals bring needed skills, create businesses and jobs, and raise output. At the same time, the pool of unskilled labor has also increased, forcing down their wages. As with other facets of globalization, increased migration benefits countries overall, but it hurts some groups. The failure to address their dislocation will allow nativists to seize the debate, creating a more permissive environment not only for protectionism but for hate crimes, as is already evident in Western Europe.

RETRAINING REDUX

WHICHEVER EXPLANATION is most important, the fact remains that technological change, free trade, migration, and other forces such as defense cuts create losers as well as winners. The rationale for open economies is that, in principle, the gains will outweigh the losses for the country as a whole; thus, the winners can afford to compensate the losers. Under GATT and Bretton Woods, this compensation took the form of such short-term measures as trade adjustment programs, which provide unemployment insurance, retraining, and even support for moving to new communities. When a robust economy was creating lots of good jobs, everyone was made better off. But that is no longer the case. Today, a worker who loses his job is likely to find a new one only at lower pay. Indeed, as *The New York Times* reported earlier this year, 65 percent of workers who ultimately find jobs after a layoff do so only at lower levels of pay, and Morris Kleiner of the University of Minnesota has found that most such workers are still earning much less even five years later.

According to an analysis of dislocated defense workers in New England, defense workers should have an easy time finding new jobs, given their skills and experience with computers, precision tools, and quality control—even if these attributes have not been tested in the context of more highly competitive enterprises. But even among these workers, one in five of those who found new jobs had wage rates that "represented a pay cut of 40 percent or more." Indeed, over 60 percent of all dislocated workers "had noticeably lower hourly earnings."[5] Their experience with retraining should also counsel caution. Some could not afford the costs associated with these programs, while others had difficulty matching training opportunities to projected new job requirements. For still others, the lack of growth prospects in even distantly related industries raised questions about whether retraining was really a good investment. Overall, as the World

---

[5]Yolanda K. Kodrzycki, "The Costs of Defense-Related Layoffs in New England," *New England Economic Review*, March/April 1995, p. 16.

Bank's 1995 *World Development Report* concluded, results are mixed regarding the value of training in helping unemployed workers find new jobs.

But even if training is a good investment, the cost of providing it to all unemployed workers is prohibitive. There are now some 34 million unemployed persons in the member countries of the Organization for Economic Cooperation and Development (OECD). If the average cost of retraining for each worker is $7,000, the total bill would be $238 billion. For the United States, with its 7 million unemployed, the total would be $49 billion. Today, the U.S. government spends about $10 billion on work-related education and training. In the current fiscal environment, it is difficult to imagine that number rising by the required amount.

On the contrary, these programs are being cut back. Since 1992, funds for labor market training and other active measures have fallen in such countries as Canada, Germany, Sweden, and the United States, the last especially ironic since Secretary of Labor Robert Reich is one of training's greatest devotees (though in fairness, he does have to contend with a Republican Congress). Incredibly, public spending for higher education has also fallen. In the United States, such expenditures were cut 10 percent in the early 1990s, and in Britain only marginally less. At the same time, in countries with federal structures, where the constituent states were expected to assume increased public burdens, local crises and fiscal stringency prevented them from taking up the slack. This is the very problem facing many Russian regions and American states.

It is odd that training has become the mom and apple pie of economists and public officials across the political spectrum when it could at best provide only a partial answer to the problems of dislocated workers, at least given the knowledge base about what works at current spending levels. Indeed, one learns in economics that policymakers should choose the most direct and efficient means for solving problems. This lesson suggests that if the concern is income inequality, policies should be adopted to close the income gap. If the concern is unemployment, more jobs should be created. Training should not be abandoned, of course, but it is not by itself a solution.

KEEPING GROWTH DOWN

IN DEVELOPING positive solutions, however, it is important to recognize that declining rates of economic growth, caused largely by a drop-off in productivity, are hurting all workers. Curiously, analysts have paid less attention to these indexes than to unemployment and inequality. But had the industrial countries continued to grow in the 1990s at their earlier postwar rates, many current headline issues would hardly attract attention. If growth had remained at the 1960s average of 3.5 percent instead of current levels of just over 2 percent, more jobs of all kinds would have been created, rectifying unemployment in Europe and obviating inequality in the United States.

In truth, this productivity slowdown remains a puzzle. Why is it happening if the industrial countries have invested heavily in technology and opened their economies to foreign competition? These things should have spurred productivity growth. At present there is no good answer, though hypotheses focus on such diverse factors as the widespread shift from manufacturing to services in the north, and the decline in educational attainment, especially in science and math, among workers in many of the industrial countries.

Between 1971 and 1978, according to the OECD, the members of the Group of Seven (G-7) enjoyed an average economic growth rate of 3.5 percent per year, and this during a period of severe oil shocks, with the consequent rise in energy prices and inflation. Since 1989, by contrast, growth has averaged 2.1 percent. For Japan, the drop has been even steeper. Its average growth between 1971 and 1978 was 4.5 percent, a number that has fallen in the 1990s to 2.4 percent. Meanwhile, between 1979 and 1994, unemployment in the OECD rose from 17.7 million and a rate of 5.1 percent to 34 million and a rate of 8 percent.

Unfortunately, this slowdown in the 1990s followed on the heels of a period of inflation, deficit spending, and increasing government debt levels around the industrial world. In the G-7 the interest payments on government debt rose from 1.6 percent of GDP in 1980 to 2.5 percent in 1990. Today the figure stands at 2.8 percent. In order to stabilize their financial affairs, states adopted stringent monetary and, more recently, fiscal policies—in short, policies deemed sustainable or credible by financial markets. These policies privileged financial stability over employment. They were the welfare state's equivalent of a grapefruit diet. The problem is that, as with all diets, they can become obsessive and cause more harm than good.

Over time, special interest groups have become entrenched around particular sets of policies, creating bureaucratic sclerosis. Restrictive economic policies—reduced deficits, reduced spending, reduced taxes, and the most exalted deity, low inflation—have favored financial interests at the expense of workers and have created an international rentier class. For anyone with money to invest, the last 20 years have been bountiful. Fiscally restrictive policies have become an ideology of this class for all practical purposes, defended in the pages of the leading newspapers and economic journals and most of the Beltway think tanks. Public officials who adopt restrictive measures are labeled "responsible" by editorialists, and the markets reward their behavior, sustaining the ideology.

The politics of financial credibility has played out somewhat differently across the industrial world. In the United States they have centered around the balanced budget debate between President Clinton and Congress. Indeed, they led to Clinton's Hoover-like statement about big government in his recent State of the Union address. Policies have targeted inflation and fiscal expansion in recent years, but the benefits of this approach have yet to be widely shared. At the same time, polling data and other evidence, such as the results of the Republican presidential primaries, suggest that the American people are becoming increasingly worried about their economic security and want the government to do something about it. And this concern is not solely a local phenomenon. What in America was once called the battle between Wall Street and Main Street has now become global.

The budget debate is a case of ideology overriding economics. In fact, there is no reason a balanced budget must always be favored over Keynesian deficit spending. As economist Robert Eisner wrote in *How Real Is the Federal Deficit?* in 1986, "Deficits can be too small as well as too large." He reminds us that when "there is slack in the economy, deficit-induced demand stimulates output and employment." It may well be the case that Clinton has gone too far in agreeing with congressional Republicans about the need to balance the budget over the next seven years.

But there is no direct correlation between deficit spending and inflation, as Japan demonstrates. During most of the postwar era Japan has had far higher deficits than the United States as a percentage of GNP, but lower inflation. The reason is Japan's credibility when it comes to maintaining monetary stability. Given Japan's high savings rate, the markets have confidence in its ability to finance long-term debt obligations. Today Japan is the only industrial country that is taking a Keynesian approach to its economic problems, and its latest growth figures suggest that fiscal expansion has been beneficial. There is, in short, no reason that moderate fiscal relaxation must generate high inflation. Moreover, to the extent that Japanese levels of inflation become somewhat higher than those in the United States, they would contribute to easing tensions over the yen-dollar exchange rate.

In contrast, leaders in Europe, where deficits are also higher than in the United States, have demanded a rapid reduction in government spending in order to meet the criteria of the Maastricht treaty on monetary union. With Germany setting the economic rules of the game according to its domestic preferences, European states that wish to participate in the planned union must reduce their budget deficits to 3 percent of GDP by 1999. In France, where deficits are now running at 5 percent of GDP, the rules mean applying the ax to the state budget. These policies reflect an obsessive fear of Europe's traditional bouts of inflation, but the major central banks have done a credible job of maintaining monetary stability. What has been the point of adopting these anti-inflationary policies if they do not permit governments some fiscal room to maneuver?

Even in Russia one can see restrictive fiscal policies dismantling earlier contracts between the state and society. Thus, under stringent IMF discipline, Russia too must reduce its budget deficit. Those hardest hit have been pensioners, the unemployed, and the poor—again, the people most in need of state services. The collapse of the social safety net in Russia explains why the Communist Party received the largest share of the vote in the December 1995 Duma elections and why its leader, Gennadi Zyuganov, may be elected the country's president in June 1996.

LOOSENING UP

TO MEET THE growing problems of working people, governments must develop a coherent package of economic policies and programs supported by international policy coordination that generates renewed growth. Such a strategy, which will require some fiscal relaxation, has some costs, but the consequences of doing nothing will be worse, since disastrous measures like protectionism and nativism are again being mentioned, even in economically literate circles.

The starting point for any policy effort of this kind is the normative assertion that the appropriate goal of economic policy is to improve the lives of the citizenry. Monetary and fiscal policies should be structured in such a way as to ensure the fundamental promise that working people can earn a living wage. This means that in every industrial country policies must be directed toward helping people cope with the consequences of economic change. Of course, the appropriate policy mix will vary. In the United States, job insecurity, income inequality, and the plight of the working poor are now chief concerns. In Europe, job creation is key. Thus the policy for Europe would permit greater fiscal relaxation and that for the United States more income redistribution.

The argument that present-day fiscal restrictions must be maintained in order to balance budgets and stabilize national economies is without merit. The critical issue on the fiscal side is how governments spend the money. Just as with corporate investment, there is a difference between investments that are likely to yield long-term benefits and those that throw money down rat holes. To take an extreme case, no American during World War II said that the investment in armaments was a bad one, and it was gladly financed through bond issues and payroll taxes. Contemporary critics who would say that spending money on labor policies is unfair to the nation's children forget that the best thing that can be bequeathed to the next generation is social peace.

An expansionary strategy must include both microeconomic and macroeconomic elements, coupled with international policy coordination. Microeconomic policies, like the expansion of education and training, are needed to provide workers with the skills that will enable them to rejoin the labor market or find better career prospects. But these policies and programs are of little value if the economy is not producing good jobs. Macroeconomic policies, like fiscal relaxation and changes in taxation, are therefore required to provide a stimulus to spur economic growth. Taken together, these micro- and macroeconomic policies should translate into a better-educated and more productive work force. Finally, international policy coordination is necessary so that countries can develop expansionary policies within a collective framework, avoiding competitive currency depreciations that in the long run hurt everyone.

Governments that wish to assist unskilled workers have four choices: protectionism, education and training, public works programs and employment subsidies, and tax policy and income transfers. All of them entail costs, which must be paid for in one way or another.

Protectionism has received both renewed attention and scrutiny since candidate Patrick Buchanan's victory in the New Hampshire presidential primary. Buchanan, an avowed "economic nationalist," would place prohibitive tariffs on a range of imports in order to protect American jobs and wages. Unfortunately, whatever the alleged benefits of protectionism, the costs would outweigh them for most workers, and national income would certainly fall. Protectionism would lead to higher prices for all products, both foreign and domestic, resulting in lower consumption and an economic slowdown. Furthermore, America's trading partners could not be expected to sit passively while they were victimized; they too would erect higher trade barriers in response, eliminating markets for U.S. exports and the high-wage jobs that go with them. Since exports are the fastest-growing segment of the economy, policies that lead to their restriction deserve condemnation. In short, protectionism is a remedy that is worse than the disease.

Increased spending on education and training appears to be the only policy intervention that meets with universal approval across the political spectrum. Over a generation, unskilled workers will respond to the economic signals and opt for more education and training. Historical evidence suggests that this process occurs in most industrial countries undergoing significant economic change.[6] But the benefits of training for dislocated workers are uncertain, and the costs of universal training would be prohibitive. Clearly, the expansion of educational opportunities should play a central role in any democratic society and should be financed—it makes for good politics and good economics. It cannot, however, provide anything resembling a near-term solution to the structural problems of unemployment and inequality.

The third approach is to increase the number of jobs through public works programs or, perhaps more effectively, employment subsidies to the private sector. Few Western countries have pursued this tack as an explicit policy since the Great Depression, but it should be remembered that the New Deal was successful in creating jobs and reducing misery. Public job creation is relatively efficient and socially productive—since it provides younger workers with needed job experience—and it can be done fairly quickly. If the government subsidizes jobs, it will get more of them. Such policies, however, must be designed carefully to avoid an unproductive substitution of subsidized for unsubsidized workers.

This approach becomes all the more compelling in light of the sharp defense drawdowns among the member states of NATO. In the United States, for example, the size of the military force has shrunk by nearly one million since 1986, closing a once-promising route to education, training,

---

[6]Jeffrey G. Williamson, *Inequality, Poverty, and History,* Cambridge: Blackwell, 1991.

experience, and responsibility for thousands of young adults. France will soon end military conscription. Alternative paths must be forged to help this population enter the workforce. Moreover, public works spending would counteract the fiscal drag of these defense cuts.

Finally, it is clear that tax policy and income transfers must play a key role in any serious effort to help working people and to finance new programs. One possible approach, combining in a sense the best of candidate Steve Forbes' flat tax and Senator Jeff Bingaman's (D-N.M.) proposal to tax financial transactions, would be to lower overall federal income tax rates— perhaps eliminating income taxes altogether for a large number of the working poor—while making them sharply more progressive up the income ladder. In the United States, the fiscal gap that resulted could then be covered by introducing a national value-added tax, at least on luxury goods. Most industrial countries already have a VAT. In principle, workers would still pay less in overall taxes, since their VAT payments would be lower than their income taxes under the current system, while the rich, who now enjoy a variety of tax loopholes, could not escape paying their fair share of the VAT. Most important, more job-related services could be provided than is now the case.

In Europe, unemployment rather than income distribution is the key problem. Additional reforms are needed there if the goal is to increase labor market flexibility, the hiring of new workers, and small business creation. Again, the policies are not a mystery, and inaction reflects a lack of political will rather than of economic knowledge. Among these reforms, reductions in employer social charges such as health care costs and greater flexibility in hiring, firing, and setting work hours are absolute necessities. Small and medium-sized enterprises in particular, which are important generators of new jobs, are being stymied by these onerous charges. Furthermore, unemployment and other benefits in most European countries are simply out of proportion, and they give the jobless little incentive to seek work. Here, the Europeans probably could learn something from the United States. Savings in these areas could provide funds for programs that create employment. Unfortunately, Europe's technocratic leaders have done a poor job of explaining the economic situation to voters and have lacked imagination in promoting new ideas.

A recent Brookings Institution study of the policies needed to restore growth in the U.S. economy, including funds for education and training and adding spending for research and development, estimates annual expenditures on the order of $80 billion, a large but not Himalayan sum. In

Ethan B. Kapstein

Europe with its far higher levels of unemployment, the costs would likely be greater. To pay for this program, the authors call for higher taxes on upper income groups, coupled with spending cuts in other areas, presumably defense. While one can disagree with the specifics, the cost estimate suggests the magnitude of the task that confronts decision-makers.

One of the main arguments against an expansionary strategy, of course, is that it is inflationary. In the current climate, inflation can be avoided if monetary discipline is maintained. But in the event, some inflation overseas, as in the Japanese case, might well suit American interests. For Europe, it may be time to reassess the costs associated with the doctrinaire German approach to monetary policy. While inflation is a scourge, so is double-digit unemployment, with its dangers to the global economy.

HANGING TOGETHER

No SINGLE formula would produce an optimal set of policy reforms. Each industrial country must find its own mix, given its particular political and economic circumstances. But these efforts will be more effective if pursued as part of an international effort. Without such policy coordination countries will either be penalized by financial markets for adopting growth-oriented policies or they will aggressively pursue beggar-thy-neighbor currency devaluations.

Effective coordination in the G-7 is not impossible; the global economy could not have been built without it. Nor is there a risk that such growth-oriented coordination would be undermined by massive capital flight to East Asia or other regions, since the United States and other Western countries still dominate the global financial marketplace. According to the OECD, in 1994 member countries were home to 90 percent of world stock market capitalization and bond issues.

A precedent for cooperation during hard times is the Bonn Summit of 1978. As the world economy was recovering from the oil crisis of 1973-74, the OECD called on governments to stimulate their economies to ensure that the growth prospects became a reality—remarkable in light of today's deflationary bias. The member countries agreed to a package of national measures that would collectively spur global growth. These included a reduction in U.S. oil imports, which led to a fall in world oil prices, and the implementation of expansionary policies in Germany and Japan. Unfortunately, the second oil crisis, caused by the Iranian Revolution, undercut most of these initiatives.

Workers and the World Economy

Why have Western countries eschewed this type of coordination in recent years? If they truly believe in globalization, they must accept that the economic performance of trading partners is converging. They should see such variables as growth rates, interest rates, and workers' wages approaching some common values. But instead, there are profound divergences in national economic performance, even in Western Europe, suggesting the continuing importance of domestic politics. This internecine competitiveness makes policy coordination difficult to achieve in the best of circumstances, but all the more so when growth is sluggish.

During the postwar decades, American leadership has time and again played a crucial role in leading the industrial countries out of the doldrums. The United States has assumed this burden not because it is magnanimous, but out of enlightened self-interest. Prosperous allies are needed for both economic and security reasons, and the OECD countries still generate by far the largest share of world trade. Today that leadership is absent. The president, perhaps pushed by Congress, seems to believe that domestic economic problems can be solved through domestic economic policies. The administration's singular focus on the international front has been export promotion. But American exports can increase only if the world economy continues to liberalize and grow.

This is an age of widespread economic insecurity, brought about by profound changes in trade, finance, and technology. For globalization to proceed, public officials in every country must give the lie to those who assert that it is anathema to workers' interests. The best way to make this case is by restoring growth and opportunity. Restrictive economic policies may have been necessary when first conceived in the 1980s to bring stability to financial markets, but they have failed too many people too long.

While the world stands at a critical time in postwar history, it has a group of leaders who appear unwilling, like their predecessors in the 1930s, to provide the international leadership to meet economic dislocations. Worse, many of them and their economic advisers do not seem to recognize the profound troubles affecting their societies. Like the German elite in Weimar, they dismiss mounting worker dissatisfaction, fringe political movements, and the plight of the unemployed and working poor as marginal concerns compared with the unquestioned importance of a sound currency and balanced budget. Leaders need to recognize the policy failures of the last 20 years and respond accordingly. If they do not, there are others waiting in the wings who will, perhaps on less pleasant terms.✿

Workers and Economists I:

First, Do No Harm

Paul Krugman

WHEN A FIRE breaks out in a single-family home, firefighters know what they have to do. Fires in private houses are all pretty much alike. But when a fire breaks out in a warehouse, the firefighters make an effort to find out what is inside before they go to work, lest they do more harm than good. For example, if the warehouse is filled with highly flammable chemicals, dousing the building with water may spread the fire. In the end, the fire department must act regardless, but it is important to act on as much information as one can get about the nature of the problem.

I offer this homily because Ethan B. Kapstein uses an analogy with firefighting to claim that the West, faced with the economic difficulties of inequality and unemployment, has been paralyzed by too much debate over causes ("Workers and the World Economy," May/June 1996). He seems to believe that economic crises are like house fires, all pretty much the same. In particular, he seems to believe that the economic woes of advanced nations in the 1990s are basically similar to the problems of the 1930s. Deficit spending was the answer then and it is the answer now. Money should, therefore, be spent like water.

PAUL KRUGMAN is Professor of Economics at the Massachusetts Institute of Technology. This article appeared in the July/August 1996 issue of *Foreign Affairs*.

Workers and Economists I: First, Do No Harm

Economic crises, however, are not all the same, and the problems of the 1990s look very little like those of the 1930s. The good news is that while there is considerable dispute about the relative importance of some factors, economists have reached enough of a workable consensus about the nature of the problem to accommodate helpful policies. The bad news is that much, although not all, of what Kapstein has to say ignores this consensus, and that some of his policy recommendations are mischievous. They would either create the risk of renewed inflation and worsen the already shaky finances of Western governments, or they would contribute to the very policy paralysis Kapstein decries.

THE NOT-QUITE CONSENSUS

THE ECONOMIC difficulties of the advanced nations are not new. Unemployment in Europe has been rising steadily since the early 1970s, while inequality in the United States began rising sharply only a few years later. Nor have they failed to receive attention. Over these 20-plus years, hundreds of conferences and thousands of academic articles and official reports have addressed them. While there is not a total consensus—there never is—a widely held middle-of-the-road position can be summarized by two propositions.

The first proposition is that the problems of wages and employment are mainly—forgive the jargon—structural rather than cyclical. A cyclical economic problem is caused by inadequate demand and can be cured by adopting a more expansionary monetary and fiscal policy—that is, spending more or taxing less. Structural economic problems cannot be solved in this way. Most economists now believe that the Great Depression was essentially cyclical; the slack in employment could have been taken up simply through an aggressive program of demand expansion. But the structural nature of Europe's unemployment was graphically demonstrated by the events of the late 1980s. The later stages of a broad business cycle recovery were marked by a noticeable increase in inflation (drastic in the case of the United Kingdom), despite the fact that the unemployment rate was still nearly nine percent. Demand had recovered, but unemployment could not fall below the nine-percent structural rate without triggering inflation.

What is wrong with trading off lower unemployment for slightly higher inflation? Not much, but that is the wrong question, because there is overwhelming evidence that inflation begets inflation. Suppose the

Federal Reserve were to push the U.S. unemployment rate down from its current 5.5 percent to 4.5 percent. In the first year the inflation rate would probably rise only from its current 3 percent to 3.5 or 4 percent. But in the next year it would be 4 or 5 percent, the year after that 5 or 6 percent, and ever upward. The point, then, is not that inflation will explode if the unemployment rate is pushed too low. It is that a sustained effort to keep unemployment below the so-called NAIRU—the non-accelerating-inflation rate of unemployment—merely by stimulating demand will lead to an upward spiral of inflation. And though high rates of inflation would be slow to materialize, they would be equally hard to get rid of. Once the economy has developed six percent inflation, to get it back down to three percent would require a severe recession. Some countries have substantial room for demand expansion, most notably Japan. For the advanced nations as a whole, however, demand expansion is not a solution; indeed, it will only add new problems.

The second and somewhat more controversial proposition of the not-quite consensus is that the growth of international trade is not the main cause of the persistent rise in European unemployment and American inequality. Rather, the main source is a decline in the internal demand for less-skilled labor, probably driven in large part by technological change biased toward highly skilled workers. While Kapstein insists that time should not be wasted debating causes, he nonetheless finds time to pick sides in the dispute here, asserting that "as a general explanation, technology is unsatisfactory. It is never clearly distinguished from other kinds of capital, and there is no reason that its introduction must in principle reduce the wages of the unskilled."

In fact, MIT's Robert Solow won a Nobel Prize in economics in large part for making it very clear why technological progress and capital accumulation are not at all the same—and how to measure the difference. Since his work, in literally thousands of empirical studies of economic change, the distinction between technology and capital has played a crucial role. (My own article in the November/December 1994 *Foreign Affairs*, "The Myth of Asia's Miracle," was motivated by this very distinction.)

But Kapstein is quite right that technology need not in principle reduce the wages of the unskilled. Whether it does so depends on the bias of the technological change—whether it is sufficiently biased toward skilled and against unskilled workers. But the claim of many economists that technological change is a major factor in recent wage trends is not based on a priori reasoning; it is an empirical proposition, based on facts. Nearly all industries (including those not exposed to international competition) have been increasing the average skill level of their work force by hiring relatively more skilled workers, despite the lower wages of unskilled workers. That indicates that recent technological change has been strongly skill-biased.

The conventional view that international trade is only a secondary source of the growth in unemployment and inequality is also an empirical proposition, and one not arrived at lightly. This is an ongoing debate, driven by technical issues rather than ideology. It is risky for nonspecialists to put their faith in an economist merely because they like the sound of what the economist says. For example, Adrian Wood's work, approvingly cited by Kapstein, has been subjected to devastating criticism; Wood's own numbers do not support his strong claims, and he arrives at large estimates of trade's effect only by finessing a basic calculation that indicates the opposite conclusion.[1]

Does the distinction between internal and international causes matter? Yes, it does. Although Kapstein forswears protectionism, it is not at all clear why. After all, if international trade is the main cause of the problem, why not use import restrictions as one line of defense? But if international trade is only 10 or 20 percent of the problem, a protectionist response will bring a whole new set of problems without resolving the ones we already have.

WHAT TO DO

SUPPOSE THE middle-of-the-road position on unemployment and inequality is correct: the main source of these problems is a structural, not cyclical, decline in the internal demand for less-skilled labor within advanced countries. One may then conclude that neither a simple policy of overall demand expansion nor one of protectionism against Third World imports is the answer. What, then, can be done?

---

[1] For a detailed dissection of Wood's work, see William Cline, *Trade Jobs, and Income Distribution*, Washington: Institute for International Economics, forthcoming. The majority view that technology is the main story while trade is a secondary factor may be wrong, but one certainly should not take sides on this subject unless one is thoroughly familiar with the technical issues involved.

Paul Krugman

This is actually not such a hard question. In the United States, which has managed to maintain relatively full employment but has experienced rising inequality, the incomes of low-wage workers need support; but that must be done, so far as possible, without raising the cost to employers of hiring those workers. The obvious answer is something like a much bigger version of the earned income tax credit—an income supplement for workers with low earnings that falls off as a worker's earnings rise, but not so rapidly as to negate pay increases and discourage work. Such a program would be subject to some abuse, but so are all government programs.

Europe has nearly the opposite problem. The poor receive relatively generous support, but not enough people are employed. What Europe needs to do is reduce the cost of employing the less skilled, so that the private sector will offer them more jobs. But it must do so without, so far as possible, reducing their incomes. In this case reducing or removing the tax burden associated with hiring low-wage labor, and possibly providing some employment subsidies, are the obvious answers.

The important point—on which I agree with Kapstein—is that it should be possible to make a large difference to the incomes of low-wage workers (in the United States) or to their prospects of employment (in Europe) without devastating effects on the budget. In the United States, the crucial thing to remember is just how poor the poor are and how rich the country is. If the United States were willing to devote, say, two percent of GDP to income supplements for the working poor, the effect would be dramatic.

So why hasn't the United States tried this policy? Surely it is not because economists have quarreled over whether trade explains 10 or 30 percent of the increase in wage disparities. A better target for Kapstein's ire might be influential figures who insist that the only way to help the poor in America is to cut taxes on the rich. But Kapstein at least seems to place most of the blame on those with what he regards as a misguided, indeed mystical, concern over budget deficits.

FEAR IS NOT THE ONLY DANGER

KAPSTEIN IMPLIES that the economic difficulties of the West are due to its governments' obsession with deficit reduction. Let me repeat that the West's economic problems have been building steadily for more than 20 years, while serious budget-cutting has begun only within the last two or three. The term "Eurosclerosis" dates not from the 1990s but from the late 1970s; European unemployment had already risen to double digits by 1985, when budget difficulties were rarely discussed. The Reagan administration took a remarkably relaxed view of unprecedented peacetime deficits during the 1980s, but that fiscal expansion did not prevent inequality in the United States from soaring.

Nor is concern about deficits the reason Western nations have been unwilling to provide more support for low-wage workers. The sums involved are small enough that if governments and voters were truly persuaded that such policies were necessary, they could quite easily be funded with new taxes or reduced benefits to middle-and upper-income families. Governments and voters are not persuaded, but that has nothing to do with the deficit.

The main reason Kapstein is eager to put aside concern about deficits seems to be that, in spite of all the evidence, he is determined to view the 1990s through the lens of the 1930s. He quotes economist Robert Eisner on the desirability of deficit-induced demand. But with the possible exception of Japan, every advanced country has plenty of room to increase demand simply by cutting interest rates. If they do not do so, it is because their central bankers think an increase in demand is unnecessary or dangerous. They might be wrong, but running budget deficits, which will merely lead those central bankers to impose still higher interest rates, will do nothing to help the situation.

Still, would a more relaxed attitude toward budget deficits do any harm? Here Kapstein's article becomes truly mischievous, by suggesting that concern about deficits is motivated entirely by ideology. Would that it were! Unfortunately, the West is past the point at which the virtues and vices of its budget deficits could be discussed in terms of uncertain macroeconomic effects. The stakes now are much cruder and more elemental: the long-term solvency of Western governments.

Debt as a percentage of national income in almost all Western nations is now comparable to the levels that historically have prevailed only at the end of major wars. But there has been no war, and instead of paying down their debts, as peacetime governments always have in the past, Western treasuries are continuing to increase their debt, for the most part faster than the increases in their tax bases. Moreover, in the current situation there are no major emergencies—no big arms races or wars in prospect, no natural disasters that require extraordinary spending. But stuff happens. If governments cannot control their budgets when it is not happening, what will they do when it does?

The demographic time bomb makes this situation particularly worrying. The budgets of advanced countries are in large part engines that transfer money from workers to retirees, a system that runs smoothly as long as the population is steadily growing, so that the working-age population is large relative to the retired population. But Western populations have not grown steadily. Baby boom was followed by baby bust, and it is therefore certain that the demands on the social insurance systems of advanced countries will greatly exceed their resources beginning only a bit more than a decade from now. Or to put it differently, to the already huge explicit debts of Western nations one should add implicit debt in the form of their unfunded promises to future retirees. In short, concern about the budget deficits of Western nations can no longer be considered a matter of ideology. These days it is a matter of straightforward accounting, and one must deliberately stick one's head in the sand to imagine otherwise.

PUBLICITY COORDINATION

THE ASPECT of Kapstein's prescriptions I found most puzzling is his insistence that a prerequisite for effective action is coordination of economic policies among the major economies. His suggestion seems to be fairly close to the textbook model for macroeconomic coordination. In that much-beloved classroom exercise, each country would like to expand its domestic demand but fears that such an expansion will worsen its trade balance or lead to a depreciation of its currency. In that case a coordinated expansion offers a way out. Increased imports are matched by increased exports, and flight capital has nowhere to go. It is a perfectly reasonable scenario in principle. It may even be a good model for the economic situation during the 1930s. But does this story about the need for coordinated expansion bear any resemblance to the current situation?

Let's get specific. Which major economies are actually constrained from expansion by concerns about the balance of payments or the reaction of international financial markets? Surely not the United States, which may huff and puff about trade conflicts but whose monetary and fiscal policies treat the trade balance and the exchange rate with benign neglect. Surely not Japan, which is worried about an excessive trade surplus, not a deficit, and which is plagued by a yen that is too strong, not too weak. Japan would actually welcome a bit of capital flight. Surely not Germany; with the deutsche mark the key currency of what remains of the European

Monetary System, Germany can expect its neighbors to match any reduction it chooses to make in its interest rates. Probably not Britain; since it stopped pegging the value of the pound in 1992, Britain has felt free to follow an independent monetary policy. If it has tightened recently, it is not because it fears the reaction of international markets, but because its domestic economy is again showing signs of inflationary pressures.

What we are left with, I guess, is France, which is indeed pursuing a more restrictive monetary policy than it would if it were not concerned about the value of the franc. But the reason for France's concern is not any inherent need to keep the franc strong—inflation is almost zero—but precisely the commitment of the French government to the Maastricht criteria. France, in other words, is the victim of too much international coordination, not too little. So Kapstein's demand for coordinated economic policy seems to arise more from his general sense that such coordination ought to be a good thing than from any consideration of the real economic situation. Still, does it do any harm?

Whatever your assessment of the economic case, there is one overwhelming empirical observation that can be made about macroeconomic policy coordination: it never happens. Well, hardly ever. Whole forests have been leveled to print reports about the Plaza, the Louvre, the Group of Seven, and so on, but it is hard to find a single case in which a major economic player has altered monetary or fiscal policy at the behest of the other major players. One often hears about the G-7 process; the reason aficionados like to talk so much about the process is that there have been so few results.

To say, as Kapstein does, that "international policy coordination is necessary so that countries can develop expansionary policies within a collective framework," is in effect to say that real action should be postponed for years while countries engage in endless rounds of content-free summitry. Perhaps if there were a compelling case for coordinated policies there might be a way to turn these photo ops into real negotiations (although recent experience in noneconomic affairs is not encouraging), but there is no such compelling case.

None of this should be taken as a counsel of inaction. There is a great deal that can be done to improve the economic situations of the ill-paid and unemployed. However, there is no reason to tie responsible, realistic proposals to raise incomes and create jobs either to irresponsible demands for bigger deficits or to unrealistic expectations about international coordination. ☯

Workers and Economists II:

Resist the Binge

Robert Z. Lawrence

KAPSTEIN IS CORRECT in saying that the problems of workers in the developed world are serious. I agree, too, that ignoring their plight could have tragic political consequences. But by overstating the effects of the world economy and ignoring the other sources of these problems, Kapstein could well promote the tragedy he seeks to avoid. I also take strong exception to his proposal that governments increase spending. Expansionary fiscal policy would severely set back the progress governments are finally making in bringing their expenditures in line with their revenues. First, expansion driven by a fiscal stimulus is not needed. To the degree that there is insufficient demand in the developed countries—in Europe and Japan, but not the United States—domestic monetary policies are quite adequate for the task. Second, demand-side expansion can do little to solve the structural supply-side problems about which Kapstein is concerned. Economic growth is fundamentally limited by the expansion of productive capacity. Any demand expansion beyond that capacity will translate purely into inflation.

WAGGING THE DOG

KAPSTEIN ARGUES strongly that serious labor market problems such as slow productivity growth, growing inequality, and rising unemployment

---

ROBERT Z. LAWRENCE is Albert L. Williams Professor of International Trade and Investment at the John F. Kennedy School of Government, Harvard University. This article appeared in the July/August 1996 issue of *Foreign Affairs*.

in the developed countries reflect the increasing influence of the world economy on local conditions. As every student of statistics knows, however, correlation should not be confused with causation. Globalization has increased at a time of poor domestic performance, but is globalization truly culpable or just an innocent bystander?

Globalization is important in Western economies. International trade and investment have expanded rapidly, but consider some facts about the United States. Eighty-eight percent of the goods and services Americans buy, they produce themselves. Eighty-two percent of Americans are employed in sectors like government, construction, nonprofit organizations, services, utilities, and wholesale and retail trade, in which international trade is barely a factor. Moreover, America's international interaction with developing countries remains even smaller. In 1994, U.S. non-oil imports from developing countries amounted to just 3 percent of GNP; exports to developing countries were just 2.5 percent. Employment in the foreign affiliates of U.S. multinationals in developing countries is less than 5 percent of overall U.S. manufacturing employment. I am not saying this interaction has not grown rapidly or even that its effect at the margin may not be greater than these numbers suggest, but to point only to trade with developing countries as the source of workers' problems is to wag a very large dog with a rather small tail.

Most problems in the developed economies would exist even if those economies were not increasingly open to trade and investment. Similarly, most of the remedies require changes in domestic policies unconstrained by international forces. By focusing on the convenient scapegoat of international trade, Kapstein gives short shrift to other important problems, some unique, some shared, that developed countries confront. He overlooks the fact that in the United States, slow domestic productivity growth in service sectors not exposed to trade has led to wage stagnation; that in Europe, sclerotic labor markets and overextended government regulations inhibit structural change, regardless of whether the source is internal or external; and that in Japan, the current recession reflects the aftermath of a splurge sparked by domestic monetary policy, and the recession's persistence stems from failures to deregulate domestic markets and deal with a domestic banking crisis. Kapstein is also too cavalier about the fact that in all countries these problems have been compounded because technological change has shifted demand away from the less-skilled and less-educated workers.

Robert Z. Lawrence

With very few exceptions, economists who have studied the impact of trade with developing countries on labor markets conclude it plays a relatively minor role.[1] In the 1980s, during which Americans experienced widening inequality in their income levels, neither the quantities of imported goods nor the changes in prices the imports caused were large enough to give trade much of a role. Even those in the United States who believe trade to be significant suggest it explains no more than a fifth of the growth in the relative wages of educated workers. Almost all economists assign a much larger role to the technological changes associated with the introduction of computers and to the changes in management practices that have skewed demand toward more skilled workers while at the same time providing disappointing increases in productivity.

Kapstein dismisses studies by me and others with the claim that trade induces technological change. He argues that "a significant share of new technology, for example, has been induced by foreign competition." In fact, research on the effects of trade on both productivity growth and research-and-development spending confirms the maxim: sometimes a kick in the pants gets you going, and sometimes it just hurts. Some firms, typically in concentrated industries with surplus profits, are spurred to innovate and to spend more on research and development. But other firms, especially those in highly competitive industries, are more likely to respond to international competition by cutting back on investment. It turns out that most trade with developing countries occurs in sectors such as clothing and footwear that are highly competitive. This suggests that when it comes to trade with developing countries, the innovation caused directly by trade is relatively small; indeed, it is more likely to be slowed by trade than sped up. Moreover, to the extent that some trade does lower the wages of unskilled workers throughout the economy, it discourages labor-saving innovation.

Kapstein's account of the role of trade is also imprecise. Does he have in mind all international trade or just trade with developing countries? Since wages in developed countries are quite similar, it must be developing countries he has in mind when he invokes the Stolper-Samuelson theory to argue that trade lowers the welfare of the least-skilled workers

---

[1]For a more extensive discussion, see my *Single World, Divided Nations? The Impact of Trade on OECD Labor Markets,* Washington: Brookings Institution, 1996.

in the developed countries. But at another point he talks about the investment-generating effects of trade in industries such as automobiles and steel, in which the developing countries are not major players.

THE GROWTH CEILING

I SHARE WITH Kapstein the view that government should assist workers in adjusting to change. Training and education are crucial in helping workers adjust, but it is impractical and unrealistic to see them as the only answer. I also concur that the tax system should be used to boost the incomes of the working poor and facilitate job turnover. Europe's strength is that it helps its poor; its problem is that its inflexible labor markets fail to create jobs. America's strength is its flexibility and job creation; its problem is that the income of the least-skilled workers has been depressed. The ideal system would combine American efficiency with European compassion. A deregulated labor market and a generous earned income tax credit would do exactly that. Let wages be freely determined in the market, but let the government safeguard the workers through the tax system.

Where I part company with Kapstein is on his call for coordinated expansionary fiscal policies. Indeed, I think his prescription of tight money and loose fiscal policies has it exactly wrong. Loosen money, perhaps, but keep fiscal policy tight. Currently, there may be some room in Europe and Japan for monetary expansion and, in my heretical view, in countries such as France even room for exchange rates to float. But soon this expansion in demand will strike the ceiling set by the supply capacity of the economy. In a fully employed economy, that capacity is equal to the rise in output per worker plus the growth of the labor force. Once that ceiling is reached, efforts to expand demand can only produce inflation. There is some controversy over whether the United States has already reached the maximum growth rate. I would err on the side of caution, but if you think more stimulus is called for, leave it up to the Federal Reserve. However, calling for bigger budget deficits and more public works programs could not be more wrongheaded. If the problem is slow productivity growth, the country surely needs more investment. But change the mix and not the size of public spending. Let fiscal policy contribute to supply growth by substituting public investment for public consumption, but not through bigger deficits. Increased government borrowing leads to higher interest rates and crowds out private investment. Public works programs delay market adjustments and fail to give workers the skills they need for viable long-run employment. Moreover, such fiscal expansion reinforces the tendency to deny the need for adjustments by piling up debt for future generations.

The simple truth is that, notwithstanding Kapstein's pronouncement, monetary and fiscal policies cannot "be structured in such a way as to ensure . . . that working people can earn a living wage." Successful fiscal and monetary policies may keep inflation low and achieve full employment, but only increased productivity in the private sector can raise the marketplace earnings of working people. If these earnings are inadequate, redistribution may have a role. But bigger government deficits will only pass the burden to future generations.@

Culture Is Destiny

A Conversation with Lee Kuan Yew

Fareed Zakaria

"ONE OF THE asymmetries of history," wrote Henry Kissinger of Singapore's patriarch Lee Kuan Yew, "is the lack of correspondence between the abilities of some leaders and the power of their countries." Kissinger's one time boss, Richard Nixon, was even more flattering. He speculated that, had Lee lived in another time and another place, he might have "attained the world stature of a Churchill, a Disraeli, or a Gladstone." This tag line of a big man on a small stage has been attached to Lee since the 1970s. Today, however, his stage does not look quite so small. Singapore's per capita GNP is now higher than that of its erstwhile colonizer, Great Britain. It has the world's busiest port, is the third-largest oil refiner and a major center of global manufacturing and service industries. And this move from poverty to plenty has taken place within one generation. In 1965 Singapore ranked economically with Chile, Argentina and Mexico; today its per capita GNP is four or five times theirs.

Lee managed this miraculous transformation in Singapore's economy while maintaining tight political control over the country; Singapore's government can best be described as a "soft" authoritarian regime, and at times it has not been so soft. He was prime minister of Singapore from its independence in 1959 (it became part of a federation with Malaysia in 1963 but was expelled in 1965) until 1990, when he allowed his deputy to succeed him. He is now "Senior Minister" and still commands enormous influence and power in the country. Since his retirement, Lee has embarked on another career of sorts as a world-class pundit, speaking his mind with impolitic frankness. And what is often on his mind is American-style democ-

FAREED ZAKARIA is Managing Editor of *Foreign Affairs*. This article appeared in the March/April 1994 issue of *Foreign Affairs*.

racy and its perils. He travels often to East Asian capitals from Beijing to Hanoi to Manila dispensing advice on how to achieve economic growth while retaining political stability and control. It is a formula that the governing elites of these countries are anxious to learn.

The rulers of former British colonies have been spared the embarrassment of building grandiose monuments to house their offices; they simply occupy the ones that the British built. So it is with Singapore. The president, prime minister and senior minister work out of *Istana* (palace), the old colonial governor's house, a gleaming white bungalow surrounded by luxuriant lawns. The interior is modern—light wood paneling and leather sofas. The atmosphere is hushed. I waited in a large anteroom for the "SM," which is how everybody refers to Lee. I did not wait long. The SM was standing in the middle of a large, sparsely furnished office. He is of medium build. His once-compact physique is now slightly shrunken. Still, he does not look 70.

Lee Kuan Yew is unlike any politician I have met. There were no smiles, no jokes, no bonhomie. He looked straight at me—he has an inexpressive face but an intense gaze—shook hands and motioned toward one of the room's pale blue leather sofas (I had already been told by his press secretary on which one to sit). After 30 awkward seconds, I realized that there would be no small talk. I pressed the record button on my machine.

FZ: With the end of the Cold War, many Americans were surprised to hear growing criticism of their political and economic and social system from elites in East Asia, who were considered staunchly pro-American. What, in your view, is wrong with the American system?

LKY: It is not my business to tell people what's wrong with their system. It is my business to tell people not to foist their system indiscriminately on societies in which it will not work.

FZ: But you do not view the United States as a model for other countries?

LKY: As an East Asian looking at America, I find attractive and unattractive features. I like, for example, the free, easy and open relations between people regardless of social status, ethnicity or religion. And the things that I have always admired about America, as against the communist system, I still do: a certain openness in argument about what is good or bad for society; the accountability of public officials; none of the secrecy and terror that's part and parcel of communist government.

But as a total system, I find parts of it totally unacceptable: guns, drugs, violent crime, vagrancy, unbecoming behavior in public—in sum the breakdown of civil society. The expansion of the right of the individual to behave or misbehave as he pleases has come at the expense of orderly society. In the East the main object is to have a well-ordered society so that everybody can have maximum enjoyment of his freedoms. This freedom can only exist in an ordered state and not in a natural state of contention and anarchy.

Let me give you an example that encapsulates the whole difference between America and Singapore. America has a vicious drug problem. How does it solve it? It goes around the world helping other anti-narcotic agencies to try and stop the suppliers. It pays for helicopters, defoliating agents and so on. And when it is provoked, it captures the president of Panama and brings him to trial in Florida. Singapore does not have that option. We can't go to Burma and capture warlords there. What we can do is to pass a law which says that any customs officer or policeman who sees anybody in Singapore behaving suspiciously, leading him to suspect the person is under the influence of drugs, can require that man to have his urine tested. If the sample is found to contain drugs, the man immediately goes for treatment. In America if you did that it would be an invasion of the individual's rights and you would be sued.

I was interested to read Colin Powell, when he was chairman of the Joint Chiefs of Staff, saying that the military followed our approach because when a recruit signs up he agrees that he can be tested. Now, I would have thought this kind of approach would be quite an effective way to deal with the terrible drug problem you have. But the idea of the inviolability of the individual has been turned into dogma. And yet nobody minds when the army goes and captures the president of another state and brings him to Florida and puts him in jail. I find that incomprehensible. And in any case this approach will not solve America's drug problem. Whereas Singapore's way, we may not solve it, but we will lessen it considerably, as we have done.

FZ: Would it be fair to say that you admired America more 25 years ago? What, in your view, went wrong?

LKY: Yes, things have changed. I would hazard a guess that it has a lot to do with the erosion of the moral underpinnings of a society and the diminution of personal responsibility. The liberal, intellectual tradition that developed after World War II claimed that human beings had arrived at this perfect state where everybody would be better off if they were allowed to do their own thing and flourish. It has not worked out, and I doubt if it will. Certain basics about human nature do not change. Man needs a certain moral sense of right and wrong. There is such a thing called evil, and it is not the result of being a victim of society. You are just an evil man, prone to do evil things, and you have to be stopped from doing them. Westerners have abandoned an ethical basis for society, believing that all problems are solvable by a good government, which we in the East never believed possible.

FZ: Is such a fundamental shift in culture irreversible?

LKY: No, it is a swing of the pendulum. I think it will swing back. I don't know how long it will take, but there's already a backlash in America against failed social policies that have resulted in people urinating in public, in aggressive begging in the streets, in social breakdown.

THE ASIAN MODEL

FZ: You say that your real concern is that this system not be foisted on other societies because it will not work there. Is there another viable model for political and economic development? Is there an "Asian model"?

LKY: I don't think there is an Asian model as such. But Asian societies are unlike Western ones. The fundamental difference between Western concepts of society and government and East Asian concepts—when I say East Asians, I mean Korea, Japan, China, Vietnam, as distinct from Southeast Asia, which is a mix between the Sinic and the Indian, though Indian culture also emphasizes similar values—is that Eastern societies believe that the individual exists in the context of his family. He is not pristine and separate. The family is part of the extended family, and then friends and the wider society. The ruler or the government does not try to provide for a person what the family best provides.

In the West, especially after World War II, the government came to be seen as so successful that it could fulfill all the obligations that in less modern societies are fulfilled by the family. This approach encouraged alternative families, single mothers for instance, believing that government could provide the support to make up for the absent father. This is a bold, Huxleyan view of life, but one from which I as an East Asian shy away. I would be afraid to experiment with it. I'm not sure what the consequences are, and I don't like the consequences that I see in the West. You will find this view widely shared in East Asia. It's not that we don't have single mothers here. We are also caught in the same social problems of change when we educate our women and they become independent financially and no longer need to put up with unhappy marriages. But there is grave disquiet when we break away from tested norms, and the tested norm is the family unit. It is the building brick of society.

There is a little Chinese aphorism which encapsulates this idea: *Xiushen qijia zhiguo pingtianxia. Xiushen* means look after yourself, cultivate yourself, do everything to make yourself useful; *Qijia,* look after the family; *Zhiguo,* look after your country; *Pingtianxia,* all is peaceful under heaven. We have a whole people immersed in these beliefs. My granddaughter has the name *Xiu-qi.* My son picked out the first two words, instructing his daughter to cultivate herself and look after her family. It is the basic concept of our civilization. Governments will come, governments will go, but this endures. We start with self-reliance. In the West today it is the opposite. The government says give me a popular mandate and I will solve all society's problems.

FZ: What would you do instead to address America's problems?

LKY: What would I do if I were an American? First, you must have order in society. Guns, drugs and violent crime all go together, threatening social order. Then the schools; when you have violence in schools, you are not going to have education, so you've got to put that right. Then you have to educate rigorously and train a whole generation of skilled, intelligent, knowledgeable people who can be productive. I would start off with basics, working on the individual, looking at him within the context of his family, his friends, his society. But the Westerner says I'll fix things at the top. One magic formula, one grand plan. I will wave a wand and everything will work out. It's an interesting theory but not a proven method.

BACK TO BASICS

FZ: You are very skeptical of government's ability to solve deeper social issues. But you're more confident, certainly than many Americans are, in the government's ability to promote economic growth and technological advancement. Isn't this a contradiction?

LKY: No. We have focused on basics in Singapore. We used the family to push economic growth, factoring the ambitions of a person and his family into our planning. We have tried, for example, to improve the lot of children through education. The government can create a setting in which people can live happily and succeed and express themselves, but finally it is what people do with their lives that determines economic success or failure. Again, we were fortunate we had this cultural backdrop, the belief in thrift, hard work, filial piety and loyalty in the extended family, and, most of all, the respect for scholarship and learning.

There is, of course, another reason for our success. We have been able to create economic growth because we facilitated certain changes while we moved from an agricultural society to an industrial society. We had the advantage of knowing what the end result should be by looking at the West and later Japan. We knew where we were, and we knew where we had to go. We said to ourselves,

"Let's hasten, let's see if we can get there faster." But soon we will face a different situation. In the near future, all of us will get to the stage of Japan. Where do we go next? How do we hasten getting there when we don't know where we're going? That will be a new situation.

FZ: Some people say that the Asian model is too rigid to adapt well to change. The sociologist Mancur Olson argues that national decline is caused most fundamentally by sclerosis—the rigidity of interest groups, firms, labor, capital and the state. An American-type system that is very flexible, laissez-faire and constantly adapting is better suited to the emerging era of rapid change than a government-directed economic policy and a Confucian value system.

LKY: That is an optimistic and attractive philosophy of life, and I hope it will come true. But if you look at societies over the millennia you find certain basic patterns. American civilization from the Pilgrim fathers on is one of optimism and the growth of orderly government. History in China is of dynasties which have risen and fallen, of the waxing and waning of societies. And through all that turbulence, the family, the extended family, the clan, has provided a kind of survival raft for the individual. Civilizations have collapsed, dynasties have been swept away by conquering hordes, but this life raft enables the civilization to carry on and get to its next phase.

Nobody here really believes that the government can provide in all circumstances. The government itself does not believe it. In the ultimate crisis, even in earthquakes and typhoons, it is your human relationships that will see you through. So the thesis you quote, that the government is always capable of reinventing itself in new shapes and forms, has not been proven in history. But the family and the way human relationships are structured, do increase the survival chances of its members. That has been tested over thousands of years in many different situations.

THE CULTURE OF SUCCESS

FZ: A key ingredient of national economic success in the past has been a culture of innovation and experimentation. During their rise to great wealth and power the centers of growth—Venice, Holland, Britain, the United States—all had an atmosphere of intellectual freedom in which new ideas, technologies, methods and products could emerge. In East Asian countries, however, the government frowns upon an open and free wheeling intellectual climate. Leaving aside any kind of human rights questions this raises, does it create a productivity problem?

LKY: Intellectually that sounds like a reasonable conclusion, but I'm not sure things will work out this way. The Japanese, for instance, have not been all that

Culture Is Destiny

disadvantaged in creating new products. I think that if governments are aware of your thesis and of the need to test out new areas, to break out of existing formats, they can counter the trend. East Asians, who all share a tradition of strict discipline, respect for the teacher, no talking back to the teacher and rote learning, must make sure that there is this random intellectual search for new technologies and products. In any case, in a world where electronic communications are instantaneous, I do not see anyone lagging behind. Anything new that happens spreads quickly, whether it's superconductivity or some new life-style.

FZ: Would you agree with the World Bank report on East Asian economic success, which I interpret to have concluded that all the governments that succeeded got fundamentals right—encouraging savings and investment, keeping inflation low, providing high-quality education. The tinkering of industrial policies here and targeting sectors there was not as crucial an element in explaining these countries' extraordinary economic growth as were these basic factors.

LKY: I think the World Bank had a very difficult job. It had to write up these very, very complex series of situations. But there are cultural factors which have been lightly touched over, which deserved more weightage. This would have made it a more complex study and of less universal application, but it would have been more accurate, explaining the differences, for example, between the Philippines and Taiwan.

FZ: If culture is so important, then countries with very different cultures may not, in fact, succeed in the way that East Asia did by getting economic fundamentals right. Are you not hopeful for the countries around the world that are liberalizing their economies?

LKY: Getting the fundamentals right would help, but these societies will not succeed in the same way as East Asia did because certain driving forces will be absent. If you have a culture that doesn't place much value in learning and scholarship and hard work and thrift and deferment of present enjoyment for future gain, the going will be much slower.

But, you know, the World Bank report's conclusions are part of the culture of America and, by extension, of international institutions. It had to present its findings in a bland and universalizable way, which I find unsatisfying because it doesn't grapple with the real problems. It makes the hopeful assumption that all men are equal, that people all over the world are the same. They are not. Groups of people develop different characteristics when they have evolved for thousands of years separately. Genetics and history interact. The Native American Indian is genetically of the same stock as the Mongoloids of East Asia—the Chinese, the Koreans and the Japanese. But one group got cut off after the Bering Straits melted away. Without that land bridge they were totally isolated in America for thousands of years. The other, in East Asia, met successive invading forces from Central Asia and interacted with waves of people moving back and forth. The two groups may share certain characteristics, for instance if you measure the shape of their skulls and so on, but if you start testing them you find that they are different, most particularly in their neurological development, and their cultural values.

Now if you gloss over these kinds of issues because it is politically incorrect to study them, then you have laid a land mine for yourself. This is what leads to the disappointments with social policies, embarked upon in America with great enthusiasm and expectations, but which yield such meager results. There isn't a willingness to see things in their stark reality. But then I am not being politically correct.

FZ: Culture may be important, but it does change. The Asian "model" may prove to be a transitional phenomenon. After all, Western countries also went through a period in the eighteenth and nineteenth centuries when they were capitalist and had limited participatory democracy. Elites then worried—as you do today—that "too much" democracy and "too many" individual rights would destabilize social order. But as these societies modernized and as economic growth spread to all sections of society, things changed. Isn't East Asia changing because of a growing middle class that demands a say in its own future?

LKY: There is acute change in East Asia. We are agricultural societies that have industrialized within one or two generations. What happened in the West over 200 years or more is happening here in about 50 years or less. It is all crammed and crushed into a very tight time frame, so there are bound to be dislocations and malfunctions. If you look at the fast-growing countries—Korea, Thailand, Hong Kong, and Singapore—there's been one remarkable phenomenon: the rise of religion. Koreans have taken to Christianity in large numbers, I think some 25 percent. This is a country that was never colonized by a Christian nation. The old customs and religions—ancestor worship, shamanism—no longer completely satisfy. There is a quest for some higher explanations about man's purpose, about why we are here. This is associated with periods of great stress in society. You will find in Japan that every time it goes through a period of stress new sects crop up and new religions proliferate. In Taiwan—and also in Hong Kong and Singapore—you see a rise in the number of new temples; Confucianist temples, Taoist temples and many Christian sects.

We are all in the midst of very rapid change and at the same time we are all groping towards a destination which we hope will be identifiable with our past. We have left the past behind and there is an underlying unease that there will be nothing left of us which is part of the old. The Japanese have solved this problem to some extent. Japan has become an industrial society, while remaining essentially Japanese in its human relations. They have industrialized and shed some of their feudal values. The Taiwanese and the Koreans are trying to do the same. But whether these societies can preserve their core values and make this transition is a problem which they alone can solve. It is not something Americans can solve for them. Therefore, you will find people unreceptive to the idea that they be Westernized. Modernized, yes, in the sense that they have accepted the inevitability of science and technology and the change in the life-styles they bring.

FZ: But won't these economic and technological changes produce changes in the mind-sets of people?

LKY: It is not just mind-sets that would have to change but value systems. Let me give anecdotal evidence of this. Many Chinese families in Malaysia migrated in periods of stress, when there were race riots in Malaysia in the 1960s, and they settled in Australia and Canada. They did this for the sake of their children so that they would get a better education in the English language because then Malaysia was switching to Malay as its primary language. The children grew up, reached their late teens and left home. And suddenly the parents discovered the emptiness of the whole exercise. They had given their children a modern education in the English language and in the process lost their children altogether. That was a very sobering experience. Something less dramatic is happening in Singapore now because we are not bringing up our children in the same circumstances in which we grew up.

FZ: But these children are absorbing influences different from your generation. You say that knowledge, life-styles, culture all spread rapidly in this world. Will not the idea of democracy and individual rights also spread?

LKY: Let's not get into a debate on semantics. The system of government in China will change. It will change in Korea, Taiwan, Vietnam. It is changing in Singapore. But it will not end up like the American or British or French or German systems. What are we all seeking? A form of government that will be comfortable, because it meets our needs, is not oppressive, and maximizes our opportunities. And whether you have one-man, one-vote or some-men, one vote or other men, two votes, those are forms which should be worked out. I'm not intellectually convinced that one-man, one-vote is the best. We practice it because that's what the British bequeathed us and we haven't really found a need to challenge that. But I'm convinced, personally, that we would have a better system if we gave every man over the age of 40 who has a family two votes because he's likely to be more careful, voting also for his children. He is more likely to vote in a serious way than a capricious young man under 30. But we haven't found it necessary yet. If it became necessary we should do it. At the same time, once a person gets beyond 65, then it is a problem. Between the ages of 40 and 60 is ideal, and at 60 they should go back to one vote, but that will be difficult to arrange.

Fareed Zakaria

FZ: Change is often most threatening when it occurs in multiethnic societies. You have been part of both a multiethnic state that failed and one that has succeeded. Malaysia was unwilling to allow what it saw as a Chinese city-state to be part of it and expelled Singapore from its federation in 1965. Singapore itself, however, exists peacefully as a multiethnic state. Is there a solution for those states that have ethnic and religious groups mixed within them?

LKY: Each state faces a different set of problems and I would be most reluctant to dish out general solutions. From my own experience, I would say, *make haste slowly*. Nobody likes to lose his ethnic, cultural, religious, even linguistic identity. To exist as one state you need to share certain attributes, have things in common. If you pressure-cook you are in for problems. If you go gently, but steadily, the logic of events will bring about not assimilation, but integration. If I had tried to foist the English language on the people of Singapore I would have faced rebellion all around. If I had tried to foist the Chinese language, I'd have had immediate revolt and disaster. But I offered every parent a choice of English and their mother tongue, in whatever order they chose. By their free choice, plus the rewards of the marketplace over a period of 30 years, we have ended up with English first and the mother tongue second. We have switched one university already established in the Chinese language from Chinese into English. Had this change been forced in five or ten years instead of being done over 30 years—and by free choice—it would have been a disaster.

FZ: This sounds like a live-and-let-live kind of approach. Many Western countries, particularly the United States and France, respectively, have traditionally attempted to assimilate people toward a national mainstream—with English and French as the national language, respectively. Today this approach is being questioned, as you know, with some minority groups in the United States and France arguing for "multiculturalism," which would allow distinct and unassimilated minority groups to coexist within the nation. How does this debate strike you as you read about it in Singapore?

LKY: You cannot have too many distinct components and be one nation. It makes interchangeability difficult. If you want complete separateness then you should not come to live in the host country. But there are circumstances where it is wise to leave things be. For instance, all races in Singapore are eligible for jobs and for many other things. But we put the Muslims in a slightly different category because they are extremely sensitive about their customs, especially diet. In such matters one has to find a middle path between uniformity and a certain freedom to be somewhat different. I think it is wise to leave alone questions of fundamental beliefs and give time to sort matters out.

Culture Is Destiny

FZ: So you would look at the French handling of their Muslim minorities and say "Go slow, don't push these people so hard."

LKY: I would not want to say that because the French having ruled Algeria for many years know the kind of problems that they are faced with. My approach would be, if some Muslim girl insists on coming to school with her headdress on and is prepared to put up with that discomfort, we should be prepared to put up with the strangeness. But if she joined the customs or immigration department where it would be confusing to the millions of people who stream through to have some customs officer looking different, she must wear the uniform. That approach has worked in Singapore so far.

IS EUROPE'S PAST ASIA'S FUTURE?

FZ: Let me shift gears somewhat and ask you some questions about the international climate in East Asia. The part of the world you live in is experiencing the kind of growth that the West has experienced for the last 400 years. The West has not only been the world's great producer of wealth for four centuries, it has also been the world's great producer of war. Today East Asia is the locus of great and unsettling growth, with several newly rising powers close to each other, many with different political systems, historical animosities, border disputes, and all with ever-increasing quantities of arms. Should one look at this and ask whether Europe's past will be East Asia's future?

LKY: No, it's too simplistic. One reason why growth is likely to last for many years in East Asia—and this is just a guess—is that the peoples and the governments of East Asia have learned some powerful lessons about the viciousness and destructiveness of wars. Not only full-scale wars like in Korea, but guerrilla wars as in Vietnam, in Cambodia and in the jungles of Malaysia, Thailand, Indonesia and the Philippines. We all know that the more you engage in conflict, the poorer and the more desperate you become. Visit Cambodia and Vietnam; *the world just passed them by.* That lesson will live for a very long time, at least as long as this generation is alive.

FZ: The most unsettling change in an international system is the rise of a new great power. Can the rise of China be accommodated into the East Asian order? Isn't that kind of growth inevitably destabilizing?

LKY: I don't think we can speak in terms of just the East Asian order. The question is: Can the world develop a system in which a country the size of China becomes part of the management of international peace and stability? Sometime in the next 20 or 30 years the world, by which I mean the major powers, will have to agree among themselves how to manage peace and stability, how to create a system that is both viable and fair. Wars between small countries won't destroy the whole world, but will only destroy themselves. But big conflicts between big powers will destroy the world many times over. That's just too disastrous to contemplate.

At the end of the last war what they could foresee was the United Nations. The hope was that the permanent five would maintain the rule of law or gradually spread the rule of law in international relations. It did not come off because of Stalin and the Cold War. This is now a new phase. The great powers—by which I mean America, Western Europe as a group if they become a union, Japan, China and, in 20 to 30 years time, the Russian republic—have got to find a balance between themselves. I think the best way forward is through the United Nations. It already has 48 years of experience. It is imperfect, but what is the alternative? You can not have a consortium of five big powers lording it over the rest of mankind. They will not have the moral authority or legitimacy to do it. Are they going to divide the world into five spheres of influence? So they have to fall back on some multilateral framework and work out a set of rules that makes it viable. There may be conflicts of a minor nature, for instance between two Latin American countries or two small Southeast Asian countries; that doesn't really matter. Now if you have two big countries in South Asia like India and Pakistan and both with nuclear capabilities, then something has to be done. It is in that context that we have to find a place for China when it becomes a major economic and military power.

FZ: Is the Chinese regime stable? Is the growth that's going on there sustainable? Is the balancing act between economic reform and political control that Deng Xiaoping is trying to keep going sustainable after his death?

LKY: The regime in Beijing is more stable than any alternative government that can be formed in China. Let us assume that the students had carried the day at Tiananmen and they had formed a government. The same students who were at Tiananmen went to France and America. They've been quarreling with each other ever since. What kind of China would they have today? Something worse than the Soviet Union. China is a vast, disparate country; there is no alternative to strong central power.

FZ: Do you worry that the kind of rapid and unequal growth taking place in China might cause the country to break up?

LKY: First, the economy is growing everywhere, even in Sichuan, in the heart of the interior. Disparate growth rates are inevitable. It is the difference between, say, California before the recession and the Rust Belt. There will be enormous stresses because of the size of the country and the intractable nature of the problems—the poor infrastructure, the weak institutions, the wrong systems that they have installed, modeling themselves upon the Soviet system in Stalin's time. Given all those handicaps, I am amazed that they have got so far.

FZ: What about the other great East Asian power? If Japan continues on the current trajectory, should the world encourage the expansion of its political and military responsibilities and power?

LKY: No. I know that the present generation of Japanese leaders do not want to project power. I'm not sure what follows when leaders born after the war take charge. I doubt if there will be a sudden change. If Japan can carry on with its current policy, leaving security to the Americans and concentrating on the economic and the political, the world will be better off. And the Japanese are quite happy to do this. It is when America feels that it's too burdensome and not worth the candle to be present in East Asia to protect Japan that it will have to look after its own security. When Japan becomes a separate player, it is an extra joker in the pack of cards.

FZ: You've said recently that allowing Japan to send its forces abroad is like giving liquor to an alcoholic.

LKY: The Japanese have always had this cultural trait, that whatever they do they carry it to the nth degree. I think they know this. I have Japanese friends who have told me this. They admit that this is a problem with them.

FZ: What if Japan did follow the trajectory that most great powers have; that it was not content simply to be an economic superpower, "a bank with a flag" in a writer's phrase? What if they decided they wanted to have the ultimate mark of a great power—nuclear weapons? What should the world do?

LKY: If they decided on that the world will not be able to stop them. You are unable to stop North Korea. Nobody believes that an American government that could not sustain its mission in Somalia because of an ambush and one television snippet of a dead American pulled through the streets in Mogadishu could contemplate a strike on North Korean nuclear facilities like the Israeli strike on Iraq. Therefore it can only be sanctions in the U.N. Security Council. That requires that there be no vetoes. Similarly, if the Japanese decide to go nuclear, I don't believe you will be able to stop them. But they know that they face a nuclear power in China and in Russia, and so they would have to posture themselves in such a way as not to invite a preemptive strike. If they can avoid a preemptive strike then a balance will be established. Each will deter the others.

Fareed Zakaria

FZ: So it's the transition period that you are worried about.

LKY: I would prefer that the matter never arises and I believe so does the world. Whether the Japanese go down the military path will depend largely on America's strength and its willingness to be engaged.

VIVE LA DIFFERENCE

FZ: Is there some contradiction here between your role as a politician and your new role as an intellectual, speaking out on all matters? As a politician you want America as a strong balancer in the region, a country that is feared and respected all over the world. As an intellectual, however, you choose to speak out forcefully against the American model in a way that has to undermine America's credibility abroad.

LKY: That's preposterous. The last thing I would want to do is to undermine her credibility. America has been unusual in the history of the world, being the sole possessor of power—the nuclear weapon—and the one and only government in the world unaffected by war damage whilst the others were in ruins. Any old and established nation would have ensured its supremacy for as long as it could. But America set out to put her defeated enemies on their feet, to ward off an evil force, the Soviet Union, brought about technological change by transferring technology generously and freely to Europeans and to Japanese, and enabled them to become her challengers within 30 years. By 1975 they were at her heels. That's unprecedented in history. There was a certain greatness of spirit born out of the fear of communism plus American idealism that brought that about. But that does not mean that we all admire everything about America.

Let me be frank; if we did not have the good points of the West to guide us, we wouldn't have got out of our backwardness. We would have been a backward economy with a backward society. But we do not want all of the West.

A CODA ON CULTURE

THE DOMINANT theme throughout our conversation was culture. Lee returned again and again to his views on the importance of culture and the differences between Confucianism and Western values. In this respect, Lee is very much part of a trend. Culture is in. From business consultants to military strategists, people talk about culture as the deepest and most determinative aspect of human life.

I remain skeptical. If culture is destiny, what explains a culture's failure in one era and success in another? If Confucianism explains the economic boom in East Asia today, does it not also explain that region's stagnation for four centuries? In fact, when East Asia seemed immutably poor, many scholars—most famously Max Weber—made precisely that case, arguing that Confucian-based cultures discouraged all the attributes necessary for success in capitalism. Today scholars explain how Confucianism emphasizes the essential traits for economic dynamism. Were Latin American countries to succeed in the next few decades, we shall surely read encomiums to Latin culture. I suspect that since we cannot find one simple answer to why certain societies succeed at certain times, we examine successful societies and search within their cultures for the seeds of success. Cultures being complex, one finds in them what one wants.

What explains Lee Kuan Yew's fascination with culture? It is not something he was born with. Until his thirties he was called "Harry" Lee (and still is by family and friends). In the 1960s the British foreign secretary could say to him, "Harry, you're the best bloody Englishman east of the Suez." This is not a man untouched by the West. Part of his interest in cultural differences is surely that they provide a coherent defense against what he sees as Western democratic imperialism. But a deeper reason is revealed in something he said in our conversation: "We have left the past behind, and there is an underlying unease that there will be nothing left of us which is part of the old."

Cultures change. Under the impact of economic growth, technological change and social transformation, no culture has remained the same. Most of the attributes that Lee sees in Eastern cultures were once part of the West. Four hundred years of economic growth changed things. From the very beginning of England's economic boom, many Englishmen worried that as their country became rich it was losing its moral and ethical base. "Wealth accumulates and men decay," wrote Oliver Goldsmith in 1770. It is this "decay" that Lee is trying to stave off. He speaks of the anxious search for religion in East Asia today, and while he never says this, his own quest for a Confucian alternative to the West is part of this search.

But to be modern without becoming more Western is difficult; the two are not wholly separable. The West has left a mark on "the rest," and it is not simply a legacy of technology and material products. It is, perhaps most profoundly, in the realm of ideas. At the close of the interview Lee handed me three pages. This was, he explained, to emphasize how alien Confucian culture is to the West. The pages were from the book *East Asia: Tradition and Transformation,* by John Fairbank, an American scholar.✿

Is Culture Destiny?

The Myth of Asia's Anti-Democratic Values

Kim Dae Jung

IN HIS INTERVIEW with *Foreign Affairs* (March/April 1994), Singapore's former prime minister, Lee Kuan Yew, presents interesting ideas about cultural differences between Western and East Asian societies and the political implications of those differences. Although he does not explicitly say so, his statements throughout the interview and his track record make it obvious that his admonition to Americans "not to foist their system indiscriminately on societies in which it will not work" implies that Western-style democracy is not applicable to East Asia. Considering the esteem in which he is held among world leaders and the prestige of this journal, this kind of argument is likely to have considerable impact and therefore deserves a careful reply.

With the collapse of the Soviet Union in 1991, socialism has been in retreat. Some people conclude that the Soviet demise was the result of the victory of capitalism over socialism. But I believe it represented the triumph of democracy over dictatorship. Without democracy, capitalism in Prussian Germany and Meiji Japan eventually met its tragic end. The many Latin American states that in recent decades embraced capitalism while rejecting democracy failed miserably. On the other hand, countries practicing democratic capitalism or democratic socialism, despite temporary setbacks, have prospered.

KIM DAE JUNG was a dissident, human rights activist, and presidential candidate during a political career of more than four decades in the Republic of Korea. He is currently Chairman of the Kim Dae Jung Peace Foundation for the Asia-Pacific Region. This article appeared in the November/December 1994 issue of *Foreign Affairs*.

Is Culture Destiny?

In spite of these trends, lingering doubts remain about the applicability of and prospects for democracy in Asia. Such doubts have been raised mainly by Asia's authoritarian leaders, Lee being the most articulate among them. They have long maintained that cultural differences make the "Western concept" of democracy and human rights inapplicable to East Asia. Does Asia have the philosophical and historical underpinnings suitable for democracy? Is democracy achievable there?

SELF-SERVING SELF-RELIANCE

Lee stresses cultural factors throughout his interview. I too believe in the importance of culture, but I do not think it alone determines a society's fate, nor is it immutable. Moreover, Lee's view of Asian cultures is not only unsupportable but self-serving. He argues that Eastern societies, unlike Western ones, "believe that the individual exists in the context of his family" and that the family is "the building brick of society." However, as an inevitable consequence of industrialization, the family-centered East Asian societies are also rapidly moving toward self-centered individualism. Nothing in human history is permanent.

Lee asserts that, in the East, "the ruler or the government does not try to provide for a person what the family best provides." He cites this ostensibly self-reliant, family-oriented culture as the main cause of East Asia's economic successes and ridicules Western governments for allegedly trying to solve all of society's problems, even as he worries about the moral breakdown of Western societies due to too much democracy and too many individual rights. Consequently, according to Lee, the Western political system, with its intrusive government, is not suited to family-oriented East Asia. He rejects Westernization while embracing modernization and its attendant changes in lifestyle—again strongly implying that democracy will not work in Asia.

FAMILY VALUES (REQUIRED HERE)

But the facts demonstrate just the opposite. It is not true, as Lee alleges, that Asian governments shy away from intervening in private matters and taking on all of society's problems. Asian governments intrude much more than Western governments into the daily affairs of individuals and families. In Korea, for example, each household is required to attend monthly neighborhood meetings to receive government directives and discuss local affairs. Japan's powerful government constantly intrudes into the business world to protect perceived national interests, to the point of causing disputes with the United States and other trading partners. In Lee's Singapore, the government stringently regulates individuals' actions—such as chewing bubble-gum, spitting, smoking, littering, and so on—to an Orwellian extreme of social engineering. Such facts fly in the face of his assertion that East Asia's governments are minimalist. Lee makes these false claims to justify his rejection of Western-style democracy. He even dislikes the one man, one vote principle, so fundamental to modern democracy, saying that he is not "intellectually convinced" it is best.

Opinions like Lee's hold considerable sway not only in Asia but among some Westerners because of the moral breakdown of many advanced democratic societies. Many Americans thought, for example, that the U.S. citizen Michael Fay deserved the caning he received from Singaporean authorities for his act of vandalism. However, moral breakdown is attributable not to inherent shortcomings of Western cultures but to those of industrial societies; a similar phenomenon is now spreading through Asia's newly industrializing societies. The fact that Lee's Singapore, a small city-state, needs a near-totalitarian police state to assert control over its citizens contradicts his assertion that everything would be all right if governments would refrain from interfering in the private affairs of the family. The proper way to cure the ills of industrial societies is not to impose the terror of a police state but to emphasize ethical education, give high regard to spiritual values, and promote high standards in culture and the arts.

LONG BEFORE LOCKE

NO ONE CAN argue with Lee's objection to "foisting" an alien system "indiscriminately on societies in which it will not work." The question is whether democracy is a system so alien to Asian cultures that it will not work. Moreover, considering Lee's record of absolute intolerance of dissent and the continued crackdown on dissidents in many other Asian countries, one is also compelled to ask whether democracy has been given a chance in places like Singapore.

Is Culture Destiny?

A thorough analysis makes it clear that Asia has a rich heritage of democracy-oriented philosophies and traditions. Asia has already made great strides toward democratization and possesses the necessary conditions to develop democracy even beyond the level of the West.

Democratic Ideals. It is widely accepted that English political philosopher John Locke laid the foundation for modern democracy. According to Locke, sovereign rights reside with the people and, based on a contract with the people, leaders are given a mandate to govern, which the people can withdraw. But almost two millennia before Locke, Chinese philosopher Meng-tzu preached similar ideas. According to his "Politics of Royal Ways," the king is the "Son of Heaven," and heaven bestowed on its son a mandate to provide good government, that is, to provide good for the people. If he did not govern righteously, the people had the right to rise up and overthrow his government in the name of heaven. Meng-tzu even justified regicide, saying that once a king loses the mandate of heaven he is no longer worthy of his subjects' loyalty. The people came first, Meng-tzu said, the country second, and the king third. The ancient Chinese philosophy of *Minben Zhengchi,* or "people-based politics," teaches that "the will of the people is the will of heaven" and that one should "respect the people as heaven" itself.

A native religion of Korea, Tonghak, went even further, advocating that "man is heaven" and that one must serve man as one does heaven. These ideas inspired and motivated nearly half a million peasants in 1894 to revolt against exploitation by feudalistic government internally and imperialistic forces externally. There are no ideas more fundamental to democracy than the teachings of Confucianism, Buddhism, and Tonghak. Clearly, Asia has democratic philosophies as profound as those of the West.

Democratic Institutions. Asia also has many democratic traditions. When Western societies were still being ruled by a succession of feudal lords, China and Korea had already sustained county prefecture systems for about 2,000 years. The government of the Chin Dynasty, founded by Chin-shih huang-ti (literally, the founder of Chin), practiced the rule of law and saw to it that everyone, regardless of class, was treated fairly. For nearly 1,000 years in China and Korea, even the sons of high-ranking officials were not appointed to important official positions unless they passed civil service examinations. These stringent tests were administered to members of the aristocratic class, who constituted over ten percent of the population, thus guaranteeing equal opportunity and social mobility, which are so central to popular democracy. This practice sharply contrasted with that of European fiefdoms of that time, where pedigree more or less determined one's official position. In China and Korea powerful boards of censors acted as a check against imperial misrule and abuses by government officials. Freedom of speech was highly valued, based on the understanding that the nation's fate depended on it. Confucian scholars were taught that remonstration against an erring monarch was a paramount duty. Many civil servants and promising political elites gave their lives to protect the right to free speech.

The fundamental ideas and traditions necessary for democracy existed in both Europe and Asia. Although Asians developed these ideas long before the Europeans did, Europeans formalized comprehensive and effective electoral democracy first. The invention of the electoral system is Europe's greatest accomplishment. The fact that this system was developed elsewhere does not mean that "it will not work" in Asia. Many Asian countries, including Singapore, have become prosperous after adopting a "Western" free-market economy, which is such an integral part of a democracy. Incidentally, in countries where economic development preceded political advancement—Germany, Italy, Japan, Spain—it was only a matter of time before democracy followed.

The State of Democracy in Asia. The best proof that democracy can work in Asia is the fact that, despite the stubborn resistance of authoritarian rulers like Lee, Asia has made great strides toward democracy. In fact, Asia has achieved the most remarkable record of democratization of any region since 1974. By 1990 a majority of Asian countries were democracies, compared to a 45 percent democratization rate worldwide.[1] This achievement has been overshadowed by Asia's tremendous economic success. I believe democracy will take root throughout Asia around the start of the next century. By the end of its first quarter, Asia will witness an era not only of economic prosperity, but also of flourishing democracy.

I am optimistic for several reasons. The Asian economies are moving from a capital- and labor-intensive industrial phase into an information- and technology-intensive one. Many experts have acknowledged that this new economic world order requires guaranteed freedom of information and creativity. These things are possible only in a democratic society. Thus Asia has no practical alternative to democracy; it is a matter of survival in an age of intensifying global economic competition. The world

---

[1]Samuel Huntington, *The Third Wave*, Norman: University of Oklahoma Press, 1991.

economy's changes have already meant a greater and easier flow of information, which has helped Asia's democratization process.

Democracy has been consistently practiced in Japan and India since the end of World War II. In Korea, Burma, Taiwan, Thailand, Pakistan, the Philippines, Bangladesh, Sri Lanka, and other countries, democracy has been frustrated at times, even suspended. Nevertheless, most of these countries have democratized, and in all of them, a resilient "people power" has been demonstrated through elections and popular movements. Even in Thailand, after ten military governments, a civilian government has finally emerged. The Mongolian government, after a long period of one-party dictatorship, has also voluntarily accepted democracy. The fundamental reason for my optimism is this increasing awareness of the importance of democracy and human rights among Asians themselves and their willingness to make the necessary efforts to realize these goals. Despite many tribulations, the torch of democracy continues to burn in Asia because of the aspirations of its people.

WE ARE THE WORLD

As ASIANS increasingly embrace democratic values, they have the opportunity and obligation to learn from older democracies. The West has experienced many problems in realizing its democratic systems. It is instructive, for example, to remember that Europeans practiced democracy within the boundaries of their nation-states but not outside. Until recently, the Western democracies coddled the interests of a small propertied class. The democracies that benefited much broader majorities through socioeconomic investments were mostly established after World War II. Today, we must start with a rebirth of democracy that promotes freedom, prosperity, and justice both within each country and among nations, including the less-developed countries: a global democracy.

Instead of making Western culture the scapegoat for the disruptions of rapid economic change, it is more appropriate to look at how the traditional strengths of Asian society can provide for a better democracy. In Asia, democracy can encourage greater self-reliance while respecting cultural values. Such a democracy is the only true expression of a people, but it requires the full participation of all elements of society. Only then will it have legitimacy and reflect a country's vision.

Kim Dae Jung

Asian authoritarians misunderstand the relationship between the rules of effective governance and the concept of legitimacy. Policies that try to protect people from the bad elements of economic and social change will never be effective if imposed without consent; the same policies, arrived at through public debate, will have the strength of Asia's proud and self-reliant people.

A global democracy will recognize the connection between how we treat each other and how we treat nature, and it will pursue policies that benefit future generations. Today we are threatening the survival of our environment through wholesale destruction and endangerment of all species. Our democracy must become global in the sense that it extends to the skies, the earth, and all things with brotherly affection.

The Confucian maxim *Xiushen qijia zhiguo pingtianxia,* which offers counsel toward the ideal of "great peace under heaven," shows an appreciation for judicious government. The ultimate goal in Confucian political philosophy, as stated in this aphorism, is to bring peace under heaven (*pingtianxia*). To do so, one must first be able to keep one's own household in order (*qijia*), which in turn requires that one cultivate "self" (*xiushen*). This teaching is a political philosophy that emphasizes the role of government and stresses the ruling elite's moral obligation to strive to bring about peace under heaven. Public safety, national security, and water and forest management are deemed critical. This concept of peace under heaven should be interpreted to include peaceful living and existence for all things under heaven. Such an understanding can also be derived from Gautama Buddha's teaching that all creatures and things possess a Buddha-like quality.

Since the fifth century B.C., the world has witnessed a series of revolutions in thought. Chinese, Indian, Greek, and Jewish thinkers have led great revolutions in ideas, and we are still living under the influence of their insights. However, for the past several hundred years, the world has been dominated by Greek and Judeo-Christian ideas and traditions. Now it is time for the world to turn to China, India, and the rest of Asia for another revolution in ideas. We need to strive for a new democracy that guarantees the right of personal development for all human beings and the wholesome existence of all living things.

A natural first step toward realizing such a new democracy would be full adherence to the Universal Declaration of Human Rights, adopted by the United Nations in 1948. This international document reflects basic respect for the dignity of people, and Asian nations should take the lead in implementing it.

The movement for democracy in Asia has been carried forward mainly by Asia's small but effective army of dedicated people in and out of political parties, encouraged by nongovernmental and quasi-governmental organizations for democratic development from around the world. These are hopeful signs for Asia's democratic future. Such groups are gaining in their ability to force governments to listen to the concerns of their people, and they should be supported.

Asia should lose no time in firmly establishing democracy and strengthening human rights. The biggest obstacle is not its cultural heritage but the resistance of authoritarian rulers and their apologists. Asia has much to offer the rest of the world; its rich heritage of democracy-oriented philosophies and traditions can make a significant contribution to the evolution of global democracy. Culture is not necessarily our destiny. Democracy is.☯

The Rise of
Illiberal Democracy

Fareed Zakaria

THE NEXT WAVE

THE AMERICAN diplomat Richard Holbrooke pondered a problem on the eve of the September 1996 elections in Bosnia, which were meant to restore civic life to that ravaged country. "Suppose the election was declared free and fair," he said, and those elected are "racists, fascists, separatists, who are publicly opposed to [peace and reintegration]. That is the dilemma." Indeed it is, not just in the former Yugoslavia, but increasingly around the world. Democratically elected regimes, often ones that have been reelected or reaffirmed through referenda, are routinely ignoring constitutional limits on their power and depriving their citizens of basic rights and freedoms. From Peru to the Palestinian Authority, from Sierra Leone to Slovakia, from Pakistan to the Philippines, we see the rise of a disturbing phenomenon in international life—illiberal democracy.

It has been difficult to recognize this problem because for almost a century in the West, democracy has meant *liberal* democracy—a political system marked not only by free and fair elections, but also by the rule of law, a separation of powers, and the protection of basic liberties of speech, assembly, religion, and property. In fact, this latter bundle of freedoms— what might be termed constitutional liberalism—is theoretically different and historically distinct from democracy. As the political scientist Philippe Schmitter has pointed out, "Liberalism, either as a conception of political liberty, or as a doctrine about economic policy, may have coincided with the rise of democracy. But it has never been immutably or unambiguously linked to its practice." Today the two strands of liberal democracy, interwoven in the Western political fabric, are coming apart in the rest of the world. Democracy is flourishing; constitutional liberalism is not.

FAREED ZAKARIA is Managing Editor of *Foreign Affairs* and a Contributing Editor for *Newsweek*.

The Rise of Illiberal Democracy

Today, 118 of the world's 193 countries are democratic, encompassing a majority of its people (54.8 percent, to be exact), a vast increase from even a decade ago. In this season of victory, one might have expected Western statesmen and intellectuals to go one further than E. M. Forster and give a rousing three cheers for democracy. Instead there is a growing unease at the rapid spread of multiparty elections across south-central Europe, Asia, Africa, and Latin America, perhaps because of what happens *after* the elections. Popular leaders like Russia's Boris Yeltsin and Argentina's Carlos Menem bypass their parliaments and rule by presidential decree, eroding basic constitutional practices. The Iranian parliament—elected more freely than most in the Middle East—imposes harsh restrictions on speech, assembly, and even dress, diminishing that country's already meager supply of liberty. Ethiopia's elected government turns its security forces on journalists and political opponents, doing permanent damage to human rights (as well as human beings).

Naturally there is a spectrum of illiberal democracy, ranging from modest offenders like Argentina to near-tyrannies like Kazakstan and Belarus, with countries like Romania and Bangladesh in between. Along much of the spectrum, elections are rarely as free and fair as in the West today, but they do reflect the reality of popular participation in politics and support for those elected. And the examples are not isolated or atypical. Freedom House's 1996-97 survey, *Freedom in the World,* has separate rankings for political liberties and civil liberties, which correspond roughly with democracy and constitutional liberalism, respectively. Of the countries that lie between confirmed dictatorship and consolidated democracy, 50 percent do better on political liberties than on civil ones. In other words, half of the "democratizing" countries in the world today are illiberal democracies.[1]

Illiberal democracy is a growth industry. Seven years ago only 22 percent of democratizing countries could have been so categorized; five years ago that

---

[1] Roger Kaplan, ed., *Freedom Around the World, 1997,* New York: Freedom House, 1997, pp. 21-22. The survey rates countries on two 7-point scales, for political rights and civil liberties (lower is better). I have considered all countries with a combined score of between 5 and 10 to be democratizing. The percentage figures are based on Freedom House's numbers, but in the case of individual countries I have not adhered strictly to its ratings. While the *Survey* is an extraordinary feat—comprehensive and intelligent—its methodology conflates certain constitutional rights with democratic procedures, which confuses matters. In addition, I use as examples (though not as part of the data set) countries like Iran, Kazakstan, and Belarus, which even in procedural terms are semi-democracies at best. But they are worth highlighting as interesting problem cases since most of their leaders were elected, reelected, and remain popular.

figure had risen to 35 percent.[2] And to date few illiberal democracies have matured into liberal democracies; if anything, they are moving toward heightened illiberalism. Far from being a temporary or transitional stage, it appears that many countries are settling into a form of government that mixes a substantial degree of democracy with a substantial degree of illiberalism. Just as nations across the world have become comfortable with many variations of capitalism, they could well adopt and sustain varied forms of democracy. Western liberal democracy might prove to be not the final destination on the democratic road, but just one of many possible exits.

DEMOCRACY AND LIBERTY

FROM THE TIME of Herodotus democracy has meant, first and foremost, the rule of the people. This view of democracy as a process of selecting governments, articulated by scholars ranging from Alexis de Tocqueville to Joseph Schumpeter to Robert Dahl, is now widely used by social scientists. In *The Third Wave,* Samuel P. Huntington explains why:

> Elections, open, free and fair, are the essence of democracy, the inescapable sine qua non. Governments produced by elections may be inefficient, corrupt, shortsighted,
> irresponsible, dominated by special interests, and incapable of adopting policies demanded by the public good. These qualities make such govern-ments undesirable but they do not make them undemocratic. Democracy is one public virtue, not the only one, and the relation of democracy to other public virtues and vices can only be understood if democracy is clearly distinguished from the other characteristics of political systems.

This definition also accords with the commonsense view of the term. If a country holds competitive, multiparty elections, we call it democratic. When public participation in politics is increased, for example through the enfranchisement of women, it is seen as more democratic. Of course elections must be open and fair, and this requires some protections for freedom of speech and assembly. But to go beyond this minimalist definition and label a country democratic only if it guarantees a comprehensive catalog of social, political, economic, and religious rights turns the word democracy into a badge of honor rather than a descriptive category. After all, Sweden has an

---

[2]*Freedom in the World: The Annual Survey of Political Rights and Civil Liberties, 1992-1993,* pp. 620-26; *Freedom in the World, 1989-1990,* pp. 312-19.

economic system that many argue curtails individual property rights, France until recently had a state monopoly on television, and England has an established religion. But they are all clearly and identifiably democracies. To have democracy mean, subjectively, "a good government" renders it analytically useless.

Constitutional liberalism, on the other hand, is not about the procedures for selecting government, but rather government's goals. It refers to the tradition, deep in Western history, that seeks to protect an individual's autonomy and dignity against coercion, whatever the source—state, church, or society. The term marries two closely connected ideas. It is *liberal* because it draws on the philosophical strain, beginning with the Greeks, that emphasizes individual liberty.[3] It is *constitutional* because it rests on the tradition, beginning with the Romans, of the rule of law. Constitutional liberalism developed in Western Europe and the United States as a defense of the individual's right to life and property, and freedom of religion and speech. To secure these rights, it emphasized checks on the power of each branch of government, equality under the law, impartial courts and tribunals, and separation of church and state. Its canonical figures include the poet John Milton, the jurist William Blackstone, statesmen such as Thomas Jefferson and James Madison, and philosophers such as Thomas Hobbes, John Locke, Adam Smith, Baron de Montesquieu, John Stuart Mill, and Isaiah Berlin. In almost all of its variants, constitutional liberalism argues that human beings have certain natural (or "inalienable") rights and that governments must accept a basic law, limiting its own powers, that secures them. Thus in 1215 at Runnymede, England's barons forced the king to abide by the settled and customary law of the land. In the American colonies these laws were made explicit, and in 1638 the town of Hartford adopted the first written constitution in modern history. In the 1970s, Western nations codified standards of behavior for regimes across the globe. The Magna Carta, the Fundamental Orders of Connecticut, the American Constitution, and the Helsinki Final Act are all expressions of constitutional liberalism.

THE ROAD TO LIBERAL DEMOCRACY

SINCE 1945 Western governments have, for the most part, embodied both democracy and constitutional liberalism. Thus it is difficult to imagine the two apart, in the form of either illiberal democracy or liberal autocracy. In fact both have existed in the past and persist in the present. Until the twentieth

---

[3]The term "liberal" is used here in its older, European sense, now often called classical liberalism. In America today the word has come to mean something quite different, namely policies upholding the modern welfare state.

century, most countries in Western Europe were liberal autocracies or, at best, semi-democracies. The franchise was tightly restricted, and elected legislatures had little power. In 1830 Great Britain, in some ways the most democratic European nation, allowed barely 2 percent of its population to vote for one house of Parliament; that figure rose to 7 percent after 1867 and reached around 40 percent in the 1880s. Only in the late 1940s did most Western countries become full-fledged democracies, with universal adult suffrage. But one hundred years earlier, by the late 1840s, most of them had adopted important aspects of constitutional liberalism—the rule of law, private property rights, and increasingly, separated powers and free speech and assembly. For much of modern history, what characterized governments in Europe and North America, and differentiated them from those around the world, was not democracy but constitutional liberalism. The "Western model" is best symbolized not by the mass plebiscite but the impartial judge.

The recent history of East Asia follows the Western itinerary. After brief flirtations with democracy after World War II, most East Asian regimes turned authoritarian. Over time they moved from autocracy to liberalizing autocracy, and, in some cases, toward liberalizing semi-democracy.[4] Most of the regimes in East Asia remain only semi-democratic, with patriarchs or one-party systems that make their elections ratifications of power rather than genuine contests. But these regimes have accorded their citizens a widening sphere of economic, civil, religious, and limited political rights. As in the West, liberalization in East Asia has included economic liberalization, which is crucial in promoting both growth and liberal democracy. Historically, the factors most closely associated with full-fledged liberal democracies are capitalism, a bourgeoisie, and a high per capita gnp. Today's East Asian governments are a mix of democracy, liberalism, capitalism, oligarchy, and corruption—much like Western governments circa 1900.

Constitutional liberalism has led to democracy, but democracy does not seem to bring constitutional liberalism. In contrast to the Western and East Asian paths, during the last two decades in Latin America, Africa, and parts of Asia, dictatorships with little background in constitutional liberalism have given way to democracy. The results are not encouraging. In the western

---

[4]Indonesia, Singapore, and Malaysia are examples of liberalizing autocracies, while South Korea, Taiwan, and Thailand are liberal semi-democracies. Both groups, however, are more liberal than they are democratic, which is also true of the region's only liberal democracy, Japan; Papua New Guinea, and to a lesser extent the Philippines, are the only examples of illiberal democracy in East Asia.

hemisphere, with elections having been held in every country except Cuba, a 1993 study by the scholar Larry Diamond determined that 10 of the 22 principal Latin American countries "have levels of human rights abuse that are incompatible with the consolidation of [liberal] democracy."[5] In Africa, democratization has been extraordinarily rapid. Within six months in 1990 much of Francophone Africa lifted its ban on multiparty politics. Yet although elections have been held in most of the 45 sub-Saharan states since 1991 (18 in 1996 alone), there have been setbacks for freedom in many countries. One of Africa's most careful observers, Michael Chege, surveyed the wave of democratization and drew the lesson that the continent had "overemphasized multiparty elections . . . and correspondingly neglected the basic tenets of liberal governance." In Central Asia, elections, even when reasonably free, as in Kyrgyzstan and Kazakstan, have resulted in strong executives, weak legislatures and judiciaries, and few civil and economic liberties. In the Islamic world, from the Palestinian Authority to Iran to Pakistan, democratization has led to an increasing role for theocratic politics, eroding long-standing traditions of secularism and tolerance. In many parts of that world, such as Tunisia, Morocco, Egypt, and some of the Gulf States, were elections to be held tomorrow, the resulting regimes would almost certainly be more illiberal than the ones now in place.

Many of the countries of Central Europe, on the other hand, have moved successfully from communism to liberal democracy, having gone through the same phase of liberalization without democracy as other European countries did during the nineteenth century. Indeed, the Austro-Hungarian empire, to which most belonged, was a classic liberal autocracy. Even outside Europe, the political scientist Myron Weiner detected a striking connection between a constitutional past and a liberal democratic present. He pointed out that, as of 1983, "every single country in the Third World that emerged from colonial rule since the Second World War with a population of at least one million (and almost all the smaller colonies as well) with a continuous democratic experience is a former British colony."[6] British rule meant not democracy—colonialism is by definition undemocratic—but constitutional

---

[5] Larry Diamond, "Democracy in Latin America," in Tom Farer, ed., *Beyond Sovereignty: Collectively Defending Democracy in a World of Sovereign States*, Baltimore: Johns Hopkins University Press, 1996, p. 73.

[6] Myron Weiner, "Empirical Democratic Theory," in Myron Weiner and Ergun Ozbudun, eds., *Competitive Elections in Developing Countries*, Durham: Duke University Press, 1987, p. 20. Today there are functioning democracies in the Third World that are not former British colonies, but the majority of the former are the latter.

liberalism. Britain's legacy of law and administration has proved more beneficial than France's policy of enfranchising some of its colonial populations.

While liberal autocracies may have existed in the past, can one imagine them today? Until recently, a small but powerful example flourished off the Asian mainland—Hong Kong. For 156 years, until July 1, 1997, Hong Kong was ruled by the British Crown through an appointed governor general. Until 1991 it had never held a meaningful election, but its government epitomized constitutional liberalism, protecting its citizens' basic rights and administering a fair court system and bureaucracy. A September 8, 1997, editorial on the island's future in *The Washington Post* was titled ominously, "Undoing Hong Kong's Democracy." Actually, Hong Kong has precious little democracy to undo; what it has is a framework of rights and laws. Small islands may not hold much practical significance in today's world, but they do help one weigh the relative value of democracy and constitutional liberalism. Consider, for example, the question of where you would rather live, Haiti, an illiberal democracy, or Antigua, a liberal semi-democracy. Your choice would probably relate not to the weather, which is pleasant in both, but to the political climate, which is not.

ABSOLUTE SOVEREIGNTY

JOHN STUART MILL opened his classic *On Liberty* by noting that as countries became democratic, people tended to believe that "too much importance had been attached to the limitation of power itself. That . . . was a response against rulers whose interests were opposed to those of the people." Once the people were themselves in charge, caution was unnecessary. "The nation did not need to be protected against its own will." As if confirming Mill's fears, consider the words of Alexandr Lukashenko after being elected president of Belarus with an overwhelming majority in a free election in 1994, when asked about limiting his powers: "There will be no dictatorship. I am of the people, and I am going to be for the people."

The tension between constitutional liberalism and democracy centers on the scope of governmental authority. Constitutional liberalism is about the limitation of power, democracy about its accumulation and use. For this reason, many eighteenth- and nineteenth-century liberals saw in democracy a force that could undermine liberty. James Madison explained in *The Federalist* that "the danger of oppression" in a democracy came from "the majority of the community." Tocqueville warned of the "tyranny of the majority," writing, "The very essence of democratic government consists in the absolute sovereignty of the majority."

The Rise of Illiberal Democracy

The tendency for a democratic government to believe it has absolute sovereignty (that is, power) can result in the centralization of authority, often by extraconstitutional means and with grim results. Over the last decade, elected governments claiming to represent the people have steadily encroached on the powers and rights of other elements in society, a usurpation that is both horizontal (from other branches of the national government) and vertical (from regional and local authorities as well as private businesses and other nongovernmental groups). Lukashenko and Peru's Alberto Fujimori are only the worst examples of this practice. (While Fujimori's actions—disbanding the legislature and suspending the constitution, among others—make it difficult to call his regime democratic, it is worth noting that he won two elections and was extremely popular until recently.) Even a bona fide reformer like Carlos Menem has passed close to 300 presidential decrees in his eight years in office, about three times as many as all previous Argentinean presidents put together, going back to 1853. Kyrgyzstan's Askar Akayev, elected with 60 percent of the vote, proposed enhancing his powers in a referendum that passed easily in 1996. His new powers include appointing all top officials except the prime minister, although he can dissolve parliament if it turns down three of his nominees for the latter post.

Horizontal usurpation, usually by presidents, is more obvious, but vertical usurpation is more common. Over the last three decades, the Indian government has routinely disbanded state legislatures on flimsy grounds, placing regions under New Delhi's direct rule. In a less dramatic but typical move, the elected government of the Central African Republic recently ended the long-standing independence of its university system, making it part of the central state apparatus.

Usurpation is particularly widespread in Latin America and the states of the former Soviet Union, perhaps because both regions mostly have presidencies. These systems tend to produce strong leaders who believe that they speak for the people—even when they have been elected by no more than a plurality. (As Juan Linz points out, Salvador Allende was elected to the Chilean presidency in 1970 with only 36 percent of the vote. In similar circumstances, a prime minister would have had to share power in a coalition government.) Presidents appoint cabinets of cronies, rather than senior party figures, maintaining few internal checks on their power. And when their views conflict with those of the legislature, or even the courts, presidents tend to "go to the nation," bypassing the dreary tasks of bargaining and coalition-building. While scholars debate the merits of presidential versus parliamentary forms of government, usurpation can occur under either, absent well-developed alternate centers of power such as strong legislatures, courts, political parties, regional governments, and independent universities and media. Latin America actually combines presidential systems with proportional representation, producing populist leaders and multiple parties—an unstable combination.

Many Western governments and scholars have encouraged the creation of strong and centralized states in the Third World. Leaders in these countries have argued that they need the authority to break down feudalism, split entrenched coalitions, override vested interests, and bring order to chaotic societies. But this confuses the need for a legitimate government with that for a powerful one. Governments that are seen as legitimate can usually maintain order and pursue tough policies, albeit slowly, by building coalitions. After all, few claim that governments in developing countries should not have adequate police powers; the trouble comes from all the other political, social, and economic powers that they accumulate. In crises like civil wars, constitutional governments might not be able to rule effectively, but the alternative—states with vast security apparatuses that suspend constitutional rights—has usually produced neither order nor good government. More often, such states have become predatory, maintaining some order but also arresting opponents, muzzling dissent, nationalizing industries, and confiscating property. While anarchy has its dangers, the greatest threats to human liberty and happiness in this century have been caused not by disorder but by brutally strong, centralized states, like Nazi Germany, Soviet Russia, and Maoist China. The Third World is littered with the bloody handiwork of strong states.

Historically, unchecked centralization has been the enemy of liberal democracy. As political participation increased in Europe over the nineteenth century, it was accommodated smoothly in countries such as England and Sweden, where medieval assemblies, local governments, and regional councils had remained strong. Countries like France and Prussia, on the other hand, where the monarchy had effectively centralized power (both horizontally and vertically), often ended up illiberal and undemocratic. It is not a coincidence that in twentieth-century Spain, the beachhead of liberalism lay in Catalonia, for centuries a doggedly independent and autonomous region. In America, the presence of a rich variety of institutions—state, local, and private—made it much easier to accommodate the rapid and large extensions in suffrage that took place in the early nineteenth century. Arthur Schlesinger Sr. has documented how, during America's first 50 years, virtually every state, interest group and faction tried to weaken and even break up the federal government.[7] More recently, India's semi-liberal democracy has survived because of, not despite, its strong regions and varied languages, cultures, and even castes. The point is logical, even tautological: pluralism in the past helps ensure political pluralism in the present.

Fifty years ago, politicians in the developing world wanted extraordinary powers to implement then-fashionable economic doctrines, like nationalization of industries. Today their successors want similar powers to privatize those very industries. Menem's justification for his methods is that they are desperately needed to enact tough economic reforms. Similar arguments are made by Abdalá Bucarem of Ecuador and by Fujimori. Lending institutions, such as the International Monetary Fund and the World Bank, have been sympathetic to these pleas, and the bond market has been positively exuberant. But except in emergencies like war, illiberal means are in the long run incompatible with liberal ends. Constitutional government is in fact the key to a successful economic reform policy. The experience of East Asia and Central Europe suggests that when regimes—whether authoritarian, as in East Asia, or liberal democratic, as in Poland, Hungary, and the Czech Republic—protect individual rights, including those of property and contract, and create a framework of law and administration, capitalism and growth will follow. In a recent speech at the Woodrow Wilson International Center in Washington, explaining what it takes for capitalism to flourish, Federal Reserve chairman Alan Greenspan concluded that, "The guiding mechanism of a free market economy. . . is a bill of rights, enforced by an impartial judiciary".

Finally, and perhaps more important, power accumulated to do good can be used subsequently to do ill. When Fujimori disbanded parliament, his approval ratings shot up to their highest ever. But recent opinion polls suggest that most of those who once approved of his actions now wish he were more constrained. In 1993 Boris Yeltsin famously (and literally) attacked the Russian parliament, prompted by parliament's own unconstitutional acts. He then suspended the constitutional court, dismantled the system of local governments, and fired several provincial governors. From the war in Chechnya to his economic programs, Yeltsin has displayed a routine lack of concern for constitutional procedures and limits. He may well be a liberal democrat at heart, but Yeltsin's actions have created a Russian super-presidency. We can only hope his successor will not abuse it.

For centuries Western intellectuals have had a tendency to view constitutional liberalism as a quaint exercise in rule-making, mere formalism that should take a

---

[7]Arthur Schlesinger, Sr., *New Viewpoints in American History*, New York: Macmillan, 1922, pp. 220-40.

back seat to battling larger evils in society. The most eloquent counterpoint to this view remains an exchange in Robert Bolt's play *A Man For All Seasons.* The fiery young William Roper, who yearns to battle evil, is exasperated by Sir Thomas More's devotion to the law. More gently defends himself.

> MORE: What would you do? Cut a great road through the law to get after the Devil?
> ROPER: I'd cut every law in England to do that!
> MORE: And when the last law was down, and the Devil turned on you— where would you hide Roper, the laws all being flat?

ETHNIC CONFLICT AND WAR

ON DECEMBER 8, 1996, Jack Lang made a dramatic dash to Belgrade. The French celebrity politician, formerly minister of culture, had been inspired by the student demonstrations involving tens of thousands against Slobodan Milos̆evi´c, a man Lang and many Western intellectuals held responsible for the war in the Balkans. Lang wanted to lend his moral support to the Yugoslav opposition. The leaders of the movement received him in their offices—the philosophy department—only to boot him out, declare him "an enemy of the Serbs," and order him to leave the country. It turned out that the students opposed Milos̆evi´c not for starting the war, but for failing to win it.

Lang's embarrassment highlights two common, and often mistaken, assumptions—that the forces of democracy are the forces of ethnic harmony and of peace. Neither is necessarily true. Mature liberal democracies can usually accommodate ethnic divisions without violence or terror and live in peace with other liberal democracies. But without a background in constitutional liberalism, the introduction of democracy in divided societies has actually fomented nationalism, ethnic conflict, and even war. The spate of elections held immediately after the collapse of communism were won in the Soviet Union and Yugoslavia by nationalist separatists and resulted in the breakup of those countries. This was not in and of itself bad, since those countries had been bound together by force. But the rapid secessions, without guarantees, institutions, or political power for the many minorities living within the new countries, have caused spirals of rebellion, repression, and, in places like Bosnia, Azerbaijan, and Georgia, war.

Elections require that politicians compete for peoples' votes. In societies without strong traditions of multiethnic groups or assimilation, it is easiest to organize support along racial, ethnic, or religious lines. Once an ethnic group is in power, it tends to exclude other ethnic groups. Compromise seems impossible; one can bargain on material issues like housing, hospitals, and handouts, but how does one split the difference on a national religion? Political competition that is so divisive can rapidly degenerate into violence. Opposition movements, armed rebellions, and coups in Africa have often been directed against ethnically based regimes, many of which came to power through elections. Surveying the breakdown of African and Asian democracies in the 1960s, two scholars concluded that democracy "is simply not viable in an environment of intense ethnic preferences." Recent studies, particularly of Africa and Central Asia, have confirmed this pessimism. A distinguished expert on ethnic conflict, Donald Horowitz, concluded, "In the face of this rather dismal account . . . of the concrete failures of democracy in divided societies . . . one is tempted to throw up one's hands. What is the point of holding elections if all they do in the end is to substitute a Bemba-dominated regime for a Nyanja regime in Zambia, the two equally narrow, or a southern regime for a northern one in Benin, neither incorporating the other half of the state?"[8]

Over the past decade, one of the most spirited debates among scholars of international relations concerns the "democratic peace"—the assertion that no two modern democracies have gone to war with each other. The debate raises interesting substantive questions (does the American Civil War count? do nuclear weapons better explain the peace?) and even the statistical findings have raised interesting dissents. (As the scholar David Spiro points out, given the small number of both democracies and wars over the last two hundred years, sheer chance might explain the absence of war between democracies. No member of his family has ever won the lottery, yet few offer explanations for this impressive correlation.) But even if the statistics are correct, what explains them? Kant, the original proponent of the democratic peace, contended that in democracies, those who pay for wars—that is, the public—make the decisions, so they are understandably cautious. But that claim suggests that democracies are more pacific than other states. Actually they are more warlike, going to war more often and with greater intensity than most states. It is only with other democracies that the peace holds.

When divining the cause behind this correlation, one thing becomes clear: the democratic peace is actually the liberal peace. Writing in the eighteenth

<hr/>

[8]Alvin Rabushka and Kenneth Shepsle, *Politics in Plural Societies: A Theory of Democratic Instability*, Columbus: Charles E. Merill, pp. 62-92; Donald Horowitz, "Democracy in Divided Societies," in Larry Diamond and Mark F. Plattner, eds., *Nationalism, Ethnic Conflict and Democracy*, Baltimore: The Johns Hopkins University Press, 1994, pp. 35-55.

century, Kant believed that democracies were tyrannical, and he specifically excluded them from his conception of "republican" governments, which lived in a zone of peace. Republicanism, for Kant, meant a separation of powers, checks and balances, the rule of law, protection of individual rights, and some level of representation in government (though nothing close to universal suffrage). Kant's other explanations for the "perpetual peace" between republics are all closely linked to their constitutional and liberal character: a mutual respect for the rights of each other's citizens, a system of checks and balances assuring that no single leader can drag his country into war, and classical liberal economic policies—most importantly, free trade—which create an interdependence that makes war costly and cooperation useful. Michael Doyle, the leading scholar on the subject, confirms in his 1997 book *Ways of War and Peace* that without constitutional liberalism, democracy itself has no peace-inducing qualities:

> Kant distrusted unfettered, democratic majoritarianism, and his argument offers no support for a claim that all participatory polities—democracies—should be peaceful, either in general or between fellow democracies. Many participatory polities have been non-liberal. For two thousand years before the modern age, popular rule was widely associated with aggressiveness (by Thucydides) or imperial success (by Machiavelli)... The decisive preference of [the] median voter might well include "ethnic cleansing" against other democratic polities.

The distinction between liberal and illiberal democracies sheds light on another striking statistical correlation. Political scientists Jack Snyder and Edward Mansfield contend, using an impressive data set, that over the last 200 years democratizing states went to war significantly more often than either stable autocracies or liberal democracies. In countries not grounded in constitutional liberalism, the rise of democracy often brings with it hyper-nationalism and war-mongering. When the political system is opened up, diverse groups with incompatible interests gain access to power and press their demands. Political and military leaders, who are often embattled remnants of the old authoritarian order, realize that to succeed that they must rally the masses behind a national cause. The result is invariably aggressive rhetoric and policies, which often drag countries into confrontation and war. Noteworthy examples range from Napoleon III's France, Wilhelmine Germany, and Taisho Japan to those in today's newspapers, like Armenia and Azerbaijan and Milos̆evi´c's Serbia. The democratic peace, it turns out, has little to do with democracy.

The Rise of Illiberal Democracy

AN AMERICAN SCHOLAR recently traveled to Kazakstan on a U.S. government-sponsored mission to help the new parliament draft its electoral laws. His counterpart, a senior member of the Kazak parliament, brushed aside the many options the American expert was outlining, saying emphatically, "We want our parliament to be just like your Congress." The American was horrified, recalling, "I tried to say something other than the three words that had immediately come screaming into my mind: 'No you don't!'" This view is not unusual. Americans in the democracy business tend to see their own system as an unwieldy contraption that no other country should put up with. In fact, the adoption of some aspects of the American constitutional framework could ameliorate many of the problems associated with illiberal democracy. The philosophy behind the U.S. Constitution, a fear of accumulated power, is as relevant today as it was in 1789. Kazakstan, as it happens, would be particularly well-served by a strong parliament—like the American Congress—to check the insatiable appetite of its president.

It is odd that the United States is so often the advocate of elections and plebiscitary democracy abroad. What is distinctive about the American system is not how democratic it is but rather how undemocratic it is, placing as it does multiple constraints on electoral majorities. Of its three branches of government, one—arguably paramount—is headed by nine unelected men and women with life tenure. Its Senate is the most unrepresentative upper house in the world, with the lone exception of the House of Lords, which is powerless. (Every state sends two senators to Washington regardless of its population—California's 30 million people have as many votes in the Senate as Arizona's 3.7 million—which means that senators representing about 16 percent of the country can block any proposed law.) Similarly, in legislatures all over the United States, what is striking is not the power of majorities but that of minorities. To further check national power, state and local governments are strong and fiercely battle every federal intrusion onto their turf. Private businesses and other nongovernmental groups, what Tocqueville called intermediate associations, make up another stratum within society.

The American system is based on an avowedly pessimistic conception of human nature, assuming that people cannot be trusted with power. "If men were angels," Madison famously wrote, "no government would be necessary." The other model for democratic governance in Western history is based on the French Revolution. The French model places its faith in the goodness of human beings. Once the people are the source of power, it should be unlimited so that they can create a just society. (The French revolution, as Lord Acton observed, is not about the limitation of sovereign power but the abrogation of all intermediate powers that get in its way.) Most non-Western countries have embraced the French model—not least because political elites like the prospect of empowering the state, since that means empowering themselves—and most have descended into bouts of chaos, tyranny, or both. This should have come as no surprise. After all, since its revolution France itself has run through two monarchies, two empires, one proto-fascist dictatorship, and five republics.[9]

Of course cultures vary, and different societies will require different frameworks of government. This is not a plea for the wholesale adoption of the American way but rather for a more variegated conception of liberal democracy, one that emphasizes both parts of that phrase. Before new policies can be adopted, there lies an intellectual task of recovering the constitutional liberal tradition, central to the Western experience and to the development of good government throughout the world. Political progress in Western history has been the result of a growing recognition over the centuries that, as the Declaration of Independence puts it, human beings have "certain inalienable rights" and that "it is to secure these rights that governments are instituted." If a democracy does not preserve liberty and law, that it is a democracy is a small consolation.

LIBERALIZING FOREIGN POLICY

A PROPER appreciation of constitutional liberalism has a variety of implications for American foreign policy. First, it suggests a certain humility. While it is easy to impose elections on a country, it is more difficult to push constitutional liberalism on a society. The process of genuine liberalization and democratization is gradual and long-term, in which an election is only one step. Without appropriate preparation, it might even be a false step. Recognizing this, governments and nongovernmental organizations are increasingly promoting a wide array of measures designed to bolster constitutional liberalism in developing countries. The National Endowment for Democracy promotes free markets, independent labor movements, and political parties. The U.S. Agency for International Development funds independent judiciaries. In the end, however, elections trump everything. If a country holds elections, Washington and the world will tolerate a great deal from the resulting government, as they have with Yeltsin, Akayev, and Menem. In an age of images and

---

[9]Bernard Lewis, "Why Turkey Is the Only Muslim Democracy," *Middle East Quarterly*, March 1994, pp. 47-48.

symbols, elections are easy to capture on film. (How do you televise the rule of law?) But there is life after elections, especially for the people who live there.

Conversely, the absence of free and fair elections should be viewed as one flaw, not the definition of tyranny. Elections are an important virtue of governance, but they are not the only virtue. Governments should be judged by yardsticks related to constitutional liberalism as well. Economic, civil, and religious liberties are at the core of human autonomy and dignity. If a government with limited democracy steadily expands these freedoms, it should not be branded a dictatorship. Despite the limited political choice they offer, countries like Singapore, Malaysia, and Thailand provide a better environment for the life, liberty, and happiness of their citizens than do either dictatorships like Iraq and Libya or illiberal democracies like Slovakia or Ghana. And the pressures of global capitalism can push the process of liberalization forward. Markets and morals can work together. Even China, which remains a deeply repressive regime, has given its citizens more autonomy and economic liberty than they have had in generations. Much more needs to change before China can even be called a liberalizing autocracy, but that should not mask the fact that much has changed.

Finally, we need to revive constitutionalism. One effect of the overemphasis on pure democracy is that little effort is given to creating imaginative constitutions for transitional countries. Constitutionalism, as it was understood by its greatest eighteenth century exponents, such as Montesquieu and Madison, is a complicated system of checks and balances designed to prevent the accumulation of power and the abuse of office. This is done not by simply writing up a list of rights but by constructing a system in which government will not violate those rights. Various groups must be included and empowered because, as Madison explained, "ambition must be made to counteract ambition." Constitutions were also meant to tame the passions of the public, creating not simply democratic but also deliberative government. Unfortunately, the rich variety of unelected bodies, indirect voting, federal arrangements, and checks and balances that characterized so many of the formal and informal constitutions of Europe are now regarded with suspicion. What could be called the Weimar syndrome—named after interwar Germany's beautifully constructed constitution, which failed to avert fascism—has made people regard constitutions as simply paperwork that cannot make much difference. (As if any political system in Germany would have easily weathered military defeat, social revolution, the Great Depression, and hyperinflation.) Procedures that inhibit direct democracy are seen as inauthentic, muzzling the voice of the people. Today around the world we see variations on the same majoritarian theme. But the trouble with these winner-take-all systems is that, in most democratizing countries, the winner really does take all.

DEMOCRACY'S DISCONTENTS

WE LIVE IN a democratic age. Through much of human history the danger to an individual's life, liberty and happiness came from the absolutism of monarchies, the dogma of churches, the terror of dictatorships, and the iron grip of totalitarianism. Dictators and a few straggling totalitarian regimes still persist, but increasingly they are anachronisms in a world of global markets, information, and media. There are no longer respectable alternatives to democracy; it is part of the fashionable attire of modernity. Thus the problems of governance in the 21st century will likely be problems *within* democracy. This makes them more difficult to handle, wrapped as they are in the mantle of legitimacy.

Illiberal democracies gain legitimacy, and thus strength, from the fact that they are reasonably democratic. Conversely, the greatest danger that illiberal democracy poses—other than to its own people—is that it will discredit liberal democracy itself, casting a shadow on democratic governance. This would not be unprecedented. Every wave of democracy has been followed by setbacks in which the system was seen as inadequate and new alternatives were sought by ambitious leaders and restless masses. The last such period of disenchantment, in Europe during the interwar years, was seized upon by demagogues, many of whom were initially popular and even elected. Today, in the face of a spreading virus of illiberalism, the most useful role that the international community, and most importantly the United States, can play is—instead of searching for new lands to democratize and new places to hold elections—to consolidate democracy where it has taken root and to encourage the gradual development of constitutional liberalism across the globe. Democracy without constitutional liberalism is not simply inadequate, but dangerous, bringing with it the erosion of liberty, the abuse of power, ethnic divisions, and even war. Eighty years ago, Woodrow Wilson took America into the twentieth century with a challenge, to make the world safe for democracy. As we approach the next century, our task is to make democracy safe for the world.✪

Response to "The Rise of Illiberal Democracy"

Marc F. Plattner

LESS THAN a quarter-century ago, democracy appeared to be confined, with a few exceptions, to North America and Western Europe. These nations had advanced industrial economies, sizable middle classes, and high literacy rates—factors that many political scientists regarded as prerequisites for successful democracy. They were home not only to free and competitive multiparty elections but also to the rule of law and the protection of individual liberties. In short, they were what had come to be called "liberal democracies."

In the rest of the world, by contrast, most countries were neither liberal nor democratic. They were ruled by a variety of dictatorships—military, single-party, revolutionary, Marxist-Leninist—that rejected free, multiparty elections (in practice, if not always in principle). By the early 1990s, however, this situation had changed dramatically, as an astonishing number of autocratic regimes around the world fell from power. They were generally succeeded by regimes that at least aspired to be democratic, giving rise to the phenomenon that Samuel P. Huntington termed the "third wave" of democratization. Today, well over a hundred countries, in every continent in the world, can plausibly claim to have freely elected governments.

Outside of Africa, few of these aspiring new democracies have suffered outright reversions to authoritarianism. But many, even among those that hold unambiguously free and fair elections, fall short of providing the protection of individual liberties and adherence to the rule of law commonly found in the long-established democracies. As Larry Diamond has put it, many of the new regimes are "electoral democracies" but not "liberal democracies." Citing Diamond's distinction, Huntington has argued that the introduction of elections

---

MARC F. PLATTNER is Co-Editor of the *Journal of Democracy*, and Co-Director of the International Forum for Democratic Studies.

in non-Western societies may often lead to victory by antiliberal forces. And Fareed Zakaria has contended that the promotion of elections around the world has been responsible for "the rise of illiberal democracy"—that is, of freely elected governments that fail to safeguard basic liberties. "Constitutional liberalism," Zakaria argues, "is theoretically different and historically distinct from democracy . . . . Today the two strands of liberal democracy, interwoven in the Western political fabric, are coming apart in the rest of the world. Democracy is flourishing; constitutional liberalism is not." Drawing upon this distinction, Zakaria recommends that Western policymakers not only increase their efforts to foster constitutional liberalism but diminish their support for elections, and suggests that "liberal autocracies" are preferable to illiberal democracies.

DECONSTRUCTING DEMOCRACY

THE BASIC distinction made by all these authors is both valid and important. Liberal democracy—which is what most people mean today when they speak of democracy—is indeed an interweaving of two different elements, one democratic in a stricter sense and the other liberal. As its etymological derivation suggests, the most basic meaning of the word "democracy" is the rule of the people. As the rule of the many, it is distinguished from monarchy (the rule of one person), aristocracy (the rule of the best), and oligarchy (the rule of the few). In the modern world, where the sheer size of states has rendered impossible the direct democracy once practiced by some ancient republics, the election of legislative representatives and other public officials is the chief mechanism by which the people exercise their rule. Today it is further presumed that democracy implies virtually universal adult suffrage and eligibility to run for office. Elections, then, are regarded as embodying the popular or majoritarian aspect of contemporary liberal democracy.

The word "liberal" in the phrase liberal democracy refers not to the matter of who rules but to the matter of how that rule is exercised. Above all, it implies that government is limited in its powers and its modes of acting. It is limited first by the rule of law, and especially by a fundamental law or constitution, but ultimately it is limited by the rights of the individual. The idea of natural or inalienable rights, which today are most commonly called "human rights," originated with liberalism. The primacy of individual rights means that the protection of the private sphere, along with the plurality and diversity of ends that people seek in their pursuit of happiness, is a key element of a liberal political order.

Liberalism and Democracy

The fact that democracy and liberalism are not inseparably linked is proven by the historical existence both of nonliberal democracies and of liberal nondemocracies. The democracies of the ancient world, although their citizens were incomparably more involved in governing themselves than we are today, did not provide freedom of speech or religion, protection of private property, or constitutional government. On the other side, the birthplace of liberalism, modern England, retained a highly restricted franchise well into the nineteenth century. As Zakaria points out, England offers the classic example of democratization by a gradual extension of suffrage well after the essential institutions of constitutional liberalism were already in place. In our own time, Zakaria offers Hong Kong under British colonial rule as an example of a flourishing of liberalism in the absence of democracy.

ALL MEN ARE CREATED EQUAL

ALTHOUGH "UNPACKING" the component elements of modern liberal democracy is a crucial first step toward comprehending its character, over-stating the disjunction between liberalism and democracy can easily lead to new misunderstanding. While many new electoral democracies fall short of liberalism, on the whole, countries that hold free elections are overwhelmingly more liberal than those that do not, and countries that protect civil liberties are overwhelmingly more likely to hold free elections than those that do not. This is not simply an accident. It is the result of powerful intrinsic links between electoral democracy and a liberal order.

Some of these links are immediately apparent. Starting from the democratic side, elections would seem to require the guarantee of certain civil liberties—the freedoms of speech, association, and assembly—if they are to be genuinely free and fair. Thus even minimalist definitions of democracy offered by political scientists usually include a stipulation that such liberties must be maintained at least to the extent necessary to make possible open electoral competition. If we begin instead with the human rights mandated by the liberal tradition, these are generally held today to include some kind of right to electoral participation. Thus Article 21 of the U.N. Universal Declaration of Human Rights states: "Everyone has the right to take part in the government of his country, directly or through freely chosen representatives . . . The will of the people shall be the basis of the authority of the government; this will shall be expressed in periodic and genuine elections which shall be by universal and equal suffrage and shall be held by secret vote or by equivalent free voting procedures." One may regard this as a formal or even merely definitional link between liberalism and electoral democracy, but it points to a more profound kinship.

For the political doctrine at the source of liberalism also contains a deeply egalitarian and majoritarian dimension. This is the doctrine that all legitimate political power is derived from the consent of individuals, who are by nature not only free but equal. In the opening pages of his Second Treatise of Government, John Locke states that men are naturally in "a state of perfect freedom," which is "a state also of equality, wherein all the power and jurisdiction is reciprocal, no one having more than another: there being nothing more evident, than that Creatures of the same species and rank promiscuously born to all the same advantages of Nature, and the use of the same faculties, should be equal one amongst another without Subordination or Subjection." The essential point is that no man has a natural claim to rule over another, and its clear corollary is that the rule of man over man can be justified only on the basis of a mutual agreement or "compact."

Now it is true that neither Locke nor his immediate successors concluded from this that democracy was the only legitimate form of government. For while they held that the consent of all is essential to the original compact that forms a political community, they also contended that the political community is free to decide where it chooses to bestow legislative power—whether it is in a democracy, an oligarchy, a monarchy, or a mix, as it was among the King, Lords, and Commons in England. Liberalism did not originally insist on democracy as a form of government, but it unequivocally insisted upon the ultimate sovereignty of the people. Thus Locke argues that if the legislature is dissolved or violates its trust, the power to institute a new one reverts to the majority of the people.

In order to grasp the distinctive character of liberal egalitarianism, it is necessary to appreciate how different modern liberal democracy is from the premodern (and truly illiberal) democracy of the ancient city. Reliance on elected representation in the legislature, the key political institution of modern liberal democracy, was understood by its proponents as a decisive departure from ancient democracy. The authors of The Federalist frequently contrast two very different kinds of "popular government." They write in favor of a "republic" ("a government in which the scheme of representation takes place"), which they argue need not be subject to the infirmities of "a pure democracy" ("a society consisting of a small number of citizens who assemble and administer the government in person," Federalist 10). In pure or direct democracies, they contend, "there is nothing to check the inducements to sacrifice the weaker party or an obnoxious individual," and therefore they "have ever been found incompatible with personal security or the rights of property." Later, in Federalist 63, acknowledging that the principle of representation was not unknown to the ancients, Madison states: "The true distinction between [ancient democracies] and the American governments lies in the total exclusion of the people in their collective capacity, from any share in the latter, and not in the total exclusion of the representatives of the people from the administration of the former" (italics in original). In short, modern liberal democracy from the outset was inclined to minimize the direct political role of the people. In this sense, Zakaria is on solid ground in stressing the anti-majoritarian aspects of liberalism.

In part, of course, the substitution of representative government for direct democracy was justified by the larger size of modern states, which made it impractical for the whole people to assemble. But this very fact had led thinkers like Montesquieu and Rousseau to conclude that democratic or republican government was possible only in a small state, and Rousseau to assert that "the moment that a people gives itself representatives, it is no longer free." There was, however, another ground used to justify representative government. In Madison's words, it "would refine and enlarge the public views by passing them through the medium of a chosen body of citizens, whose wisdom may best discern the true interest of their country and whose patriotism and love of justice will be least likely to sacrifice it to temporary or partial considerations." In other words, elected representatives are expected to be superior to the average citizen. In the ancient democracies, by contrast, most public officials were chosen by lot. In The Politics, Aristotle characterizes lot as the democratic mode of choosing officials, and election as the oligarchic mode. Montesquieu reiterates this judgment, adding, "The suffrage by lot is a method of electing that offends no one, but animates each citizen with the pleasing hope of serving his country." Where elections are used instead, those chosen tend to be richer, better educated, and more talented than most of their fellow citizens. In this light, representative or electoral democracy, besides largely eliminating the people from direct participation in self-government, also seems to constitute an aristocratic deviation from political equality.

BY AND FOR THE PEOPLE

YET THERE is another sense in which modern liberal, representative democracy is much more egalitarian than was ancient democracy. In the latter, the citizens entitled to participate in public affairs invariably represented a relatively small percentage of the overall population. Not only were large numbers of slaves and resident aliens excluded, but women had no role in political affairs.

Marc F. Plattner

Preliberal democracy, the direct democracy of the ancient city, was not based on any concept of the fundamental, natural equality of all human beings. It is true, of course, that modern representative government for a long time excluded the poor and all women from political participation, and in the United States even coexisted with slavery. But it is no less true that these kinds of exclusions were always in tension with the underlying principle of liberalism—namely, that all human beings are by nature free and equal. The historical development of this principle inevitably transformed liberalism into liberal democracy.

It is one thing to claim that the majority of people in a traditional and hierarchical society have somehow given their tacit consent to a political arrangement in which they are excluded from having any voice. Popular sentiment in seventeenth-century England, if there had been a way of measuring it, might well have approved of a monarchical political system. But as the principle that all men are created equal gained currency, and as the educational and economic situation of the common people continued to improve, it was only to be expected that some of them would begin to demand the vote. And once they began to do so, how could it any longer be claimed that they consented to a political order in which they had no say? Popular sovereignty without popular government may be coherent in theory and even sustainable in practice for a time. Over the long run, however, popular sovereignty can hardly fail to lead to popular government.

Thus it is not surprising that throughout the Western world, liberal, con- stitutional regimes became more and more democratic during the nineteenth and twentieth centuries. The share of legislative power wielded by monarchs or unelected bodies receded until it had virtually disappeared. At the same time, suffrage was gradually broadened. Property qualifications and exclusions on the basis of race or sex were eliminated, to the point where "universal and equal suffrage" was endorsed by the world community in 1948 as a human right.

The moral grounds for extending suffrage are succinctly stated by John Stuart Mill in his Considerations on Representative Government, published in 1861. "It is a personal injustice," Mill argues, "to withhold from anyone, unless for the prevention of greater evils, the ordinary privilege of having his voice reckoned in the disposal of affairs in which he has the same interest as other people . . . No arrangement of the suffrage, therefore, can be permanently satisfactory in which any person or class is peremptorily excluded, in which the electoral privilege is not open to all persons of full age who desire to obtain it." On these grounds Mill also argues for the extension of the franchise to women. Yet this does not prevent him from arguing against granting the vote to illiterates and to recipients of parish relief (i.e., welfare); he also proposes that multiple votes be allotted to the educated and professional classes. Today, such departures from universality and equality in the allocation of the franchise seem shockingly "elitist." No arguments for "the prevention of greater evils" are reckoned as sufficiently powerful to overbalance the injustice of denying any citizen an equal vote.

MAKING DEMOCRACY WORK

THERE IS another respect in which Mill's Representative Government is repugnant to contemporary sensibilities—namely, its justification of colonialism. For Mill, representative government "is the ideal type of a perfect government," but it is not applicable under all social conditions. In particular, it is ill suited to "barbarous" or "backward" peoples, who are likely to need some form of monarchical or (preferably) external rule to bring them toward the state of civilization in which they might become fit for representative government.

In part, Mill's argument in favor of colonialism is grounded in a dubious doctrine of historical progress (or of "modernization," as we would say today). Yet there is another basis for Mill's contention that representative government is not applicable under all conditions that is not easily dismissed. As he puts it, "representative, like any other government, must be unsuitable in any case in which it cannot permanently subsist." If people do not value representative government, if they are unwilling to defend it, if they are unable to do what it requires, then they will not be able to maintain it. Thus it would be vain to expect that it would serve them well.

The concern with making democracy able to maintain itself, with training and spurring the people to do what is needed to make democracy work, is certainly not outdated. It is at the heart of most programs of "democracy assistance" now being provided to new democracies by Western governments, international and regional organizations, and nongovernmental organizations alike. It is at the root of the central concern today of political scientists who study new democracies—the problem of consolidation, or how to bring a democratic regime to the point where its breakdown becomes extremely unlikely. And it explains the widespread attention to issues of citizenship and civil society today, not only in new democracies but in long-established ones as well. These concerns reflect the irreducible fact that making self-government work is not easy. A democratic government can be given to any people, but not every people can maintain it. But what is to be done in the case of a people that is not, at least for the time being, capable of making democracy work? Mill's answer to this question was colonial rule. What is ours? That is the question implicitly raised by Zakaria's article.

Marc F. Plattner

The difficulty in answering it points to an acute tension within the modern democratic tradition between the liberal doctrine of just or legitimate government and the practical requirements of popular government. (In The Social Contract, Rousseau says that "all legitimate government is republican." But later in the same work he says that "freedom is not a fruit of every climate, and it is not therefore within the capacity of every people.") The principle that all men are born free and equal, and that no one has a right to rule them without their consent, has now swept the world. As I have argued above, this has inevitably come to be understood as meaning that they cannot be ruled without their clearly expressed consent, in the form of an election. Yet the experience of past ages and of many lands suggests that this principle cannot be effectively put into practice everywhere and immediately. The failure in the 1960s of so many of the democracies bequeathed by the departing colonial powers once again demonstrated the fact that under certain conditions democracy is unlikely to endure. But if democratic government is required everywhere in principle, what course can a good liberal democrat follow where it appears unable to work in practice? This conundrum largely accounts for the alternating cycles of euphoria and despair about the prospects for the spread of liberal democracy.

How does Zakaria suggest that this dilemma be resolved? He contends, first, that constitutionalism, the rule of law, and the protection of individual liberty are more essential than representative government. Accordingly, he recommends that, rather than encouraging the introduction of elections in many developing countries, Western policy should favor the establishment of "liberal autocracy." As noted above, the prime example of liberal autocracy that he presents is nineteenth-century Europe, where the introduction of constitutional liberalism by monarchical governments preceded democratization. It has often been remarked that the sequence of first liberal constitutionalism, then gradual democratization, can have advantages in accustoming people to the requirements of self-government. But is this a practical strategy today?

During the nineteenth and early twentieth centuries, democratization proceeded in a context in which more traditional principles of social hierarchy still had a considerable hold over the popular imagination. The idea of equality had not been fully accepted as the preeminent principle of political legitimacy. Monarchy and aristocracy still prevailed in most of Europe, so that even a limited legislative role for an assembly elected with a restricted suffrage could seem like progress toward popular government. Today the situation is dramatically different. There are only a few countries—principally Islamic monarchies—in which anything like traditional rule still holds sway. In these cases, perhaps the nineteenth-century European model can to some extent be emulated. Elsewhere, existing autocracies—or the regimes that aspiring democracies have replaced—are generally ideological rather than traditional regimes and espouse some kind of egalitarian doctrine of their own. In a post-communist or formerly one-party socialist regime, what principle could be accepted as a basis for restricting suffrage? And what legitimate mechanism other than election could be used for deciding who will rule?

The only example in the contemporary world of liberal autocracy that Zakaria explicitly cites is British-ruled Hong Kong. Yet he certainly does not seem prepared to recommend a revival of colonialism. Earlier in this decade, there was a flurry of discussion of the problem of "failed states"—former client states of the superpowers during the Cold War that threatened to collapse once the support of their patron had been withdrawn. Amid the talk of a new world order, there seemed to be some inclination to have the "international community" intervene in such cases, in effect reviving something like colonial rule under the aegis of the United Nations. Whatever the merits or the feasibility of this idea, the fiasco of the U.S. attempt at political (as opposed to humanitarian) intervention in Somalia, along with the proliferation of states that might have been candidates for such costly international reconstruction operations, quickly made it clear that the political will for this kind of policy was lacking.

The practical model that Zakaria seems to have in mind is the economically successful (at least until recently) autocracies of East Asia. Yet it would surely be questionable to assert that these autocracies are genuinely constitutional or liberal, a fact that Zakaria himself seems to recognize by characterizing Indonesia, Singapore, and Malaysia not as "liberal" but only as "liberalizing" autocracies. It would be implausible indeed to claim that these states more reliably protect individual rights or have more independent and impartial judiciaries than the Latin American democracies that Zakaria describes as "illiberal." Even the Singaporeans themselves, while claiming to practice democracy, acknowledge that their regime, to quote Singapore's U.N. Ambassador, Bilahari Kausikan, "has never pretended or aspired to be liberal." Thus, despite Zakaria's talk of constitutionalism and individual rights, he seems to wind up taking the much more familiar view that authoritarian capitalist development is the most reliable road to eventual liberal democracy.

The economic achievements of these East Asian autocracies have certainly been impressive, but so have been the economic achievements of East Asian democracies, beginning with Japan. This is not the place to enter into the complex and hotly contested argument about to what extent, if at all, authoritarian rule has been responsible for Asian economic development. What is clear, however, is that in the rest of the world the overall record of autocracies in promoting economic development, let alone the growth of constitutional liberalism, has been poor. As Mill noted, the same shortcomings that make a people poorly prepared for representative government are also likely to be found in its unelected rulers. Wise and benevolent despots are the exception, not the rule.

A LOOK INSIDE THE BALLOT BOX

IT WAS only to be expected that, as countries around the world replaced their autocratic regimes with freely elected ones, they would encounter serious difficulties in making democracy work. Self-government is indeed difficult, and holding elections is merely one step in a long and arduous process that, in the best case, will culminate in a consolidated liberal democracy. Electorates can make bad choices as well as good or (most often) mediocre ones. Demagogues can use electoral campaigns to appeal to voters' worst instincts, including ethnic or religious intolerance (although the number of new democracies in which candidates have succeeded on the basis of such appeals is far fewer than might have been expected). But in any case, how often can elections themselves be plausibly cited as the cause of problems that would not have been just as likely to persist or arise under a nonelected government? African voters, for example, may often cast their ballots along ethnic or tribal lines, but in how many African countries have dictatorial governments achieved real ethnic accommodation, rather than merely the domination of some groups by others? Most new democracies are undoubtedly confronting severe challenges, but almost none of these would be overcome by abolishing elections.

It is also true that, beyond peacefully getting rid of a bad and unpopular government (which is no small accomplishment), elections by themselves do not solve most other political problems. For this and other reasons, prudence counsels against hastily pushing elections on a fairly stable, decent, and moderate nondemocratic regime, especially in a country where the strongest opposition forces are not themselves well disposed toward liberal democracy. This, however, is a lesson that most Western governments, inherently inclined toward diplomatic caution, hardly need to be taught. In fact, their adherence to such a policy is a frequent complaint of those who accuse Western governments of being too friendly with nondemocratic governments, especially in the Arab world.

There are arguably cases where elections have made things worse, as in Angola in 1992, where Jonas Savimbi's refusal to accept his defeat in a

U.N.-supervised election led to a violent escalation of that country's civil war. Yet despite some serious setbacks, most recently in Cambodia, the overall record of attempts to use internationally supervised elections as a method of conflict resolution for countries embroiled in civil strife has been surprisingly positive. This relatively recent innovation, first attempted in Nicaragua in 1990, combines peacemaking with democracy-building, but is driven primarily by the former goal. Thus elections are often held under extraordinarily difficult circumstances and at times that would not have been chosen if democracy-building were the only goal. Nonetheless, such elections have not only brought a number of bloody civil wars to a halt, but in countries like Mozambique and El Salvador have had positive political results as well. Even if such countries today are merely illiberal democracies, they are manifestly much better off than if they were still racked by civil war. Afghanistan, a country that did not undergo an electoral process and faces continuing civil war and the rule of an extremist and intolerant Islamist government, does not present a very attractive alternative model.

In more typical cases of democratic transition, where an authoritarian government either is overthrown or negotiates an agreement with domestic opposition forces on the creation of a new regime, the timing of "founding elections" can be a matter of critical importance for the success of an emerging democracy. In such cases there is room for reasonable disagreement about how soon to hold elections. Amid the devastated political landscape of the post-Mobutu Congo, for example, even those committed to trying to move the country in a democratic direction are divided about both the practicability and the desirability of conducting early elections. At the same time, it is difficult to see how dispensing with elections would lead the Kabila government to move toward "constitutional liberalism," or how such unaccountable rule would be preferable to "illiberal democracy."

IF AT FIRST YOU DON'T SUCCEED

IN SUCH unfavorable situations, of course, electoral democracies may simply be unable to endure. The history of democratization is replete with failed attempts. That is why the pattern discerned by Huntington is also characterized by "reverse waves," periods when democratic breakdowns far outnumber democratic transitions. But the overall trend, nonetheless, is for more and more countries to become and remain democratic. Moreover, the historical record shows that countries that have had an earlier experience with democracy that failed are more likely to succeed in a subsequent attempt than countries with no previous democratic experience. So even if democracy breaks down, it can leave a legacy of hope for the future.

Now that a growing number of countries lacking the standard social and economic "prerequisites" for democracy have gained the privilege of electing their own leaders, it is not surprising that these new regimes often have serious deficiencies with respect to accountability, the rule of law, and the protection of individual liberties. There is every reason for Western nations to do all they can to assist these countries in improving their electoral democracies and turning them into liberal democracies. It is precisely the illiberal democracies that Zakaria maligns that are likely to be the most receptive audience for the promotion of constitutional liberalism that he recommends. For the road to constitutional liberalism in today's world runs not through unaccountable autocracies but through freely elected governments.

Women and the Evolution of World Politics

Francis Fukuyama

CHIMPANZEE POLITICS

IN THE world's largest captive chimp colony at the Burger's Zoo in Arnhem, Netherlands, a struggle worthy of Machiavelli unfolded during the late 1970s. As described by primatologist Frans de Waal, the aging alpha male of the colony, Yeroen, was gradually unseated from his position of power by a younger male, Luit. Luit could not have done this on the basis of his own physical strength, but had to enter into an alliance with Nikkie, a still younger male. No sooner was Luit on top, however, than Nikkie turned on him and formed a coalition with the deposed leader to achieve dominance himself. Luit remained in the background as a threat to his rule, so one day he was murdered by Nikkie and Yeroen, his toes and testicles littering the floor of the cage.

Jane Goodall became famous studying a group of about 30 chimps at the Gombe National Park in Tanzania in the 1960s, a group she found on the whole to be peaceful. In the 1970s, this group broke up into what could only be described as two rival gangs in the northern and southern parts of the range. The biological anthropologist Richard Wrangham with Dale Peterson in their 1996 book *Demonic Males* describes what happened next. Parties of four or five males from the northern group would go out, not simply defending their range, but often penetrating into the rival group's territory to pick off individuals caught alone or unprepared. The murders were often grisly, and they were celebrated by the attackers with hooting and feverish excitement. All the males and several of the females in the southern group were eventually killed, and

FRANCIS FUKUYAMA is Hirst Professor of Public Policy at George Mason University. His book, *The Great Disruption*, will be published in 1999.

the remaining females forced to join the northern group. The northern Gombe chimps had done, in effect, what Rome did to Carthage in 146 B.C.: extinguished its rival without a trace.

There are several notable aspects to these stories of chimp behavior. First, the violence. Violence within the same species is rare in the animal kingdom, ususally restricted to infanticide by males who want to get rid of a rival's offspring and mate with the mother. Only chimps and humans seem to have a proclivity for routinely murdering peers. Second is the importance of coalitions and the politics that goes with coalition-building. Chimps, like humans, are intensely social creatures whose lives are pre-occupied with achieving and maintaining dominance in status hierarchies. They threaten, plead, cajole, and bribe their fellow chimps to join with them in alliances, and their dominance lasts only as long as they can main-tain these social connections.

Finally and most significantly, the violence and the coalition-building is primarily the work of males. Female chimpanzees can be as violent and cruel as the males at times; females compete with one another in hierarchies and form coalitions to do so. But the most murderous violence is the province of males, and the nature of female alliances is different. According to de Waal, female chimps bond with females to whom they feel some emotional attachment; the males are much more likely to make alliances for purely instrumental, calculating reasons. In other words, female chimps have relationships; male chimps practice realpolitik.

Chimpanzees are man's closest evolutionary relative, having descended from a common chimp-like ancestor less than five million years ago. Not only are they very close on a genetic level, they show many behav-ioral similarities as well. As Wrangham and Peterson note, of the 4,000 mammal and 10 million or more other species, only chimps and humans live in male-bonded, patrilineal communities in which groups of males routinely engage in aggressive, often murderous raiding of their own species. Nearly 30 years ago, the anthropologist Lionel Tiger suggested that men had special psychological resources for bonding with one another, derived from their need to hunt cooperatively, that explained their dominance in group-oriented activities from politics to warfare. Tiger was roundly denounced by feminists at the time for suggesting that there were biologically based psychological differences between the sexes, but more recent research, including evidence from primatology, has confirmed that male bonding is in fact genetic and predates the human species.

Women and the Evolution of World Politics

IT IS ALL too easy to make facile comparisons between animal and human behavior to prove a polemical point, as did the socialists who pointed to bees and ants to prove that nature endorsed collectivism. Skeptics point out that human beings have language, reason, law, culture, and moral values that make them fundamentally different from even their closest animal relative. In fact, for many years anthropologists endorsed what was in effect a modern version of Rousseau's story of the noble savage: people living in hunter-gatherer societies were pacific in nature. If chimps and modern man had a common proclivity for violence, the cause in the latter case had to be found in civilization and not in human nature.

A number of authors have extended the noble savage idea to argue that violence and patriarchy were late inventions, rooted in either the Western Judeo-Christian tradition or the capitalism to which the former gave birth. Friedrich Engels anticipated the work of later feminists by positing the existence of a primordial matriarchy, which was replaced by a violent and repressive patriarchy only with the transition to agricultural societies. The problem with this theory is, as Lawrence Keeley points out in his book *War Before Civilization*, that the most comprehensive recent studies of violence in hunter-gatherer societies suggest that for them war was actually more frequent, and rates of murder higher, than for modern ones.

Surveys of ethnographic data show that only 10-13 percent of primitive societies never or rarely engaged in war or raiding; the others engaged in conflict either continuously or at less than yearly intervals. Closer examination of the peaceful cases shows that they were frequently refugee populations driven into remote locations by prior warfare or groups protected by a more advanced society. Of the Yanomamö tribesmen studied by Napoleon Chagnon in Venezuela, some 30 percent of the men died by violence; the !Kung San of the Kalahari desert, once characterized as the "harmless people," have a higher murder rate than New York or Detroit. The sad archaeological evidence from sites like Jebel Sahaba in Egypt, Talheim in Germany, or Roaix in France indicates that systematic mass killings of men, women, and children occurred in Neolithic times. The Holocaust, Cambodia, and Bosnia have each been described as a unique, and often as a uniquely modern, form of horror. Exceptional and tragic they are indeed, but with precedents stretching back tens if not hundreds of thousands of years.

It is clear that this violence was largely perpetrated by men. While a small minority of human societies have been matrilineal, evidence of a primordial matriarchy in which women dominated men, or were even relatively equal to men, has been hard to find. There was no age of innocence. The line from chimp to modern man is continuous.

It would seem, then, that there is something to the contention of many feminists that phenomena like aggression, violence, war, and intense competition for dominance in a status hierarchy are more closely associated with men than women. Theories of international relations like realism that see international politics as a remorseless struggle for power are in fact what feminists call a gendered perspective, describing the behavior of states controlled by men rather than states per se. A world run by women would follow different rules, it would appear, and it is toward that sort of world that all postindustrial or Western societies are moving. As women gain power in these countries, the latter should become less aggressive, adventurous, competitive, and violent.

The problem with the feminist view is that it sees these attitudes toward violence, power, and status as wholly the products of a patriarchal culture, whereas in fact it appears they are rooted in biology. This makes these attitudes harder to change in men and consequently in societies. Despite the rise of women, men will continue to play a major, if not dominant, part in the governance of postindustrial countries, not to mention less-developed ones. The realms of war and international politics in particular will remain controlled by men for longer than many feminists would like. Most important, the task of resocializing men to be more like women—that is, less violent—will run into limits. What is bred in the bone cannot be altered easily by changes in culture and ideology.

THE RETURN OF BIOLOGY

WE ARE living through a revolutionary period in the life sciences. Hardly a week goes by without the discovery of a gene linked to a disease, condition, or behavior, from cancer to obesity to depression, with the promise of genetic therapies and even the outright manipulation of the human genome just around the corner. But while developments in molecular biology have been receiving the lion's share of the headlines, much progress has been made at the behavioral level as well. The past generation has seen a revival in Darwinian thinking about human psychology, with profound implications for the social sciences.

For much of this century, the social sciences have been premised on Emile Durkheim's dictum that social facts can be explained only by prior social facts and not by biological causes. Revolutions and wars are caused by social facts such as economic change, class inequalities, and shifting alliances. The standard social science model assumes that the human mind is the terrain of ideas, customs, and norms that are the products of man-made culture. Social reality is, in other words, socially constructed: if young boys like to pretend to shoot each other more than young girls, it is only because they have been socialized at an early age to do so.

The social-constructionist view, long dominant in the social sciences, originated as a reaction to the early misuse of Darwinism. Social Darwinists like Herbert Spencer or outright racists like Madsen Grant in the late nineteenth and early twentieth centuries used biology, specifically the analogy of natural selection, to explain and justify everything from class stratification to the domination of much of the world by white Europeans. Then Franz Boas, a Columbia anthropologist, debunked many of these theories of European racial superiority by, among other things, carefully measuring the head sizes of immigrant children and noting that they tended to converge with those of native Americans when fed an American diet. Boas, as well as his well-known students Margaret Mead and Ruth Benedict, argued that apparent differences between human groups could be laid at the doorstep of culture rather than nature. There were, moreover, no cultural universals by which Europeans or Americans could judge other cultures. So-called primitive peoples were not inferior, just different. Hence was born both the social constructivism and the cultural relativism with which the social sciences have been imbued ever since.

But there has been a revolution in modern evolutionary thinking. It has multiple roots; one was ethology, the comparative study of animal behavior. Ethologists like Konrad Lorenz began to notice similarities in behavior across a wide variety of animal species suggesting common evolutionary origins. Contrary to the cultural relativists, they found that not only was it possible to make important generalizations across virtually all human cultures (for example, females are more selective than males in their choice of sexual partners) but even across broad ranges of animal species. Major breakthroughs were made by William Hamilton and Robert Trivers in the 1960s and 1970s in explaining instances of altruism in the animal world not by some sort of instinct towards species survival but rather in terms of "selfish genes" (to use Richard Dawkins' phrase) that made social behavior in an individual animal's interest. Finally, advances in neurophysiology have shown that the brain is not a Lockean tabula rasa waiting to be filled with cultural content, but rather a highly modular organ whose components have been adapted prior to birth to suit the needs of socially oriented primates. Humans are hard-wired to act in certain predictable ways.

The sociobiology that sprang from these theoretical sources tried to provide a deterministic Darwinian explanation for just about everything, so it was perhaps inevitable that a reaction would set in against it as well. But while the term sociobiology has gone into decline, the neo-Darwinian thinking that spawned it has blossomed under the rubric of evolutionary psychology or anthropology and is today an enormous arena of new research and discovery.

Unlike the pseudo-Darwininsts at the turn of the century, most contemporary biologists do not regard race or ethnicity as biologically significant categories. This stands to reason: the different human races have been around only for the past hundred thousand years or so, barely a blink of the eye in evolutionary time. As countless authors have pointed out, race is largely a socially constructed category: since all races can (and do) interbreed, the boundary lines between them are often quite fuzzy.

The same is not true, however, about sex. While some gender roles are indeed socially constructed, virtually all reputable evolutionary biologists today think there are profound differences between the sexes that are genetically rather than culturally rooted, and that these differences extend beyond the body into the realm of the mind. Again, this stands to reason from a Darwinian point of view: sexual reproduction has been going on not for thousands but hundreds of millions of years. Males and females compete not just against their environment but against one another in a process that Darwin labeled "sexual selection," whereby each sex seeks to maximize its own fitness by choosing certain kinds of mates. The psychological strategies that result from this never-ending arms race between men and women are different for each sex.

In no area is sex-related difference clearer than with respect to violence and aggression. A generation ago, two psychologists, Eleanor Maccoby and Carol Jacklin, produced an authoritative volume on what was then empirically known about differences between the sexes. They showed that certain stereotypes about gender, such as the assertion that girls were more suggestible or had lower self-esteem, were just that, while others, like the idea that girls were less competitive, could not be proven one way or another. On one issue, however, there was virtually no disagreement in the hundreds of studies on the subject: namely, that boys were more aggressive, both verbally and physically, in their dreams, words, and actions than girls. One comes to a similar conclusion by looking at crime statistics. In every known culture, and from what we know of virtually all historical time periods, the vast majority of crimes, particularly violent crimes, are committed by men. Here there is also apparently a genetically determined age specificity to violent aggression: crimes are overwhelmingly committed by young men between the ages of 15 and 30. Perhaps young men are everywhere socialized to behave violently, but this evidence, from different cultures and times, suggests that there is some deeper level of causation at work.

At this point in the discussion, many people become uncomfortable and charges of "biological determinism" arise. Don't we know countless women who are stronger, larger, more decisive, more violent, or more competitive than their male counterparts? Isn't the proportion of female criminals rising relative to males? Isn't work becoming less physical, making sexual differences unimportant? The answer to all of these questions is yes: again, no reputable evolutionary biologist would deny that culture also shapes behavior in countless critical ways and can often overwhelm genetic predispositions. To say that there is a genetic basis for sex difference is simply to make a statistical assertion that the bell curve describing the distribution of a certain characteristic is shifted over a little for men as compared with women. The two curves will overlap for the most part, and there will be countless individuals in each population who will have more of any given characteristic than those of the other sex. Biology is not destiny, as tough-minded female leaders like Margaret Thatcher, Indira Gandhi, and Golda Meir have proven. (It is worth pointing out, however, that in male-dominated societies, it is these kinds of unusual women who will rise to the top.) But the statistical assertion also suggests that broad populations of men and women, as opposed to exceptional individuals, will act in certain predictable ways. It also suggests that these populations are not infinitely plastic in the way that their behavior can be shaped by society.

FEMINISTS AND POWER POLITICS

THERE IS by now an extensive literature on gender and international politics and a vigorous feminist subdiscipline within the field of international relations theory based on the work of scholars like Ann Tickner, Sara Ruddick, Jean Bethke Elshtain, Judith Shapiro, and others. This literature is too diverse to describe succinctly, but it is safe to say that much of it was initially concerned with understanding how international politics is "gendered," that is, run by men to serve male interests and interpreted by other men, consciously and unconsciously, according to male perspectives. Thus, when a realist theorist like Hans Morganthau or Kenneth Waltz

Francis Fukuyama

argues that states seek to maximize power, they think that they are describing a universal human characteristic when, as Tickner points out, they are portraying the behavior of states run by men.

Virtually all feminists who study international politics seek the laudable goal of greater female participation in all aspects of foreign relations, from executive mansions and foreign ministries to militaries and universities. They disagree as to whether women should get ahead in politics by demonstrating traditional masculine virtues of toughness, aggression, competitiveness, and the willingness to use force when necessary, or whether they should move the very agenda of politics away from male preoccupations with hierarchy and domination. This ambivalence was demonstrated in the feminist reaction to Margaret Thatcher, who by any account was far tougher and more determined than any of the male politicians she came up against. Needless to say, Thatcher's conservative politics did not endear her to most feminists, who much prefer a Mary Robinson or Gro Harlem Brundtland as their model of a female leader, despite—or because of—the fact that Thatcher had beaten men at their own game.

Both men and women participate in perpetuating the stereotypical gender identities that associate men with war and competition and women with peace and cooperation. As sophisticated feminists like Jean Bethke Elshtain have pointed out, the traditional dichotomy between the male "just warrior" marching to war and the female "beautiful soul" marching for peace is frequently transcended in practice by women intoxicated by war and by men repulsed by its cruelties. But like many stereotypes, it rests on a truth, amply confirmed by much of the new research in evolutionary biology. Wives and mothers can enthusiastically send their husbands and sons off to war; like Sioux women, they can question their manliness for failing to go into battle or themselves torture prisoners. But statistically speaking it is primarily men who enjoy the experience of aggression and the camaraderie it brings and who revel in the ritualization of war that is, as the anthropologist Robin Fox puts it, another way of understanding diplomacy.

A truly matriarchal world, then, would be less prone to conflict and more conciliatory and cooperative than the one we inhabit now. Where the new biology parts company with feminism is in the causal explanation it gives for this difference in sex roles. The ongoing revolution in the life sciences has almost totally escaped the notice of much of the social sciences and humanities, particularly the parts of the academy concerned with feminism, postmodernism, cultural studies, and the like. While there are some feminists who believe that sex differences have a natural basis, by far the majority are committed to the idea that men and women are psychologically identical, and that any differences in behavior, with regard to violence or any other characteristic, are the result of some prior social construction passed on by the prevailing culture.

THE DEMOCRATIC AND FEMININE PEACE

ONCE ONE views international relations through the lens of sex and biology, it never again looks the same. It is very difficult to watch Muslims and Serbs in Bosnia, Hutus and Tutsis in Rwanda, or militias from Liberia and Sierra Leone to Georgia and Afghanistan divide themselves up into what seem like indistinguishable male-bonded groups in order to systematically slaughter one another, and not think of the chimps at Gombe.

The basic social problem that any society faces is to control the aggressive tendencies of its young men. In hunter-gatherer societies, the vast preponderance of violence is over sex, a situation that continues to characterize domestic violent crime in contemporary postindustrial societies. Older men in the community have generally been responsible for socializing younger ones by ritualizing their aggression, often by directing it toward enemies outside the community. Much of that external violence can also be over women. Modern historians assume that the Greeks and Trojans could not possibly have fought a war for ten years over Helen, but many primitive societies like the Yanomamö do exactly that. With the spread of agriculture 10,000 years ago, however, and the accumulation of wealth and land, war turned toward the acquisition of material goods. Channeling aggression outside the community may not lower societies' overall rate of violence, but it at least offers them the possibility of domestic peace between wars.

The core of the feminist agenda for international politics seems fundamentally correct: the violent and aggressive tendencies of men have to be controlled, not simply by redirecting them to external aggression but by constraining those impulses through a web of norms, laws, agreements, contracts, and the like. In addition, more women need to be brought into the domain of international politics as leaders, officials, soldiers, and voters. Only by participating fully in global politics can women both defend their own interests and shift the underlying male agenda.

The feminization of world politics has, of course, been taking place gradually over the past hundred years, with very positive effects. Women have won the right to vote and participate in politics in all developed countries, as well as in many developing countries, and have exercised that right with increasing energy. In the United States and other rich countries, a pronounced gender gap with regard to foreign policy and national security issues endures. American women have always been less supportive than American men of U.S. involvement in war, including World War II, Korea, Vietnam, and the Persian Gulf War, by an average margin of seven to nine percent. They are also consistently less supportive of defense spending and the use of force abroad. In a 1995 Roper survey conducted for the Chicago Council on Foreign Relations, men favored U.S. intervention in Korea in the event of a North Korean attack by a margin of 49 to 40 percent, while women were opposed by a margin of 30 to 54 percent. Similarly, U.S. military action against Iraq in the event it invaded Saudi Arabia was supported by men by a margin of 62 to 31 percent and opposed by women by 43 to 45 percent. While 54 percent of men felt it important to maintain superior world wide military power, only 45 percent of women agreed. Women, moreover, are less likely than men to see force as a legitimate tool for resolving conflicts.

It is difficult to know how to account for this gender gap; certainly, one cannot move from biology to voting behavior in a single step. Observers have suggested various reasons why women are less willing to use military force than men, including their role as mothers, the fact that many women are feminists (that is, committed to a left-of-center agenda that is generally hostile to U.S. intervention), and partisan affiliation (more women vote Democratic than men). It is unnecessary to know the reason for the correlation between gender and antimilitarism, however, to predict that increasing female political participation will probably make the United States and other democracies less inclined to use power around the world as freely as they have in the past.

Will this shift toward a less status- and military-power-oriented world be a good thing? For relations between states in the so-called democratic zone of peace, the answer is yes. Consideration of gender adds a great deal to the vigorous and interesting debate over the correlation between democracy and peace that has taken place in the past decade. The "democratic peace" argument, which underlies the foreign policy of the Clinton administration as well as its predecessors, is that democracies tend not to fight one another. While the empirical claim has been contested, the correlation between the degree of consolidation of liberal democratic institutions and interdemocratic peace would seem to be one of the few nontrivial generalizations one can make about world politics. Democratic peace theorists have been less persuasive about the reasons democracies are pacific toward one another. The reasons usually cited—the rule of law, respect for individual rights, the commercial nature of most democracies, and the like—are undoubtedly correct. But there is another factor that has generally not been taken into account: developed democracies also tend to be more feminized than authoritarian states, in terms of expansion of female franchise and participation in political decision-making. It should therefore surprise no one that the historically unprecedented shift in the sexual basis of politics should lead to a change in international relations.

THE REALITY OF AGGRESSIVE FANTASIES

ON THE other hand, if gender roles are not simply socially constructed but rooted in genetics, there will be limits to how much international politics can change. In anything but a totally feminized world, feminized policies could be a liability.

Some feminists talk as if gender identities can be discarded like an old sweater, perhaps by putting young men through mandatory gender studies courses when they are college freshmen. Male attitudes on a host of issues, from child-rearing and housework to "getting in touch with your feelings," have changed dramatically in the past couple of generations due to social pressure. But socialization can accomplish only so much, and efforts to fully feminize young men will probably be no more successful than the Soviet Union's efforts to persuade its people to work on Saturdays on behalf of the heroic Cuban and Vietnamese people. Male tendencies to band together for competitive purposes, seek to dominate status hierarchies, and act out aggressive fantasies toward one another can be rechanneled but never eliminated.

Even if we can assume peaceful relations between democracies, the broader world scene will still be populated by states led by the occasional Mobutu, Miloševi´c , or Saddam. Machiavelli's critique of Aristotle was that the latter did not take foreign policy into account in building his model of a just city: in a system of competitive states, the best regimes adopt the practices of the worst in order to survive. So even if the democratic, feminized, postindustrial world has evolved into a zone of peace where struggles are more economic than military, it will still have to deal with those parts of the world run by young, ambitious, unconstrained men. If a future Saddam Hussein is not only sitting on the world's oil supplies but is armed to the hilt with chemical, biological, and nuclear weapons, we might be better off being led by women like Margaret Thatcher than, say, Gro Harlem Brundtland. Masculine policies will still be required, though not necessarily masculine leaders.

The implications of evolutionary biology for the hot-button issue of women in the military is not as straightforward as one might think. The vast majority of jobs in a modern military organization are in the enormous support tail that trails behind the actual combat units, and there is no reason that women cannot perform them as well if not better than men. While men have clearly evolved as cooperative hunters and fighters, it is not clear that any individual group of women will perform less well than any individual group of men in combat. What is much more problematic is integrating men and women into the same combat units, where they will be in close physical proximity over long periods of time. Unit cohesion, which is the bedrock on which the performance of armies rests, has been traditionally built around male bonding, which can only be jeopardized when men start competing for the attention of women. Commanders who encourage male bonding are building on a powerful natural instinct; those who try to keep sexual activity between healthy 20-year-old men and women in check through "zero tolerance" policies and draconian punishments are, by contrast, seeking to do something very unnatural. Unlike racial segregation, gender segregation in certain parts of the military seems not just appropriate but necessary.

THE MARGARET THATCHERS OF THE FUTURE

THE FEMINIZATION of democratic politics will interact with other demographic trends in the next 50 years to produce important changes. Due to the precipitous fall in fertility rates across the developed world since the 1960s, the age distribution of countries belonging to the Organization of Economic Cooperation and Development will shift dramatically. While the median age for America's population was in the mid-20s during the first few decades of the twentieth century, it will climb toward 40 by 2050. The change will be even more dramatic in Europe and Japan, where rates of immigration and fertility are lower. Under the U.N. Population Division's low-growth projections, the median age in Germany will be 55, in Japan 53, and in Italy 58.

The graying of the population has heretofore been discussed primarily in terms of the social security liability it will engender. But it carries a host of other social consequences as well, among them the emergence of elderly women as one of the most important voting blocs courted by mid-21st century politicians. In Italy and Germany, for example, women over 50, who now constitute 20 percent of the population, will account for 31 percent in 2050. There is no way, of course, of predicting how they will vote, but it seems likely that they will help elect more women leaders and will be less inclined toward military intervention than middle-aged males have tradition-ally been. Edward Luttwak of the Center for Strategic and International Studies has speculated that the fall in family sizes makes people in advanced countries much more leery of military casualties than people in agricultural societies, with their surpluses of young, hotheaded men. According to demographer Nicholas Eberstadt, three-fifths of Italy's offspring in 2050 will be only children with no cousins, siblings, aunts, or uncles. It is not unreasonable to suppose that in such a world tolerance of casualties will be even lower.

By the middle of the next century, then, Europe will likely consist of rich, powerful, and democratic nations with rapidly shrinking populations of mostly elderly people where women will play important leadership roles. The United States, with its higher rates of immigration and fertility, will also have more women leaders but a substantially younger population. A much larger and poorer part of the world will consist of states in Africa, the Middle East, and South Asia with young, growing populations, led mostly by younger men. As Eberstadt points out, Asia outside of Japan will buck the trend toward feminization because the high rate of abortion of female fetuses has shifted their sex ratios sharply in favor of men. This will be, to say the least, an unfamiliar world.

LIVING LIKE ANIMALS?

IN WRANGHAM and Peterson's *Demonic Males* (said to be a favorite book of Hillary Rodham Clinton, who has had her own to contend with), the authors come to the pessimistic conclusion that nothing much has changed since early hominids branched off from the primordial chimp ancestor five million years ago. Group solidarity is still based on aggression against other communities; social cooperation is undertaken to achieve higher levels of organized violence. Robin Fox has argued that military technology has developed much faster than man's ability to ritualize violence and direct it into safer channels. The Gombe chimps could kill only a handful of others; modern man can vaporize tens of millions.

While the history of the first half of the twentieth century does not give us great grounds for faith in the possibility of human progress, the situation is not nearly as bleak as these authors would have us believe. Biology, to repeat, is not destiny. Rates of violent homicide appear to be lower today than during mankind's long hunter-gatherer period, despite gas ovens and nuclear weapons. Contrary to the thrust of postmodernist thought, people cannot free themselves entirely from biological nature. But by accepting the fact that people have natures that are often evil, political, economic, and social systems can be designed to mitigate the effects of man's baser instincts.

Take the human and particularly male desire to dominate a status hierarchy, which people share with other primates. The advent of liberal democracy and modern capitalism does not eliminate that desire, but it opens up many more peaceful channels for satisfying it. Among the American Plains Indians or the Yanomamö, virtually the only way for a man to achieve social recognition was to be a warrior, which meant, of course, excelling at killing. Other traditional societies might add a few occupations like the priesthood or the bureaucracy in which one could achieve recognition. A modern, technological society, by contrast, offers thousands of arenas in which one can achieve social status, and in most of them the quest for status leads not to violence but to socially productive activity. A professor receiving tenure at a leading university, a politician winning an election, or a CEO increasing market share may satisfy the same underlying drive for status as being the alpha male in a chimp community. But in the process, these individuals have written books, designed public policies, or brought new technologies to market that have improved human welfare.

Of course, not everyone can achieve high rank or dominance in any given status hierarchy, since these are by definition zero-sum games in which every winner produces a loser. But the advantage of a modern, complex, fluid society is, as economist Robert Frank has pointed out, that small frogs in large ponds can move to smaller ponds in which they will loom larger. Seeking status by choosing the right pond will not satisfy the ambitions of the greatest and noblest individuals, but it will bleed off much of the competitive energy that in hunter-gatherer or agricultural societies often has no outlet save war. Liberal democracy and market economies work well because, unlike socialism, radical feminism, and other utopian schemes, they do not try to change human nature. Rather, they accept biologically grounded nature as a given and seek to constrain it through institutions, laws, and norms. It does not always work, but it is better than living like animals.@